THE KNIGHTS TEMPLAR
IN BRITAIN

This book is dedicated to the memory of
Madeline and Rodney Howick, with love

THE KNIGHTS TEMPLAR IN BRITAIN

EVELYN LORD

PEARSON
Longman

Harlow, England • London • New York • Boston • San Francisco • Toronto
Sydney • Tokyo • Singapore • Hong Kong • Seoul • Taipei • New Delhi
Cape Town • Madrid • Mexico City • Amsterdam • Munich • Paris • Milan

Pearson Education Limited

Edinburgh Gate
Harlow CM20 2JE
Tel: +44 (0)1279 623623
Fax: +44 (0)1279 431059
Website: www.pearsoned.co.uk

Hardback edition published in Great Britain in 2002
This paperback edition published 2004

© Pearson Education Limited 2002, 2004

The right of Evelyn Lord to be identified as Author of this work has been asserted by her
in accordance with the Copyright, Designs and Patents Act 1988.

ISBN 1 405 80163 8

British Library Cataloguing in Publication Data
A CIP catalogue record for this book can be obtained from the British Library

Library of Congress Cataloging in Publication Data
A CIP catalog record for this book can be obtained from the Library of Congress

10 9 8 7 6 5 4 3 2 1
08 07 06 05 04

Typeset in 11/13.5pt Garamond by 35
Printed and bound in Great Britain by Clays Ltd, Bungay, Suffolk

The Publishers' policy is to use paper manufactured from sustainable forests.

CONTENTS

CONTENTS

LIST OF ABBREVIATIONS

BL	British Library
HMSO	Her/His Majesty's Stationery Office
NAS	National Archives of Scotland
NMR	National Monuments Record
RCHAMS	Royal Commission on Historical and Ancient Monuments for Scotland
RCHME	Royal Commission on Historical Monuments for England
RS	Rolls Series
SNL	Scottish National Library
TNA	The National Archives (formerly known as the Public Records Office)
VCH	Victoria County History

NAME EVIDENCE AND ITS USES

Often the only evidence the historian has about the tenants living on the medieval manor is their names. An analysis of these can help to build up a picture of life on the manor and the people who farmed it. The surnames can be divided into locative names, those that refer to either a location outside the manor or a geographical feature within it, names that refer to a trade, names that show whose son the tenant was, tenants who are referred to only by their first names, and names that refer to some distinguishing feature of the individual such as Redhead or Whiteleg. The *1185 Inquest* provides the names of a great number of Templar tenants, and in some cases these can be compared with later lists of tenants such as those found in *The Hundred Rolls* or the *1308 inventories*.

Locative names can tell the historian whether the tenant has originated from elsewhere providing indirect evidence of spatial mobility. Trade names give information about the character of the manor or holding, such as whether there was a textile industry as well as farming carried on there, and can also give information on the type of trade and industry found in towns. Although in the preface to the *1185 Inquest* Lees suggests that a tenant with a trade name did not necessarily follow that trade, McKinley's work in the 1980s and 90s shows that as surnames were still developing in the 12th century it would be likely that tenants with occupational names at that time were practising that trade.[1]

[1] Lees, B.A., (1935), *Records of the Templars in the Twelfth Century*, London: British Academy, xxviii, lxxxii; McKinley, R. (1990), *A History of British Surnames*, London: Longman, 131–150.

ACKNOWLEDGEMENTS

I would like to acknowledge with gratitude the Board of Continuing Education of the University of Cambridge for arranging a sabbatical so that this book could be written, and all my colleagues at the Board. Members of Wolfson College for constructive criticism and conversation during the process of writing, and Professor Jonathan Riley-Smith of Emmanuel College for help and encouragement. The staff of Cambridge University Library, the Scottish National Library, the National Archives of Scotland, the National Archives, Kew, the Hertfordshire County Record Office, the Scottish Royal Commission on Historical and Ancient Monuments, the National Monuments Records in London, the library of Corpus Christi College, Cambridge, and the Usher Gallery, Lincoln, have all played their part in the completion of this project.

Especial thanks to Dr Joseph Elders of the Temple Dinsley Archaeological Project, to Mrs P. Willis and the staff of the Order of St John's Library and Museum, to Mr Philip Judge who drew the maps and plans from scraps of paper sent to him, and to Heather McCallum of Pearson Education.

Lastly, but by no means least, thanks to my family, who have supported me through this project. Gabriel Lord who assessed the cabalistic theories, Edward Lord who provided hospitality in

Scotland and mended the central heating at a critical point in the creative process, and to Philip and Katie who listened.

Thanks to the following institutions for providing reproductions and permission to reproduce these: The British Library, plates 1.1, 8.1, 9.3; the Master and Fellows of Corpus Christi College, Cambridge, plates 1.2, 1.3; The Conway Library, Courtauld Institute of Art, plate 1.3; English Heritage, NMR, plates 2.2–2.4, 2.6; Crown copyright: The Royal Commission of Ancient and Historical Monuments of Scotland, plates 7.1–7.3; Lincolnshire County Council, Usher Gallery, Lincoln, plate 4.1; and the National Archives, plate 2.1; The Trustees of the Wallace Collection, plate 11.1.

PREFACE

The Knights Templar arrived in the British Isles in 1128 when Hugh de Payens, the first Grand Master, came to recruit crusaders. As well as acquiring manpower he was also given estates and manors. Eventually the Templars were to become major landholders in the British Isles. It is with them this book is concerned; with their churches, preceptories, farms and buildings, and their relationship with kings, princes, prelates and peasants.

Interwoven with the account of the Templars in the British Isles is their life as soldiers of the cross in the east. There have been many books describing their heroic exploits in the struggle to keep the Holy Land in Christian hands, but few have addressed their more mundane, but albeit necessary, role in the west of supplying money and resources for the fight in the east. This book aims to redress this by a comparative study of their lives as knights, monks, farmers, financiers and royal advisers in the British Isles. Using primary sources and excavation reports, it reconstructs the world of the British Templars. The result is an account of two hundred years of endeavour set against the background of political events and civil wars.

Central to the book are issues of concern to the historian of the Middle Ages, on the standard of living and diet, agriculture and the treatment of women. These are discussed within the context of the Templars' activities on land and sea, and the Templars are set firmly within the context of medieval society and their place in the local community. The book shows how the Order's influence on town and countryside has persisted in place-names, folklore and legends, and it discusses the colourful theories about the Order that these have produced.

The central section of the book is arranged geographically by region. Starting with London and its suburbs, the reader is then taken on a circular tour of the Templar properties in England, travelling eastwards to Essex and completing the circle in Kent, before moving on to Ireland and Scotland. During the tour, the Templars' property and buildings are discussed, along with their farming methods, their relationship with their neighbours and place in society, and the provenance of their tenants. Comparative material is drawn from nearby manors, and personalities such as William Marshal and Hubert de Burgh play their part in the narrative.

From the Templars in the countryside the book moves to the role of the Templars in public life as royal councillors, treasurers and tax collectors, roles that helped to bring about their downfall when secular lords clashed with the Pope in a power struggle, with the Templars caught in the middle. The trial of the Templars and events leading up to it are discussed in detail, and contemporary opinions on their guilt and the verdict of history are considered. Finally, the way in which the Templars have been portrayed in fact and fiction, and some of the colourful theories about them and their treasure, are examined.

To encourage readers to undertake in-depth local studies that a general work such as this cannot hope to do, there is an appendix on the Templar sources in the PRO and a gazetteer is included so that the reader can visit some of the sites mentioned in the text. Overall, this book will engage anyone who is interested in medieval history, as well as the local historian and the undergraduate working on medieval society.

GLOSSARY

Advowson   The right to appoint a priest to a benefice, for example to a parish church.

Assart   A clearing of woodland. The trees were felled and pulled up by the roots and the land dug and cultivated. If five tree stumps were allowed to remain, this 'was a waste, and an outrage' (Dialogue of the exchequer). A licence was needed to assart.

Ballistas   A military engine made of wood with cords or thongs stretched tight to form a catapult that will hurl missiles.

Boon work   Labour service with food supplied.

Busses   2–3 masted medieval ships.

Carucate   120 acres of land in the Danelaw.

Close Rolls   Registered copies of letters and documents of the court of Chancery.

Common land   Land on which communal grazing was allowed and permission given to collect brushwood, furze or turf. *Commoning* was the act of grazing animals on communal land.

Corrodian   A pensioner of a religious house.

Cottar   A tenant holding a cottage.

Crenellate   To fortify.

Croft   Enclosed land attached to, or close to, a house.

Custumal   A record of the customs of a manor.

Demesne   Land put aside for the lord's own use.

Distrain To take goods in satisfaction of a debt.

Escheat A property reverting to the Treasury.

Extent A survey and valuation of a manor.

Fee A lordship.

Feet of Fines A judgement on title to land.

Hide 120 acres of land. A term used outside the Danelaw.

Interdict The official withdrawal of religious offices and privileges.

Jointure The estate settled on a wife in the event of a husband dying first.

Justiciar A royal official, premier justice of England.

Librate A piece of land worth £1 a year.

Mark A unit of currency worth 13s 4d.

Messuage A house.

Oyer and *Terminer* A writ or summons.

Pannage The right to let swine grub for food in a wood or forest.

Patent Rolls Registered copies of Letters Patent.

Paternoster Our father, that is the Lord's Prayer in Latin.

Perches Land measure of $5\frac{1}{2}$ yards.

Purgatory The place where souls departing this life went to be cleansed by temporary suffering. The suffering could be shortened by masses and gifts to the church.

Purpestre Encroachment by seizing land.

Scutage Money collected when the army was needed.

Socage A type of tenure that included obligatory attendance at the lord's court.

Soke The right of jurisdiction over a specified free area.

Tallage A tax, toll or customs levy.

Toft A plot of land attached to the house.

Township A settlement and taxable unit, mostly used in the north and midlands.

Vill A settlement and taxable unit.

Villein An unfree tenant who held land by rendering service to the landlord.

Virgate   A measurement of arable land, usually of 30 acres.

Warren   An enclosed piece of land appropriated to the breeding of rabbits or game. Right of warren was permission to enclose and construct a warren, and to keep beasts and hawks to catch the rabbits or game.

Waste   An uncultivated piece of land. An assart with tree stumps remaining in it was difficult to cultivate and so became waste.

EVENTS IN THE HOLY LAND

Templar Castles in the Holy Land

Date completed

1139	Baghras, Darbask, Destroit, La Roche Guillaume, La Roche de Roussel, Port Bonnet
1152	Castle Arnold, Castle Blanc, Tortosa
1160	Amman, Quarantere, The Red Cistern, Safad, Saffron, Toron
1178	Chastellet
1218	Atlit
1260	Beaufort

CHAPTER ONE

THE KNIGHTS TEMPLAR: KNIGHTLY MONKS OR MONKISH KNIGHTS?

In the year 1128 'Hugh of the Knights Templar came from Jerusalem to the king in Normandy; and the king received him with great ceremony and gave him great treasures of gold and silver, and sent him thereafter to England, where he was welcomed by all good men. He was given treasures by all, and in Scotland too; and by him much wealth entirely in gold and silver was sent to Jerusalem. He called for people to go to Jerusalem. As a result more people went, either with him, or after him, than ever before since the time of the first crusade, which was in the day of pope Urban: yet little was achieved by it. He declared that a decisive battle was imminent between Christians and the heathen, but, when all the multitudes got there, they were pitiably duped to find it was nothing but lies.'[1] This is the first mention of the Knights Templar in the British Isles.

In order to trace the origins of the Order we must cross the sea to the Holy Land and go back in time to 1099 when Jerusalem was 'liberated' from the infidels by the First Crusade, and placed under the Christian rule of the Latin Kingdom of Jerusalem. The liberation of Jerusalem had a parallel spiritual liberating effect on Western Christendom that became focused on visiting the holy sites associated with the life of Christ. Pilgrims flocked to the Holy Land. They went to satisfy a spiritual hunger, they went as sightseers and tourists, they went to bring home holy relics, but above all they went to gain absolution from their sins through visiting the holy shrines. Alas, the enthusiastic but ill-prepared pilgrims were a prey for robbers, Saracens and wild animals. Many never returned to tell of their adventures. They died of exhaustion and privation or were slaughtered as they travelled the recognised pilgrim routes. At Eastertide 1119, 300 pilgrims were killed and 60 taken prisoner by the Saracens as they took the road from Jerusalem to the River Jordan.[2] Such tragic loss of life could not be allowed to continue. William, Archbishop of Tyre, wrote that a group of nine 'holy and pious knights dedicated themselves to the protection of pilgrims. Since they had neither a church nor a fixed place of abode, the king [Baldwin II of Jerusalem] granted them a dwelling place in his own palace on the north side of the Temple of the Lord'. The holy and pious knights who were given a dwelling in the Temple precincts became the Knights Templar.[3]

Walter Map, Archdeacon of Oxford and a clerk in the English royal household, writing in the 1170s, embroidered this account, adding dramatic details:

There was a certain knight called Paganus after a village in Burgundy of the same name, who went on pilgrimage to Jerusalem. There he was told that pagans were in the habit of attacking Christians who went to the horse-pool for water and that the Christians were often slain. He tried as far as he could to defend them, hiding then darting out in the nick of time . . .

The Saracens were amazed, and encamped on the spot in such numbers that no one could dream of facing them, and the reservoir was abandoned. But Paganus was no coward and procured a means of help for God and himself. He obtained from the regular canons of the Temple a large hall within the precincts of the Temple of the Lord, and there sufficing himself with humble attire and spare diet devoted all his expenditure to arming and horsing a band of companions.[4]

The third major source on the origins of the Templars, Matthew Paris, the monk of St Albans, writing *c.* 1236–59, suggests that the nine knights took up monastic vows to gain remission for their sins and then roamed the country hunting infidels.[5] A fourth source is Michael the Syrian, considered to be unreliable.

All three reliable sources above were written after the event and relied on oral and hearsay evidence to reconstruct the early years of the Templars. William of Tyre, who died in 1186, was the closest in time and place to the beginnings of the Order. Paris is the furthest removed, whilst Map wrote to entertain. He is probably the least reliable, especially as he had a cavalier attitude towards chronology, starting his work with a quotation from St Augustine: 'In time I exist, and of time I speak. What time is I know not.'[6]

Both William of Tyre and Matthew Paris disliked the Templars, seeing them as rivals for ecclesiastical power and resenting their special relationship with the Pope. Entries in their chronicles reflect these attitudes, showing the Templars as proud, arrogant and unreasonably wealthy. Christian defeats in the Holy Land were blamed on this pride. The bias in Paris's account must be seen within the context in which he lived. He was a Benedictine who wished to maintain his Order's status, and he had a personal animosity towards the Pope. Sophie Menache and Helen Nicholson suggest that part of Paris's handling of the Templars was due to a hardening of attitudes towards the military orders in the thirteenth century when he was writing, and interpreting his chronicles depends on an understanding of how he viewed history and his perception of events. Nicholson likens Paris's accounts of the Templars to 'tabloid journalism'. Menache suggests that we take the accounts as evidence of thirteenth-century attitudes rather than historical accuracy. C.G. Addison, writing in the nineteenth century, also bids the reader beware of Paris's version of the Templars, and accuses him of prejudicing subsequent generations against the Order.[7]

Nicholson suggests that there is some doubt about the date that the Order was founded, whilst Barber notes that although most sources give this as 1118, it was more likely to have been 1119, after the massacre of the pilgrims at the pool.[8]

HUGH DE PAYENS

Little is known about Hugh de Payens, the first Grand Master of the Templars. He came from Payens, a village in Champagne on the left bank of the Seine, and was a vassal of the Count of Champagne. It is possible that he was in the Holy Land, having joined the First Crusade after the death of his wife. According to Scottish and Freemason tradition, his wife was Katherine St Clair, who came from the French branch of the Scottish Sinclair family. As the Sinclair family were to become the Grand Masters of Scottish Freemasonry, this would be a convenient link with the past.

Founder knights

The founder knights were:

Godfrey of St Omer (Picardy)
Geoffrey Bisot or Bisol
Payen Montdidier (Picardy)
Archimbaud de St Armand (possibly Picardy)
Andre de Montbard (he *may* have been related to Bernard of
    Clairvaux and came from either Burgundy or Champagne)
Rossol or Roland
Gondamar

It is probable that they had travelled to the Holy Land as a group. Hugh died in *c.* 1136 and was succeeded as Grand Master by Robert of Craon.

THE TEMPLARS' AIMS

Was the original intent of the Templars to protect pilgrims, or was their prime aim to lead a monastic life? William of Tyre writes that they dedicated themselves to God, taking vows of chastity, poverty and obedience, and then the Patriarch and other bishops enjoined them for the remission of their sins 'that as far as their strength permitted, they should keep the roads and highways safe from the menace of robbers and highwaymen, with especial regard for the protection of pilgrims'.[9] As the founder members came from a warrior class and were trained in arms they may have suggested this role for themselves, but the Patriarch could have seen this as a way of harnessing their warlike energies. Bernard of Clairvaux described them as 'superbly trained to war', but Peter Partner, in his book *The Murdered Magicians*, quotes an early letter from Hugh de Payens in which he declares that the knights wanted to work for God rather than others.[10]

How did outsiders perceive the Templars in their early years? Was it as knights or as brothers of a religious order? One way of answering these questions is to look at the way in which the Order is described in the charters granting them lands and rents. Although there are problems with this method, as the descriptions may show how the scribe rather than donor perceived the Order, it does give some background on contemporary perceptions. The charters that have been used are those in the Marquis D'Albon's *Cartulaire General de l'Ordre du Temple*. The Marquis collected evidence from across Europe and printed it in 1913. For the earliest period there are 21 relevant charters (Charters IV–XXIX). One is a grant to 'God and the Brothers of the Temple' and another to 'Master Hugh and the Poor Knights of the Temple, present and future . . .'. The rest have no mention of the members of the Order as brothers or members of a religious order. The number of grants increased dramatically in 1130 to 127 (Charters XXX–CCII). Of these, 20 refer to the Order as 'brothers and knights'. One makes a distinction between knights and brothers, giving land to 'Lord God, the Holy Knights of the Temple of Solomon and the Brothers of the same', adding another dimension to the problem. It is noticeable that English grants invariably refer to the 'Knight Brothers of the Temple'. In the 1120s one charter refers to the Order's poverty, and two in the 1130s (Charters CXIV, CCXILX–CCLVI, CCCCL–CCCCLXXXVI). A grant from the Templars dated 30 August 1140 shows how they referred to themselves. It starts 'In the Name of God, we, Brothers of Jerusalem, Knights of the Temple of Solomon', indicating perhaps that the members of the Order saw themselves first as monks and second as knights.

The charters also enable us to understand some of the reasons for making grants to the Order. In the 1120s five grants were made for the sake of the soul of the donor and his or her family, past, present and future, and two were made in memory of a son. The other charters did not state the reason behind the grant. In the 1130s, in 24 cases it was for the soul of the donor and the donor's family, and in eight cases the grants were for the redemption of the donor's sins and absolution. Only two grants were specifically made in order to help the defence of the Holy Land.

What conclusions can we draw from this sample? It would seem that to those granting land and rents to the Templars they were recognised mainly as knights rather than monks. The image of a knight would have been one the donors could relate to and understand from their own experience. The idea of poverty in relation to the Order was not uppermost in the minds of the donors, and the promotion of the Order's poverty may have been for the purpose of acquiring property. The legendary poverty of the Order has been assumed from them calling themselves poor knights, and from their seal, which represents two knights on one horse (Plate 1.1). Of course this may represent fellowship rather than poverty.

Plate 1.1 Two Templars on one horse with the banner of Beausant, as illustrated by Matthew Paris
The British Library. BL Royal Ms 14, fol. 42v

The reasons for making grants to the Order were primarily personal and concerned with the spiritual health of the donor and the donor's family, ancestors and successors, rather than with the defence of the Holy Land and the protection of pilgrims. The indirect result of the grants were resources that could help in this, but the direct aim of many of the donors was self-preservation and deliverance from the pain of Purgatory. Although it has been argued that feudal society was not based solely on obligations to family and kin, but depended on the wider obligation of overlord and vassal, charters such as these examples show that within the private sphere obligation to the family and its spiritual well being was of great importance.[11]

The idea of a military order of monks was a totally new concept that went against the precepts of monastic life that forbade the spilling of blood. The foundation of the Templars created a body of men who saw fighting the infidel as an act of devotion. Whilst the monk spent his life in the monastery in continual prayer and praise to God, the monkish knight spent his day fighting for the glory of God. The Knights Templar were permanently at war, and war became a version of prayer for them.

The image of knighthood was transformed by this, from one which fought for personal vengeance and material gain to one which fought for Christian ideals. We should not forget that the original founders of the Order came from the knightly class. War was their business and defined their self-image. The Knights Templar and the other military orders added piety to a knight's code, and began the modification of war for gain to a just war that defended the Holy Church, the weak and the helpless, and the pursuit of justice. Professor Riley-Smith suggests the foundation of the Templars transformed the crusading ideal to a different plane.[12]

THE KNIGHTS AND THE TEMPLE

One fact that chroniclers and their interpreters agree on is that the original knights took up residence in the Temple of Solomon. Theoderic, a German monk visiting the Holy Land between 1169 and 1174, described their residence as being like a church, supported by pillars rising to a circular roof. Inside this, stacks of arms, clothing and food were kept. Below the hall were the stables built by King Solomon: 'They are next to the Palace, and their structure is remarkably complex. They are erected with vaults, arches, curved roofs, and according to our estimation we should bear witness that they will hold 10,000 horses with their grooms. A single shot from a cross-bow would hardly reach from one end of the building to the other, either in length or breadth.'[13]

Events in the Holy Land were to draw the knights from their seclusion. The First Crusade had taken Jerusalem and the Holy Land; the problem was how to prevent it being overrun by the infidel again. Manpower and resources were desperately needed. In 1127, to boost recruitment and gain recognition for their Order, the Templars came west.

THE TEMPLARS IN THE WEST

Hugh de Payens and five of his colleagues left the Holy Land for France and the Council of Troyes in 1127, where Hugh was to plead for papal recognition of the Order. He had a powerful advocate in the Cistercian St Bernard of Clairvaux, and was to gain the support of European princes. Although a new foundation, the Order was following a precedent put forward by Gregory VII (1073–85) that violence was valid if used to defend the Church, and developed by Urban II (1088–99) that fighting for God justified violence. St Bernard went further. He wrote 'when the knight of Christ kills a malefactor the act is not homicide, but if I may say so, malicide'.[14] Hugh put his case to the Council on 13 January 1129. He outlined the way in which the Order conducted itself in the cloister but emphasised that, unlike traditional orders, they spent their time outside the cloister fighting for God.

The simple precepts by which the Order lived in Jerusalem became the basis for the Order's Rule, given to them at the Council of Troyes. Although the Rule followed the standard monastic Rule of St Benedict, the organisation of the Templars mirrored that of the Cistercians. It exists in four French and six Latin texts. The French texts include lists of fairs and feasts and a number of individual statutes. Over the years it was added to and the composite Rule starts with the statutes drawn up in 1129. These are followed by the Hierarchical Statutes written in about 1165, penances, rules covering day-to-day life, the administration of the

Order and additional penances which Judi Upton-Ward dates to between 1257 and 1267. Finally there is an account of the initiation ceremony.[15]

The Rule starts with an introduction from the Council of Troyes, describing how Hugh came to them and told them about the Order. Those who heard Hugh are listed, and then it states that the Rule is given to the Poor Knights of Christ of the Temple, with the consent of the Pope and the Patriarch of Jerusalem. Although the Rule included the standard monastic statutes, provisions had to be made for when the Templar was on active service and could not attend divine office. It also had to take into account the fighting man's need to possess arms, equipment and horses.

The religious side of the Templar's life in the cloister was divided into attending the offices of night and day, fasting, and observing silence. On campaign, if it was not possible to hear the divine office, the Templar had to say 13 paternosters for matins, seven for each hour and nine for vespers.[16]

The monastic side of the Templar's life followed standard procedure. The knights slept fully clothed in dormitories with the lights on, they had to maintain silence and observe prayers. Whilst in the house they should not quarrel with other brothers, gossip or spread rumours. Absolute obedience to the Grand Master was required at all times.

Discipline was carried out, as in other monastic foundations, through the ordinary chapter, at which all brothers who had sinned or infringed the Order's rules were required to confess and do penance. Brothers could accuse each other of infringements, but only in the privacy of the chapter house, and a brother could be expelled from the Order for revealing its secrets, and for joining through simony (buying or selling entrance to the order), killing a Christian, theft, desertion in the time of battle, or desertion to the Saracen, and for sodomy.[17] Lesser crimes included disobedience, striking another brother, having contact with a woman, charging

into battle without permission and giving away the Order's possessions. For these crimes the brother lost his habit, was put in irons,
and worked with the slaves until his penance was over, or kept his
habit, was given corporal punishment and required to eat off the
floor like a dog.[18]

The Rule shows who could join the Order and how reception
should take place. Unlike other orders there was no novitiate term,
and no children were allowed to join. This reflected the Order's
purpose. It needed trained fighting men and, in order to facilitate
this, excommunicated knights were allowed to join provided they
had been absolved by a bishop. Associate members were also
encouraged to join, serving for a specified term, and usually
making a donation for the privilege.

The initiate to the Order underwent a rigorous examination as
to his background. He had to declare that he was in good health
and had no secret illness, that he was free from debts, and if he was
married that his wife was dead or in a convent. He had to prove
that he was a freeman, as the Rule forbade accepting serfs or slaves
into the Order. These provisions reflect the nature of the Order. A
fighting man had to be unencumbered and in good health, and the
emphasis on being free added to the exclusivity of the Order, and
its relationship to the social structure of the time. The hierarchical
section of the Rule explains this, and indicates that the knights
were in a minority, with other ranks of sergeants, squires and servants providing the back-up services, whilst the body of the Templars'
army was formed by Turcopoles, a light cavalry of Arabic extrac-
tion who were accustomed to the Saracens' fighting methods. Arab
interpreters may have been employed by the Templars. This was to
lead to accusations of fraternising with the enemy.

Once accepted, the Rule stated that the initiate knelt with both
hands on the Gospels and took vows that promised his life to God
and Lady St Mary. The Templar mantle was placed round his neck
'And the one who makes him a brother should raise him up and

kiss him on the mouth; and it is customary for the chaplain to kiss him also'.[19] These kisses were to be misinterpreted and used as ammunition with other accusations by those who wanted to destroy the Order in the fourteenth century.

A number of *retrais* or individual statutes give us information about the Templars on campaign. These detail how many horses and servants each rank of the Order should have, what equipment they could use, and where their tents were to be pitched. For example, Clause 169 states: 'The turcopolier brother should have four horses . . . he should have a small tent and the same rations as he receives in the convent; and pack animals to carry the rations, and the tent, and his cauldron . . .'[20]

The Templar Rule is an excellent illustration of feudal society in practice, but with a religious gloss. It reflects the world picture of their mentor, St Bernard of Clairvaux, who thought that every man had his own place in society. The knight was bound to preserve this orderly *status quo* or confusion would follow. But the knight was a member of a military aristocracy with a code of aggression. The military orders helped to harness this aggressive energy for good by focusing it on a common external enemy, the infidel.

Although the Patriarch of Jerusalem had been instrumental in the foundation of the Order, at the Council of Troyes the overall commander of the knights became the Pope, and the Templars owed allegiance only to him. This created an international organisation crossing national frontiers, and negating any obligation to secular lords. It was a dangerous political precedent, and it was compounded by the privileges that successive popes gave to the Templars. Two papal bulls, *Omne datum optimum, Milites Templi*, issued by Innocent II and confirmed by subsequent popes, set out the Order's privileges.

The privileges included freedom from paying tithes to the Church, licence to receive priests into the Order who could celebrate mass and give absolution, licence to have their own consecrated graveyards and to be able to bury anyone who asked in these. They were promised financial support from papal taxes. Permission was given to build towns, churches and cemeteries in deserted places. No bishop could excommunicate a Templar and when a country was under an interdict the Templars were allowed to open a church once a year so that their priests could celebrate mass and give absolution to the parishioners.[21] Most secular lords with Templar preceptories in their domains exempted the Order from local or national taxes. As a result, the Templars became unpopular as the local population struggled to pay papal taxes, church tithes and demands from their overlords, whilst the Templars grew rich at what seemed like their expense. In the early 1180s William of Tyre wrote that their possessions were the equal of kings, and they were neglecting humility, and carrying off booty from the Holy Land.[22]

Some idea of the extent of papal taxation and the hardship this caused to the general population in the British Isles can be judged from the tax levied by Gregory X in 1275, which was assessed as a tenth of the value of all lay and clerical property except that of the military orders. In 1276 petitions were sent to the Pope claiming that the tax was crushing the people of England. The Pope retaliated by threatening to excommunicate any who failed to pay and to exercise the right to distrain on their goods. To make matters worse, the tax collectors took an oath of honesty at the Temple church, and the final collections were delivered there for safe-keeping.[23]

THE STANDARD AND THE HABIT

Prior to receiving official papal recognition the Templars had no distinctive habit. Clause 17 commanded that the knights should wear white mantles and cloaks to show that they had come from the darkness of evil to the light of purity. Their robes were to be plain, with no decoration, but in summer 'we mercifully rule that, because of the great intensity of the heat which exists in the east, from Easter to All Saints, through compassion and no way as a right, a linen shirt shall be given to any brother who wishes to wear it'.[24]

The addition of the red cross to the robes came later. William of Tyre reports that 'It was in the time of Pope Eugenius III (1145–53), it is said that they began to sew on their mantles crosses of red cloth so that they might be distinguished from others. Not only the knights, but also inferior brethren called sergeants, wore the sign.'[25] The sergeants wore black surcoats with brown or black mantles over these. The red cross was an eight-pointed straight cross.

The knights and sergeants were told to keep themselves neat with short hair, but not to shave their beards. There were practical reasons for this on campaign, and they were described as having visages bronzed by the sun and the wind.

The Templars' arms and armour changed as technology and fashions in armaments changed. The early knights wore a hauberk or coat of mail with a white surcoat over this, and a padded leather jerkin underneath, chain mail hose covering the legs and iron shoes, and a conical helmet. They carried a shield, lance, and a Turkish mace, and were equipped for the campaign with three knives – a dagger, a bread knife and a pocket knife.

The Rule describes the distinctive black and white Templar banner, the Beausant or Piebald banner (Plate 1.2). This was a pennant divided into two horizontally with the black above and the white below, sometimes with the red cross emblazoned on the white area.[26] The interpretation of the banner is open to debate. Does it represent the triumph of good over evil, or the two classes within the Templars, the white of the knights and the black of the sergeants? No matter what it represented, the banner was the rallying

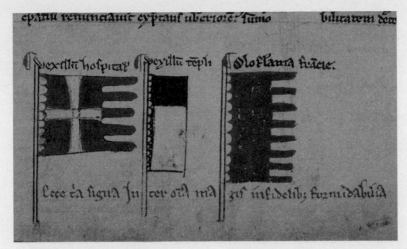

Plate 1.2 Templar banners
Corpus Christi, Cambridge Ms 16f 142e
Reproduced by permission of the Master and Fellows of Corpus Christi
College, Cambridge

point for the Templars on campaign. It was so important to them
that a duplicate was carried furled on a lance should the first fall in
battle.

DE LAUDE NOVAE MILITIAE
('IN PRAISE OF THE NEW KNIGHTHOOD')

Despite papal approval of the Order there were still those who
questioned the relevance of a religious order that shed blood as a
matter of course. In order to silence detractors, salve the consciences of his knights, and boost recruitment, Hugh de Payens
asked St Bernard to write an exhortation for the Order. The treat-
ise begins with an exhortation that Malcolm Barber suggests had
a profound influence on contemporaries and on later generations
as it created an image of knighthood harnessed to fight against

infidels and evil.[27] The exhortation shows the Templars as blessed martyrs justified in slaying the infidel. Safe in the knowledge that they fought the battle of the Lord, they could strike with confidence. Their lifestyle was shown to be joyful, sober and obedient. It included an itinerary of the Holy Land and its sites that the Templars would guard for pilgrims, thus whetting the appetite of pilgrims who wished to go there, and adding to the Templars' role of protectors of the Holy Places.[28]

Thanks to St Bernard's promotion of the Order, by the time Hugh de Payens died in c. 1136 the Order was well established. In 1149 they had been consigned the city of Gaza and its surrounding district in perpetuity. 'This charge the brothers, brave men and valiant warriors have faithfully and wisely guarded.'[29] Theoderic, recording his observations in the 1170s, saw Judaean villages revived by the Templars, and notes the strong castles and fortresses they had built.[30] Their deeds in the Holy Land were recorded by contemporaries, both Christian and Arab. They remarked on their courage in battle and siege, but also noted their arrogance towards others.[31]

THE HOLY LAND AND THE BRITISH ISLES

It could be argued that this book is about the Templars in the British Isles so that a discussion on their exploits in the Holy Land is superfluous. This would be to underestimate the grip that the struggle to keep the Holy Land in Christian hands had on western minds, and it would fail to take into account the vast drain of resources that the crusades had on the western economy, sucking in men and money. The Templars took great care to keep the west informed on what was happening in the Holy Land so that it could see what was happening to the men and material being shipped out there. Letters describing victories and defeats, and pleas for aid, were sent to the British Isles, copied by scribes and distributed around religious houses. Thus we find a letter in the annals of Burton on Trent abbey written by the Patriarch of Jerusalem in 1219 giving details of the Siege of Damietta. In 1259–60 the Grand Master of the Templars sent a letter to the west about the incursion of the Tartars, which was copied and circulated. This describes the Tartars as terrible and fearful (Plate 1.3). It tells that Damascus was taken, and it asked for urgent aid.[32]

Accounts of the disastrous Battle of Hattin in 1187, which decimated the Christian army and resulted in the death in battle and execution of Templar prisoners by Saladin, appears in Ralph of Coggeshall's *Chronicon Anglicorum*. News from the Holy Land helped to keep the struggle with the infidel in public minds, and papal taxation hit their purses. An example of this was *The Ordinance of the Saladin Tithe, 1188*, which levied a tax on one-tenth of the revenue and movables except arms, and the horses and arms of a knight or a cleric. The money was collected in each parish in the presence of the parish priest, the rural dean, a Knight Templar and a Knight Hospitaller, a servant of the king, and a clerk, a servant of the baron and a clerk of the bishop. A jury of six men attested that the right amount had been collected. Excommunication was the punishment for those not paying.

Appeals to go on crusades were preached from pulpits and market crosses. In 1188 Gerald of Wales accompanied Archbishop Baldwin on a journey through Wales to persuade men to take up the cross. About 3,000 men responded, all of them, according to Gerald, 'highly skilled in the use of spear and arrow, most experienced in military affairs and only too keen to attack the enemies of our faith. They were all sincerely and warmly committed to Christ's service.'[33]

The removal of manpower to the Holy Land was a direct effect of the involvement of the west. These men went to gain salvation, responding to a rhetoric that promised absolution and redemption to them. Redemption and salvation from their sins

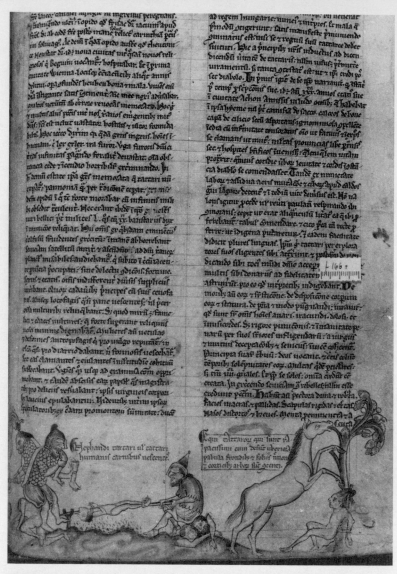

Plate 1.3 The Terrible Deeds of the Tartars, as illustrated by Matthew Paris Corpus Christi, Cambridge Ms 16f 166r. Reproduced by permission of the Conway Library, Courtauld Institute of Art and Master and Fellows of Corpus Christi College, Cambridge

were the ultimate aims of the first Templars, but as their numbers, wealth and power grew, they were perceived as losing these aims and becoming proud and worldly. The secrecy surrounding the Order began to raise speculations. Fact and fiction were to mingle, leading to accusations and the Order on trial.

CHAPTER TWO

THE TEMPLARS IN THE BRITISH ISLES: LONDON AND ITS SUBURBS

THE TEMPLARS AND LOCAL ORGANISATION

As the Templars acquired property outside the Holy Land, an organisation was needed to manage this, and to make sure that profits and resources from western estates were sent east. Other monastic foundations provided a model for the way in which this could be organised. The Cistercians had outlying granges managed by lay brethren who would send produce to the motherhouse. But the outlying estates of each Cistercian abbey were responsible only to that abbey and so had a limited sphere of action. Each Templar estate was the overall responsibility of the Grand Master and the chapter in Jerusalem, and was held in trust for the support of the knights of the Temple in Jerusalem.[1]

In order to facilitate the collection and transport of funds, to manage the estates, receive and admit recruits into the Order, and solicit gifts, each linguistic area was formed into a province with its own Master. Each province was subservient to the Grand Master in Jerusalem and a Visitor was nominated by the Grand Master to travel to each province to inspect it. Evidence from the trial in 1309 revealed that the Visitor Himbert Peraut had been in England in 1270 and was present at the provincial chapter at Temple Dinsley in Hertfordshire when the last English Master, William de la More, was received into the Order.[2]

It is not clear who appointed the Master of England. This may have been the Grand Master or the provincial chapter. There is evidence from France that on appointment the provincial Master took an oath of obedience to the Pope, the Grand Master and the Order, and promised to be faithful to the overlord of the province of which he was Master.

Although based primarily in London the Master was peripatetic, visiting other preceptories around the country. The overall government of the Order in the provinces was through the provincial chapters that, by the end of the thirteenth century, were usually held outside London at Temple Dinsley in Hertfordshire. The location of the provincial chapters in the first half of the thirteenth century can be traced through gifts of venison and wine made by Henry III to the Master for consumption at the chapter. Dinsley, Bruer in Lincolnshire, and Garway in Herefordshire all hosted chapters at this time.[3]

Masters of the Temple in England

The Masters of the Temple in England were:

1140	Hugh of Argentine
1150	Osto
1155–64	Richard de Hastings
1180–85	Geoffrey Fitz-Stephen
	William of Newham
1200–18	Aymer St Mawr
1218–28	Alan Martel
1229–48	Robert de Sandford
1259–60	Amadeus de Morestello
1264	Ambesard
1273–4	Guy de Forester
1276–90	Robert de Turville
1291–95	Guy de Forester

1296–98   Brian de Jay
1298–1312   William de la More

T.W. Parker includes Himbert Peraut, but this is a misunderstanding of the evidence given at the trial. Himbert Peraut was the Visitor. As the senior member of the Order present, he received new members to the Order at the provincial chapters they attended.[4]

Within each province were baileys under the overall control of the provincial Master. These were administrative and economic areas. The English baileys, in the order in which they appear in the 1185 inquest of lands, were: London, Kent, Warwick, Weston in Hertfordshire, Lincolnshire (sub-divided into Lindsey, Caburn, Tealby, Goulceby, the Soke of Bolingbroke and South Witham, which extended into Leicestershire and Rutland), Ogerston (which covered Huntingdonshire and Northamptonshire) and Yorkshire. There were other important estates in the 1185 inquest that were not included in baileys. These were in Essex, Oxfordshire, Berkshire, Gloucestershire, Herefordshire, Somerset and Wiltshire.[5] Map 2.1 shows the distribution of Templar preceptories and hospitals in the British Isles.

Within each bailey were preceptories that were enclosed conventual precincts. Jonathan Riley-Smith suggests that these would have included living quarters, a church and a cemetery.[6] As far as is known, there were no Templar castles in the British Isles, although the preceptories were defended by strong walls and a gatehouse. Surrounded by the demesne estates and their tenants, these were the interface between the Templars and the local community. The markets and fairs founded by the Order were part of this, as were the manorial courts that their tenants were obliged to attend.

Inside the preceptory, as specified by the Rule, the inhabitants were divided between knights, sergeants, chaplains and free servants, each dining at his own table and wearing a different livery. Evidence from the corrodians or pensioners given after the Order

Map 2.1 Templar preceptories and hospitals in the British Isles

was suppressed shows that often lay persons served with the Templars for many years and were rewarded with an honourable pension of food for life at the free servants table, a winter gown and a summer tunic and a small annuity.

Were the preceptories receiving houses for knights who were to fight in the Holy Land? The best evidence to answer this comes from the trial. This shows that few of those arrested in the British Isles had served overseas. The majority who were arrested were elderly, having been received into the Order as long as 40 years before, but several had only short terms of service, one had been received only 11 days before his arrest.

Did knights go overseas and return to their home province for rest and recuperation or retirement? One or two testimonies suggest this, but most would appear to have spent their whole time in the British Isles. However, the largest establishment broken up in 1308 was the hospital at Denny in Cambridgeshire that seems to have been a retirement home for elderly brothers and the sick and infirm. Skeletal evidence from excavations on the site shows that many of them suffered from degenerative bone diseases and arthritis,[7] and in the list of prisoners from Denny is one brother described as 'insane'.[8] But this evidence comes from the end of the Order's life and we do not know how many of those received in the British Isles left never to return, dying at the Siege of Damietta or the Battle of Hattin. The trial evidence also shows how few of the inhabitants of the preceptories belonged to the knightly class. The majority were sergeants or chaplains, and all were sparsely spread across the countryside with most of the 34 houses only having one or two occupants. This meant that the Templars must have relied heavily on lay people to administer and work their large estates, and run their markets and fairs. But each preceptory ought to have contained at least a preceptor and a chaplain. Many did not and the numbers arrested do not reflect the amount of property occupied by the Templars. Archaeological excavations have indicated that there were large complexes of buildings within the preceptory enclosure, and that often these were re-modelled several times. All of this activity needed an extensive labour force, organisation and capital.

The importance of the Templars to the local community and its economy is reflected in the survival of the word Temple in place-names. In Scotland, for example, Balantrodoch in Lothian was renamed Temple, and there are many examples of Temple being added to the original settlement name, such as Cressing Temple (Essex), Temple Hirst (Yorkshire), or Temple Guiting (Gloucestershire). Elsewhere we can trace the actual land the Templars owned through modern place-names. A good example of this is Temple Meads in Bristol, now the site of the Great Western Station.

SOURCES ON THE TEMPLARS IN THE BRITISH ISLES

In Yorkshire the commissioners who made an inventory of the possessions in the Templars' preceptories in 1308 found in Temple Cowton a chest containing all the charters pertaining to the Templars' Yorkshire estates, whilst in Faxfleet another chest was found with the Templars' Scottish deeds and records of other estates. These chests were locked and handed over to the exchequer. Eventually, and after much dispute, the Templars' archives were given to the Knights Hospitaller who were granted the majority of the Templars' lands.

Much of the evidence about their estates created by the Templars themselves is lost, but fortunately some major sources have survived. One was the Inquest of Lands of 1185 (Plate 2.1). The Inquest was taken at the request of Geoffrey Fitz-Stephen, who wanted to know the extent of the Order's holdings. This has echoes of the reason for the Domesday Inquest and, like Domesday evidence, was collected from sworn jurors and collated centrally. The survey lists the donor of the land, its tenants and the rents and services they owed. It includes the Templars' mills, and the churches of which they held the advowson. It is crammed full of local information about the size of holdings, the rent and the type of tenure that can be linked to other records and to the physical landscape.

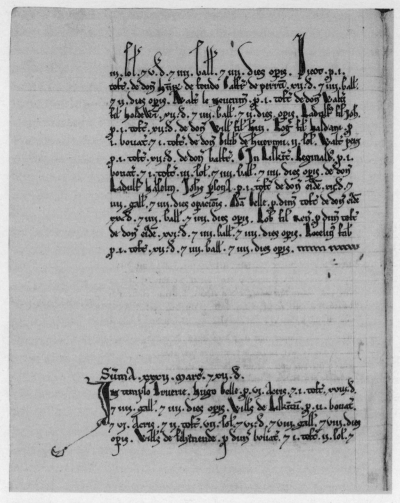

Plate 2.1 Folio 46v of the 1185 Inquest of Lands, showing the conclusion of the entry for Rauceby and Riskinton, Lincolnshire and the start of the entry for Temple Bruer
TNA E 164/16
Courtesy of The National Archives

The inquest itself ended up in the exchequer archives and is in The National Archives,[9] but a full printed transcript was published by Beatrice Lees in 1935.

We then move on 120 years to the Templars' final days. Following the arrests of the brothers in 1308, inventories were taken of the goods and chattels found in the local preceptories. From these we can get some idea of the size of the preceptory and what possessions were in it. The estates were put into the hands of commissioners to manage. They had to return accurate accounts of profits from produce and expenses on affairs to the exchequer. From 1308 to 1312 there are detailed accounts of how the Templar estates were being farmed, what livestock was kept, and what the estate was worth each year. These documents are in the PRO E358/18/19/20, E142/10–20, and E142/89–112 (see Appendix on Templar records in TNA).

There are summary records of the evidence given at the trial of the Templars that contain much indirect evidence about length of service and procedures. After the suppression of the Order, those who were owed pensions or corrodies claimed these. Evidence was taken on when and where the pensions were agreed, why they were issued, and what they received. Both the trial and the corrodies exist in printed versions published in the eighteenth century by David Wilkins and Henry Cole, but both versions are still in the original Latin.

Filling in the missing 100-odd years is possible by detective work using official records such as the *Charter*, *Close* and *Patent Rolls* that can be found in printed calendars. Details of land transactions involving the Templars are in the *Feet of Fines*, often reproduced by local record societies, and the amounts given to the Templars as royal alms will be found in the *Pipe Rolls*. The *Hundred Rolls* have details about the Order's rights and privileges, and lists of tenants and rents paid which can be compared to the 1185 Inquest, although not all of the Templars' property is covered. For the local historian, the quest for information about the Templars and the local community need not stop there. By linking series of documents it is possible to gain a greater understanding of where in a settlement the Templars' property lay and how this meshed with other property. Back projection can help to locate the Order's estates. One starting point might be the tithe map. Much Templar land remained exempt from tithes into the nineteenth century, and should be marked as such on the tithe map. Enclosure maps giving field-names will also help, and the maps associated with the 1910 Land Survey will help to locate individual holdings through field-names and earthworks.

Sale catalogues and estate maps can take the information back into the sixteenth century, and the Knights Hospitaller records provide a valuable link into the fifteenth and fourteenth centuries. If the preceptory became a farm or private house, probate inventories from the sixteenth–eighteenth centuries may reveal its structure, as will sites and monuments records, and excavation reports. These show that even a small preceptory could contain a complicated plan. Place- and field-names will show where Temple land once lay, as will earthworks.

Medieval chronicles will help to put the Order into their historical context. Although we cannot make the Templars come alive, nor reconstruct their life-style, these sources help us to understand their role, and their place in society.

LONDON IN THE TIME OF THE TEMPLARS

By the time of the Domesday Inquest in 1086 London was the largest city in the British Isles, and firmly established as the political, economic and administrative capital of England, and the country's major port. By the end of the thirteenth century it had a population of around 800,000 crammed within its walls, practising over 200 different crafts and trades as well as offering all manner of services. London sucked in goods and people from all over the country and from abroad.

The city of London was a network of 126 small parishes dominated by St Paul's Cathedral and 13 great conventual churches. These lay within 26 wards inside and outside the city walls. Tiers of local government controlled the city at ward level, parish level and city level with the Lord Mayor and the Aldermen being the top tier. Added to this were the important and influential livery companies. The Bishop of London controlled the religious life of the city.

The Thames was the main highway to and through the city and the city's main sewer, with the River Fleet and other tributaries draining effluent into it. Before the nineteenth-century embankments were built the Thames flowed swiftly, and this helped to shift the muck downstream at high tide. The Thames and the Fleet powered numerous corn, saw and fulling mills, making the riversides into industrial areas.

The city was crowded, polluted and noisy, with the sound of bells, street cries, and the bellowing of livestock being driven through the streets. Life took place in public on the streets. Butchers slaughtered on the streets and threw the waste on to the local midden, goods of all sorts were sold on the street, and a variety of industrial activity took place. For example, the Templars themselves owned two open forges on Fleet Street, and a corn and fulling mill on the Fleet.

London was vibrant with life and it was fully urbanised, satisfying all criteria for defining urbanisation suggested by Clark and Slack for the early modern period. It had a large, densely-packed population, a complex social structure and sophisticated local politics, it had a well-developed and diversified economic system, and a social, cultural and economic influence well beyond its immediate hinterland.[10] From its hinterland came goods, wagons heavily laden with corn or fleeces, wine in jars from Gascony (still an English possession), herds of cows, chickens, baskets of butter and eggs, cheeses by the cart-load, and people. A tax list of London's citizens from 1292 shows that tax payers came from France, Italy, Flanders, Germany, Wales, Scotland and Ireland and every county in England. The trades represented in the ward where the Temple was situated included barbers, hatters, chandlers, coopers, brewers, carpenters, a bookbinder, and a silk woman.[11] Luxury goods and essential craftsmen lay cheek by jowl with the Temple, which was an enclosed enclave within the polyglot hurly-burly of the city.

THE TEMPLARS IN LONDON

There is no documentary evidence to show how soon after Hugh de Payens visited the British Isles in 1128 that the Templars had an establishment in London. Lees suggests that this was in hand prior to Hugh returning to the Holy Land, but admits that this is an assumption as the first documentary evidence we have for a London establishment is 1144.[12] By that date we know that the Templars had been granted estates in Essex and elsewhere, and would have needed some sort of central organisation to run these. Also, a document dated between 1135 and 1148 confirms a grant by King Stephen of property in London.

As a conventual order the Templars needed space for an enclosure with cloisters, a church, hall and dormitory, and as a military order they needed somewhere to exercise themselves and their horses. Space was already at a premium in the city, and newcomers such as the Templars had to build outside the walls. Their first London establishment was in the parish of St Andrew Holborn. This became known as the Old Temple and was in the vicinity of what is now Southampton Buildings at the north end of Chancery Lane. The location is shown in Figure 2.1. John Stow wrote that the greater part of the Old Temple was pulled down in 1595 by a Master Roper. Addison claimed that part of the foundations of

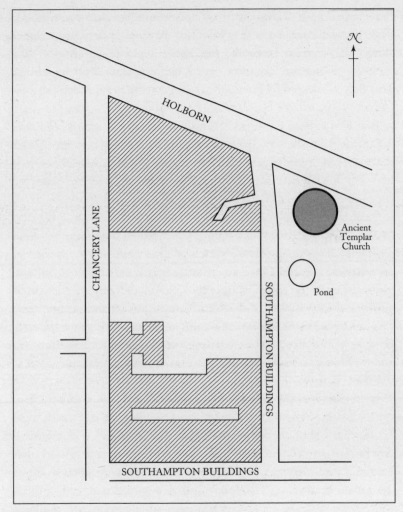

Figure 2.1 Location of the Old Temple
(Adapted from Williams, 1927)

the chapel were found in 1700, adjoining Southampton Buildings. Excavations in 1875 on the site of the London and County Bank, 324–5 High Holborn, produced a plan of a circular wall 20 inches in diameter and five-and-a-half feet thick with six arches. This was considered by the excavators to be the nave of the Templar chapel.[13]

We know that the Old Temple was set within its ditched compound and had its own graveyard by 1144 when the Order inadvertently became involved in the squabble between Stephen and Matilda. When Geoffrey de Mandeville, one of Matilda's supporters, was mortally wounded at the Siege of Burwell Castle, Cambridgeshire, the mantle of the Templars was thrown over him as he lay dying. Geoffrey had plundered Ramsey Abbey and had been excommunicated for this act, so could not be buried in consecrated ground. Once the mantle had been thrown over him he became the Templars' property. They placed his body in a lead coffin and took it back to the Old Temple, where they either hung it on a tree in the orchard or placed it in the ditch by the graveyard. Here it remained until the excommunication was reversed in 1163 and de Mandeville was reburied in the Templars' new graveyard at the New Temple.

In 1161, when the Templars ran out of space on this site, they sold it to the Bishop of Lincoln for 100 marks and a yearly rent of 7s. The charter that transferred the property contained a description of what the bishop was buying so we know what buildings it contained. On the north side, the site reached as far as the public road (High Holborn) and it was enclosed with a ditch and a bank that ran southwards as far as the garden. On the west of the site was a stable and a garden, beyond this was the church and the cemetery, other buildings included a kitchen, and bake- and brewhouses.[14] The site must also have contained a hall and a dormitory, and a bridge across the ditch. There is no mention of a cloister, and the lack of space to build a proper monastic precinct may have been one of the reasons for the Templars' move. The model for monastic precincts were those of the Benedictine and Cistercian abbeys. These were usually planned around an inner and outer courtyard, set within a walled enclosure guarded by a substantial gatehouse. Within the inner precinct were the church, the cloisters, refectory, dormitories, and the abbot's lodgings. The outer precinct housed the infirmary, guest chambers, kitchen, brewhouse, fish ponds and orchards. Only the New Temple aspired to this model. Excavations of Templar preceptories in the British Isles show these to have been more in the nature of fortified monastic farms, in the mode of the Cistercian grange than a monastery. One characteristic of Templar architecture was the church with a round nave, presumed to have been modelled on Solomon's Temple. This does not mean that all Templar churches had round naves, or that all churches with round naves once belonged to the Templars. There were probably more round churches in the twelfth century than have survived until today, as in the thirteenth century there was a general rebuilding of churches when the Romanesque apsoidal chancels and round naves were squared off. Re-modelling of churches and other buildings has been traced on several Templar sites, showing that they were cognisant with architectural fashions and new building techniques.

THE NEW TEMPLE

The New Temple was the heart of the Templars' operations in the British Isles. They moved there in about 1161 when the sale of the Old Temple was completed. The new site had a river frontage to the south and met Fleet Street in the north. It is assumed that the site was acquired from the Earl of Leicester as it was part of the Leicester fee in London, but there is no documentary evidence to support this. Like the Old Temple, it lay outside the city walls. In order to picture the river frontage when the New Temple was built we have to remove the Embankment and the modern road and see the river gate of the Temple leading directly on to the Templars' pier with their boats tied up beside it.

The Temple site today belongs to the societies of the Inner and Middle Temple, and although apart from the church little medieval fabric remains, it is still an enclosed space much as it would have been in the Templars' day. The cloisters may be modern but they occupy the same site as those of the Templars, and from the inventory taken in 1307 when the Templars were arrested we can reconstruct the location of other buildings on the site. In the fourteenth century the southern wall of the cloister was formed by the outer wall of the Knights' Hall. This stood where the Inner Temple Hall stands today. There is a small amount of medieval masonry in the west wall of the Inner Temple Hall. Outside the hall door stood a chapel that the inquisitor of 1308 called the Chapel of Blessed Mary, but which later writers suggest was dedicated to St Thomas. This was demolished in 1826. Omitted from the inventory but situated within the Temple compound was the Bishop of Ely's chamber in the north-west corner of the cloisters. The Ely bishopric had acquired this site in 1108–9, and had built an inn on it that became the bishop's lodging when he was in London. When the Templars acquired the site, some arrangement must have been made with the then bishop. For a plan of the Temple see Figure 2.2.

The cloister court is still visible on the 1677 Ogilby map of London, and the 1308 inventory shows that the complex of buildings outside the cloister included a cellar and a storehouse with a chamber over it, a kitchen, stable and brewery. In the inner precinct were the dormitory, the Master's wardrobe, and separate chambers for the Order's officials. Livestock in the compound included five horses, one diseased, and 30 pigs with their piglets with hay worth 76s 8d, rye, oats and malt in a granary which was sold for 40s, and the produce of the garden and the orchard worth

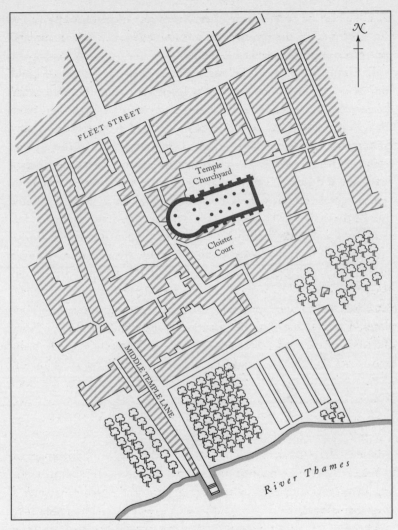

Figure 2.2 Plan of the New Temple precinct

60s. The list of expenses included the wages of those employed by the Order up to the time of the arrests. Adam the Mason received 4d a day. As he alone was recorded as a mason, he was probably employed for repairs to the fabric rather than on any major building work. There were six servants, each receiving 3d a day, a gardener who earned 2d a day and a porter who was paid one and a halfpenny a day. This does not seem like a large staff to run such a substantial establishment that included the knights and servants, eight chaplains and six clerks. Where are the cooks and domestic servants, the grooms, and the labourers?

The goods listed in the 1308 inventory show a rich assortment:

Goods	Value
In the cellar	
1 long and 4 canvas cloths	8s
4 maple cups with silver feet	2 marks
10 maple cups without feet	40s
22 silver spoons	20s
2 silver cups	16s
2 cross-bows	3s
4 cups	5s
3 coffers	2s
4 tankards	8d
In the chamber over the dispensary	
Iron work for a cart	4s
3 pair of traces for one window	12d
Ironwork for a window	3s
3 stone of hemp	18d
2 tables	12d
2 spoons	6d
3 pieces of old lead	3s
Iron for a mill	12d
1 iron fork	6d

In the Kitchen

2 great brass pots	40s
7 brass pots	58s
5 pitchers, 5 brass pots, and 1 great brass plate in the furnace, 1 brass mortar	£4 7s 6d
2 grid irons	2s
2 dishes of iron for frying	2s
1 iron fork	6d
1 iron tripod	2s

In the Stable

1 palfrey of John de Stokes, the Treasurer	4 marks
1 palfrey of William de la More, the Master	100s
2 horses of Brother Michael, the Preceptor	4 marks
1 cart horse, 2 horses for the mill	20s
2 mills	4 marks

In the Brewery

1 lead	40s
1 lead	30s
7 vats, 15 casks, 9 empty hogsheads, 1 pipe, 3 tuns	30s
Oven utensils	20s
20 hoops	2s 6d
2 pieces of lead	16d
1 press	20s
1 great trestle table	5s
4 sleeping tables (used for malting)	6s 8d
4 tables and 8 trestles	40d
2 andirons	2s
1 barrel	2s
1 bowl	1s

In the Wardrobe of the Master

1 gold buckle	5s
11 pieces of Birmingham	22s

6 pieces of Birmingham	36s
5 pieces of Birmingham	40s
3 bed-coverings	£6
1 hanging	1 mark
1 gown	half a mark
1 pelisse of budge (lambs' fur)	5s
1 covering for a bench and a little flask	5s
1 cross-bow without bolts	half a mark

In a canvas sack

3 over-tunics of fur, 1 white cloak belonging to Brother William de Scurlag	40s
1 bread basket	half a mark
2 books	6s
2 barrels	2s
1 cloth cloak, 2 cloths	10s
1 pair of boots	2s
2 bowls	3s
1 wash hand basin	6d
1 vestment	1 mark
Covering for a bench	6d

In the Chamber of Brother John de Stokes, the Treasurer

1 scarlet coverlet	half a mark
1 mat	4s
1 double linen sheet	18d
2 linen sheets	2s
2 veils	3s
1 cloak and 1 curtain	2s
1 hooded tunic and 2 pairs of boots	4s
2 coverings for a bench, 1 little flask, 5 cushions	3s
1 cross-bow	2s
1 sack for clothes and 1 trunk	2s

1 wash hand basin and 1 basin	12d
1 maple cup	40d
1 andiron and 1 iron fork	6d
1 cup	2s

In the Dormitory

1 scarlet coverlet	half a mark
4 linen sheets, 1 canvas sheet, 1 blanket	half a mark
2 robes	20s
1 mantel	half a mark
1 cloth, 2 towels, 1 ewer, 1 wash hand basin, 1 casket	3s
1 coverlet, 2 pairs of linen and 1 canvas sheet, 1 blanket	10s
1 sack for garments, 1 trunk of Brother Michael Baskerville	3s
1 mantel	2s
1 casket	12d
2 tunics	3s
1 cap	half a mark
1 clothes back, 1 ewer, 1 wash hand basin, 1 sword, 1 axe from Ireland and of Brother William de Hertford	1 mark
1 coverlet, 2 pairs of linen sheets, 1 blanket, 1 canvas 1 marksheet, 1 casket, 1 over tunic, 1 ewer, 1 wash hand basin, 1 clothes bag 1 cap, 1 sword of Brother Thomas de Staund	1 mark

In the Chamber of Brother Thomas de Burton

1 coverlet, 2 carpets, 4 pairs of linen sheets, 1 coverlet for a bed, 3 towels, 1 robe of baret (woollen cloth) 1 robe of say for summer wear, 3 hoods, 3 pairs of linen cloths, 1 basin, 1 wash hand basin, 1 casket, 1 clothes sack and 1 mantel	40s

In the Chamber of the Prior

1 counterpane, 1 trundle bed	10s
4 cushions	18d
3 carpets from the chapel of the Blessed Mary but found in the prior's chamber	20s

In the Chamber of Brother Richard de Herdwick

1 coverlet, 2 pairs of linen sheets, 1 bread platter, 1 canvas sheet, 2 corslets, 2 forms, 1 pair of boots, 1 trunk, 1 clothes bag, 1 great pouch	1 mark
2 silver cups with covers	1 mark
12 silver spoons	10s
1 pair of stools	5s
1 mantel three-fold	5s
1 bound casket, 1 sword, and one chest	4s
1 sealed chest with the charters and muniments of the house.[15]	

The New Temple contained the richest assemblage of goods of all the Templar preceptories. We can see from the inventory that the occupants were ready for travel with each having a clothes bag and a trunk, but what is perplexing is the lack of arms and armour in the list. This consists of a corslet, two swords, an Irish axe, and four cross-bows, one incomplete. We have to assume that the brothers were allowed to take their arms with them when they were arrested, and we know that the Master, preceptor, the treasurer and others were allowed their own possessions in prison, and had access to their own mounts.

The focus of the New Temple was its church (Plate 2.2). Building started on this in 1166. The Great Church or The Round, now the nave, was completed in 1185, dedicated to the Virgin Mary and consecrated by the Patriarch of Jerusalem. A plan of the church can be seen in Figure 2.3. The church that we see today is a reconstruction, owing to its partial destruction by incendiary bombs on

Plate 2.2 The exterior of the Temple Church, London
Reproduced by permission of English Heritage, NMR

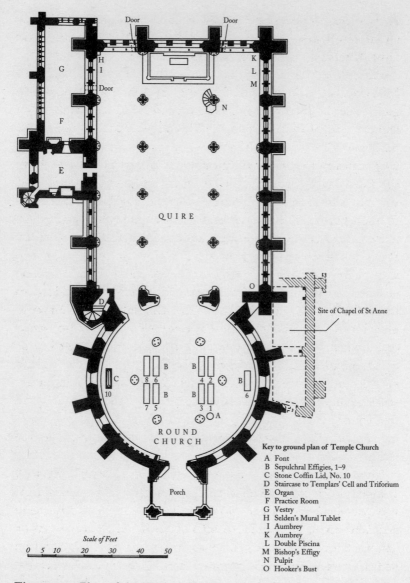

Figure 2.3 Plan of the Temple Church (Baylis, 1900)

Key to ground plan of Temple Church

A Font
B Sepulchral Effigies, 1–9
C Stone Coffin Lid, No. 10
D Staircase to Templars' Cell and Triforium
E Organ
F Practice Room
G Vestry
H Selden's Mural Tablet
I Aumbrey
K Aumbrey
L Double Piscina
M Bishop's Effigy
N Pulpit
O Hooker's Bust

10 May 1941. These destroyed the wooden roof and created such an inferno that some of the stone columns split. The church was virtually rebuilt and reconsecrated in 1954.[16]

Prior to its destruction by German bombs, other alterations had taken place. In 1678 the Chapel of St Anne was blown up by gunpowder in order to stop a disastrous fire spreading to the main church. All the buildings in the cloister were destroyed at this time, partly because the Thames was frozen and beer had to be used instead of water to put the fire out and partly because when the Lord Mayor arrived with his sword of state and retinue he was not allowed entry so refused to send any help. Alterations to the church in the seventeenth and eighteenth centuries reflected changes in taste and liturgical conventions. Sir Christopher Wren added wainscoting and box pews, and a pulpit festooned with cherubs. In the eighteenth century, as architectural fashion changed, so battlements, buttresses and a belfry were added to make the church more 'Gothic'. The Gothic idioms were continued by Robert Smirke in the 1825 restoration. Smirke also started on essential repairs to the interior, but money ran out before he could complete his work. In 1840 the Inner and Middle Temple societies underwrote a major restoration that removed the wainscoting, the pews and an organ screen, and scrubbed away all the whitewash that had been put on the walls during the preceding centuries. This revealed traces of gold and silver paint on the ceilings.[17]

The church we see today is bare of painting and ornament, stripped down to its stone ribs (Plate 2.3). In the Templars' time it would have been a riot of colour, light and sound, with eight chaplains taking it in turns to say perpetual masses for the dead. The 1308 inventory shows that part of it was carpeted and that on its five altars stood candlesticks and sacred vessels in silver, gilt and ivory. The interior was hung with banners, and the whole impression would have been one of opulence.

Plate 2.3 Interior of the Temple Church, London
Reproduced by permission of English Heritage, NMR

Plate 2.4 The west door of the Temple Church, London
Reproduced by permission of English Heritage, NMR

Diverse vestments and relics were found in the vestry. The relics were contained in a gilt case and included the sword which killed St Thomas a Becket, and two crosses on which were sections of the wood from the cross on which Christ was crucified. The appraisers felt that they could not give a value to the relics.

The earliest architectural feature surviving today is the great processional west door (Plate 2.4), which is a seven-arched Norman doorway with dog-toothed decoration and statues in its niches. The whole may have been coloured. The doorway is protected by a deep porch that connected it to the cloisters. Similar doorways can be seen at Dunstable Priory, St Albans Abbey and Ely Cathedral and are probably the work of local craftsmen rather than foreign sculptors. The statues on the doorway are thought to be Templars, but this cannot be proved. All are beardless, and some wear tunics which button at the neck, a fashion that did not emerge until after the suppression of the Templars.[18]

The choir or oblong was consecrated on Ascension Day 1240 in the presence of Henry III. This is in the Early English style with pointed lancet windows, and a roof supported on polished Purbeck marble columns. It has three aisles and five bays, with a squared-off east end. Excavations during the 1950s' restoration discovered what might have been the Templars' treasury underneath the church. This was an under-croft lying beneath the south aisle, and was clearly earlier than 1240 as the choir was built on top of it. It consisted of a chamber 42 feet long and 13 feet wide with a stone bench running round the walls above which were lockers that once had wooden doors. Once it had three windows but these appeared to have been walled up at an early date. There was evidence that the walls had once been decorated with rectangular lines and large and small circles in black.[19] If this was the treasury, this could be the remnants of a counting system, a permanent exchequer on the wall. If the underground chamber did not house the treasury, was it the Templars' secret chapter room, or the cellar mentioned in the inventory?

The most poignant links with the Templars in the church are the effigies of knights lying in the Round. These are probably not Templars themselves but associates of the Order who took its mantle in order to be buried in the Templars' precincts. One of the effigies is probably William Marshal, although not necessarily the one bearing his name today.

William Marshal's association with the Order went back a long way. He had fought with them in the Holy Land during his youth and had promised to die under the Templars' mantle and had purchased two silk cloths for the purpose. His household almoner was a Templar, Brother Geoffrey, and he drew up Marshal's final will that left the Templars the manor of Upleden (Upleaden).

GILBERT MARSHAL
Fourth Earl of Pembroke (died1241)

Plate 2.5 Gilbert Marshal

The hagiographical account of William's last hours in the *Histoire de Guillaume Marshall* says that the Master of the Templars, Aimery de St Maur, was sent for, and the Templars' mantle was laid across William as he had instructed. His body was carried to Reading Abbey for a mass and was then taken to Staines where the great barons of England joined the cortege. After a mass at Westminster Abbey he was interred in the Temple Church beside his old friend Aimeric de St Maur who had died in the meantime. Less

Plate 2.6 Effigy in Temple Church, possibly Geoffrey de Mandeville
Reproduced by permission of English Heritage, NMR

charitable accounts suggest that William chose to die wearing a Templar's mantle because he had been excommunicated by the Bishop of Ferns through a dispute over land and would otherwise have been forbidden a burial in consecrated ground.[20]

Evocative as these effigies are, they not in their original positions in the church, and neither do they rest near the bones they represent. Seven of them probably belong to the stone coffins discovered in 1827 and reburied under the centre of the Round. Not only is there a mystery about the provenance of the effigies, but also about the original number. Stow, writing in 1598, described eight effigies. By 1728 a ninth had been added. Stow writes that the four cross-legged effigies are William Marshal and his sons. It is possible that some of the effigies represent the Marshal family, and that another may be Geoffrey de Mandeville. None of them bear any Templar emblems or insignia so they are likely to have been associate knights.

THE TEMPLARS AND THEIR NEIGHBOURS

The Templars compound was an enclave that was not subject to the laws of the land nor to the city of London; and their church being extra-parochial was beyond the authority of the Bishop of London. Immediately outside their premises the Templars owned mills, shops, houses and market stalls. In 1159 Henry II granted them a mill on the Fleet by Baynard's Castle with a house on Fleet Bridge. A plot of land was added to this by Robert Fitzwalter.[21] A mill, whether used for fulling, corn or sawing, was an important asset as a landlord's tenants were obliged to use his mill or pay a fine. Water mills needed a good head of water to work well, and there was great competition for this resource in medieval London. In 1306 a petition was sent to Parliament by the Earl of Lincoln complaining that by diverting the water of the Fleet to their mill at Baynard's Castle the Templars had lowered the flow of the river so that boats could no longer use it. The Fleet was notorious for its filth and diverting the flow added to this. Earlier in the thirteenth century there had been complaints that the Templars had planted willows beside the Fleet, impeding access by boat, and by 1307 they had built a quay on it as well.[22]

In Fleet Street the Templars owned two forges, and a number of houses on plots of land varying from a few feet to an acre. These were often let on repairing leases. For example, on 12 June 1303 a lease for life for 12s per annum was granted to Robert le Dorturer and his wife Emma of a messuage and one acre of land in Holborn. Robert had to agree to attend the Templars' court every three weeks and to repair the cottage's roof at his own expense, and when he died his heirs were to pay the Master 6s 8d as death duty. In all, the Templars held 18 tenements in Fleet Street and a further nine close by in the Leicester Fee. These were rented by fairly affluent citizens, paying between 6d and 19s a year for rent. A little further south in the village of Charing and in New Street, where they had other properties, their tenants were craftsmen and trades-people often occupying market stalls and shops.[23]

Using the London Eyres, records of the Mayors' courts and the London Hustings, it is possible to get a picture of life in the streets surrounding the New Temple. This was often violent and always colourful and sometimes involved the Templars. In 1272 Simon le Waleys, the servant of a papal nuncio staying at the Temple, was involved in a street brawl with Lawrence the Barber who was killed. Simon fled and was declared an outlaw. In the same year Walter Van of Wandsworth was drowned whilst crossing the Thames in a boat. Seizing their chance, the Templars impounded the boat worth 10s and kept it. In 1276 William Ashby went to sell silks to Maud, the wife of Adam de Linton, a near neighbour of the Templars. Adam and his servant hid whilst the business was being transacted and at a crucial point leapt out and killed William. This was pre-sumably a case of adultery as Maud and her maid were arrested and taken to Newgate gaol where they died. Meanwhile the Templars seized Adam's goods and hustled him into the Temple precincts where he worked as a clerk for them. Eventually Adam was found not guilty of murder and pardoned. Adam was within his rights claiming sanctuary in the Temple, as this was one of the Order's privileges. As he is described as Master Adam throughout the proceedings, he was probably a lawyer, and may have been one of the attorneys employed by the Templars.

Another near neighbour of the Temple was a brothel. On 20 March 1301 two men assaulted Adam de Coteler as he stood at the door of the brothel. He ran into the house and they pursued him, so that he had to escape from a window. Later the same two men, much the worse for drink, were involved in a brawl with the Bishop of Durham's men at the Temple Bar.[24]

Within the New Temple precincts themselves there was a more peaceful atmosphere, with some of the inhabitants being pensioners of the Order rewarded with board, lodging, clothes and an annuity for their loyal service. We know most about the corrodies at the end of the Templars' existence because after the Order was suppressed they claimed their allowances and royal commissioners took inquests into these. These gave the date and place that an agreement between the Order and the pensioner was made, and what it entailed. For example, one of the pensioners of the New Temple was Roger Love who was given a pension for loyal service as a clerk to the Order. He was to receive food at the clerk's table for life, a robe in the livery of the free servants and a stipend. In return, the Templars would receive any goods he owned when he died. Others entered into agreements whereby the Templars maintained them in return for a gift of property or rents. In 1306 Michael de la Greene was given food for life at the New Temple, promised a robe at Christmas in the free servants livery, a summer tunic and a pension of 5s a year. When he was too old and infirm to eat in the hall he was to be served in his room. For this he gave six acres of land and eight of meadow and a messuage with a further 20 acres in Wycombe. During the trial period the corrodies were paid from the Templars' estates, and once their property was given to the Hospitallers they became liable for these pensions.[25]

THE TEMPLARS AND THE SUBURBS

London in the Templars' time was surrounded by fields and marshes on both sides of the river. Directly opposite to the New Temple and outside the city's authority was Southwark. Here an autonomous and thriving commercial centre developed around a number of manors and manorial courts that were ideally situated to exploit the trade on its way across the river to the city. Southwark consisted of five parishes and five manors, the most important of which was owned by the Bishop of Winchester. In 1113 a manor facing the river and bordered by willows, known as Wideflete or Withyflete (Willow ditch), was granted to Bermondsey Abbey. They leased it to the Templars in 1166 for a rent of 10 marks a year. The date is significant as it coincides with the move from Holborn to the New Temple, and meant that the Templars controlled both banks of the river at this point. From their pier on the north bank they could despatch messengers to the south, and in return wheat, hay, withies and reeds could be ferried across for use at the New Temple (see Map 2.2 for the Templars' possessions in the suburbs).

The Templars' manor adjoined the large manor and palace of the Bishop of Winchester. As it was liable to flood, it was surrounded by drainage ditches and embankments. In 1308 the manor included a house and five mills in need of repair and a sixth that was ruinous. There was about a hide of land plus an acre of arable and meadows that lay outside the ditches in Southwark field and Lambeth marshes. The ruinous condition of the manor in 1308 could be the result of the arrest of the Templars and the removal

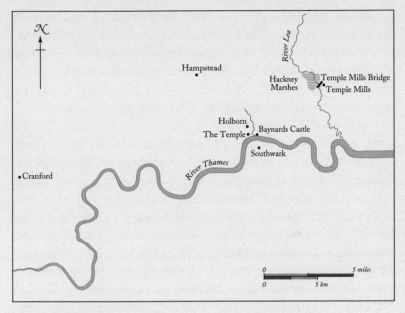

Map 2.2 Templar possessions in London and its suburbs

of their authority or it could represent long-term decay. Given the small number of Templars arrested not only in London but across the whole of the British Isles, it would seem that the Order was in disarray and this was reflected in the state of its holdings. Despite instructions to the commissioners who took over the manor on the king's behalf, nothing was done, and when the Hospitallers took over the manor the mills had disappeared.

At the time the Templars leased the manor Southwark was beginning to develop into a fully-fledged urban centre, although still retaining large agricultural manors on the riverbank. Many of the area's inhabitants were involved with the river, either as watermen or boat builders, whilst labourers could earn good wages working on London Bridge and the new building projects struggling to keep up with a rising demand on both sides of the river. Competition for labour was fierce and this too may have contributed to the state of the manor in 1308. The better survival of records for the Bishop of Winchester's neighbouring manor shows that crops of rye, barley, peas, beans and leeks were grown, and that nettles, reeds, willows and reeds were sold from the manor. The manor also included a large hay meadow. Under similar conditions the Templars' manor probably grew the same crops and added to its profits by the sale of its natural resources. The six water mills were probably a mixture of corn and fulling mills. It is possible that grain from the Templars' country estates was brought here by river to be milled into flour for the London market.

The manor of Wideflete became the manor of Paris Gardens, noted in the sixteenth century for its bear-baiting arena. In the seventeenth century it became known as the Holland Leaguer and was still an island surrounded by drainage ditches, containing a gatehouse, manor house and access to a ferry called the Cats Ditch.[26]

To the east of London lay an isolated area of low-lying marshes and bogs drained by the River Lea and known as Hackney Marshes. Despite its waterlogged condition, this area had excellent soil for arable crops and lush water meadows, as well as a good head of water to drive mills. William Hastings made the Templars a gift of about 110 acres on the marshes some time before the 1185 inquest was taken. The Templars kept 24 acres for themselves and divided the rest between 13 tenants in blocks of five and ten acres for rents of 1s 6d or 3s and the performance of labour service during hay-making. A further four tenants rented part of the boggy part of the marshes for 2s and a pound of pepper, plus labour during hay-making. The value of the Hackney estate in 1185 was 80s 8d.[27]

The 1308 inventory shows how land values had risen in this area. Meadow was leased for 3s 4d and the total value of the manor had risen to £16 18s 4d, of which nearly 40 per cent came from fines levied in the manorial court. The tenants were still required to mow the demesne meadows, but these had been cut to 12 acres and the customary tenants could commute their labour service for 7d an acre mown.[28]

The Templars had a mill on the Lea with a channel deflecting water from the river to drive it. They also constructed a bridge across the river that until 1758 was the only crossing of the Lea at this point. Both of these sites can be traced today through place-name evidence. Temple Mill lies under the A106 and Temple Bridge marks the eastern interchange of the A106 where it joins Ruckholt Road.

Channelling the Lea for their own purposes shows the Templars to have been aggressive landholders, whilst the rise in value of the land reflects two trends. One is the rise in population, creating a demand for land and resources; the other the creation of a landless class of labour who could be employed to work for wages that enabled the commutation of labour service into cash. In so far as the Templars were concerned, this was an ideal arrangement as it avoided the need to market the produce of the demesne and converted their holdings into money that could be sent to help the Order's efforts overseas. However, the Templars were not alone in this area of commuting labour services to cash or cutting the amount of the demesne. Exactly the same process took place on the Bishop of London's estates in Hackney and Stepney, but at a later date, between 1318 and 1362. The time lag may indicate that the Templars were in the vanguard of change, but it is more likely to have been a pragmatic and more convenient way for them to farm at a time when the Order lacked personnel to manage its estates.[29]

To the west of London the Templars held the manor of Cranford (St John) on the Bath Road. Again this was a low-lying manor on heavy soil and was surrounded by the River Crane. The Templars were responsible for the upkeep of the bridge across the river. They acquired this manor in about 1240 from Joan Hakepit who had been given it as part of her dowry. Two years later John le Chapeler and his wife added a house and a virgate of land to it in return for a pension and food for life from the Templars. The whole manor was leased out in 1308.[30] This is another example of the Templars preferring money rents to farming and managing the land for themselves.

In addition to this manor the Templars also had 40 acres of land in Hendon, acquired in 1243 and known as Temple Croft, and an estate in Hampstead that was given to them by Henry II sometime between 1185 and 1199. The Hampstead estate linked what is now Lisson Grove and Marylebone. In 1275 it contained at least 140 acres of wood. In 1308 the Lisson end of the estate was planted with 14 acres of peas and 35 acres of oats, and in 1338 100 acres of arable had been planted, with three acres of meadow let out to Thomas Larcher on a life lease. During the 70 years the Templars held the estate there had been considerable woodland clearance and conversion of this land to arable. With hungry London on its doorstep, this would have been a logical and lucrative development.[31]

Between 1185 and 1338 evidence from the 1185 Templars' inquest and the 1338 Hospitallers Inquest shows that the value of land in London rose by 37.5 per cent. Landlords in general kept less of their demesne in hand and commuted labour services into cash, whilst woodland was cleared and converted into arable to produce corn to feed the growing urban population. Yet the survey taken in 1308 shows that the Templars' property was unkempt and ruinous. Did this reflect the Order's gradual demise and slackening grasp on affairs, or is this part of a general trend that is related to the growth of a free peasantry no longer dependent on the customary tenancies but able to buy and sell in the land market as they wished? These questions may be answered in the subsequent chapters on the Templars in the countryside.

CHAPTER THREE

THE TEMPLARS AND THE
COUNTRYSIDE: EASTERN ENGLAND

The Templar estates in the British Isles were welded on to an ancient landscape where most settlements already existed and most land was already apportioned. The Templars relied on the munificence of existing landowners to give them estates, and on their own efforts to improve and add to these. It is no coincidence that the land given to the Templars was often on the poorer soils, low-lying marshlands or densely wooded areas that had to be cleared before the land could be planted. The cleared and drained land meant that new settlements had to be built for the labour needed to work the land. In Lincolnshire, for example, seven settlements founded after Domesday were associated with Templar land. These included the settlement around the important preceptory of Temple Bruer.

The Templars already had experience in reclaiming waste in the Holy Land where they had restored Judaean villages destroyed by the Romans to productivity.[1] They were encouraged in their efforts to reclaim the waste by successive popes. Alexander IV, for example, sent a bull out in 1256 giving the Order permission to build towns, churches and cemeteries in desert places.[2] The desert places included the west as well as the east. George Duby gives examples of the Templars organising settlements in the Lyonnais of France,[3] and, as will be shown, the same process went on in the British Isles.

The improvement and clearance of land was a characteristic of land owners in the thirteenth century, especially monastic landlords. The *Annals of Dunstable Augustinian Priory* in Bedfordshire record that they were improving their land in the 1230s, and embarked on a new building programme on their farms in the 1250s. Prior to the 1230s the priory claimed that one-twentieth of its revenues were sent to the Holy Land. By 1230 they were putting more of their income back into their estates. This represented a hardening of attitude towards the struggle to keep the Holy Land in Christian hands, and the necessity to increase production as the population increased.

It has been argued by Michael Postan that the medieval economy of the British Isles was dominated by population trends. In the thirteenth century and the first half of the fourteenth century the population rose faster than the production of food. In order to increase food production, marginal land was brought into production, and existing holdings were split into smaller and smaller units. Demand for food sent up prices and profits for the landlords, whilst the exhaustion of the supply of land created a landless class of peasants who were available as wage labour, and who needed to be fed from those who had land. This advanced the development of the cash economy and led to a decrease in land held for labour service rather than cash rent, and helped to break down feudal society into one based on a market and money economy (see Figure 3.1).[4]

The aim of the Templars' farming activities in the west was mainly to raise money and resources to be sent to the east. The fighting arm of the Order needed a constant supply of manpower to replace those killed in action, as well as horses, harness, arms, armour and fodder. From 1207 these could be sent east in the Order's own fleet based at Marseilles.[5] Each preceptory was obliged to send a proportion of its annual income to Jerusalem. For farms in the British Isles far divorced from the theatre of war this was in

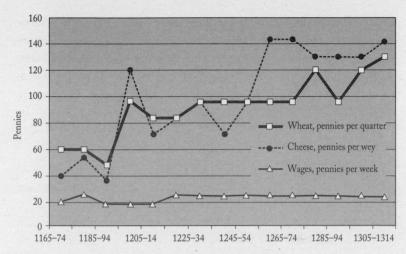

Figure 3.1 Cost of living, 1165–1308

the form of ready money. The need to raise cash should be reflected in farming practices with a trend that kept only a small amount of demesne in hand with the maximum amount of land on each estate being leased out for a money rent, and for labour service to be commuted to cash as well.

There is evidence from other landlords that whether or not the demesne was kept in hand was connected to economic and market forces. Our best evidence for this comes from the long series of extents and accounts that have survived for monastic and episcopal estates. In general these indicate that in the early fourteenth century it was more profitable to rent out the demesne, with a fall in the amount of demesne in hand on these estates of 30.7 per cent between 1269 and 1310.[6] Leasing the demesne for a cash rent changed the structure of local society. Instead of customary labour working the lord's land, the farmer who leased it hired labour instead, and the old ties of obligation were eroded.

The Templars' farm management had another force to deal with as well. Events in the Holy Land and the long shadow of the infidel had to be taken into account. Key dates to watch for are as follows:

Good news from the east

1148–49	The Second Crusade
1149	The grant of Gaza to the Templars
1153	The Fall of Ascalon to the Christians
1189	The Third Crusade
1218	The Fifth Crusade, Siege of Damietta
1240	The Crusade of Richard of Cornwall
1271	The Crusade of the Lord Edward

Bad news from the east

1187	Battle of Hattin
1244	Defeat at La Forbie
1291	The Fall of Acre and the evacuation of the Holy Land

Barber gives the fatality figures for major defeats in the Holy Land:

1164	60 out of 64 knights killed at Harim
1187	290 knights killed at Cresson and Hattin
1237	20 out of 120 knights killed at the Siege of Darbask
1244	277 out of 300 knights killed at La Forbie
1250	280 knights killed at Mansourah

These heavy casualties meant a constant demand for new recruits and for money to replace horses and arms. This should be reflected in farming practices as the Templars tried to maximise their profits, for example changing from arable to sheep in order to export the lucrative fleeces. As they had a special licence to export wool, this would appear to be a feature of their planning.

Changes in agriculture are not necessarily the result of population pressure or external affairs but of events beyond human control.

Bad weather could ruin a harvest, animal plagues could decimate the livestock. Two years after the Templars settled in the British Isles the country was hit by a catastrophic animal plague.

In the same year (1130), over the whole of England, murrain among the cattle and pigs was worse than any within living memory; so that in a village where ten or twelve ploughs were in use, not a single one was left: and a man who owned two or three hundred pigs found himself with none. After that the hens died and then meat and cheese and butter were in short supply . . .[7]

Similar disasters followed throughout the thirteenth century. There was a sheep plague in 1243, a poor harvest in 1253, an equine plague in 1254, a scarcity of corn in 1255, with high prices, and in 1258 another bad harvest followed by a long, wet autumn. In 1270 there were bad weather and poor harvests again, and a decade later sheep plague reappeared, whilst in 1294 a late harvest led to scarcity and starvation for many.[8]

Local conditions also played a part in the way the Templars farmed their land. Soil type, topography and climate meant that different methods were the practical and pragmatic result. Some areas were better for pasturing livestock, others for growing crops. The geography of the area could influence the settlement pattern and the communications route, and help to produce a local identity. Were the Templars part of this, farming as their neighbours did, following the same customs and integrating into the local community? Or did they stand outside the local community, set apart, safe within their precincts, guarded by royal and papal privileges?

The following chapters will look at these questions. They are divided into regions and, in order to compare like with like, examples of estates from the same region have been chosen for comparison. We must remember, however, that the Templars were not professional farmers. They were soldier monks dedicated to a way of life that combined contemplation with bloodshed, and the conventual life with action in the field. They came from a section of society used to command rather than to labour, and for the practical organisation of their farms they relied on the brother sergeants and the free servants, as well as the agricultural professionals such as the reeve, shepherd, ploughman and herdsman to keep their land fully productive and making a profit for the defence of the Holy Land.

ESSEX

The following sections cover the counties of Essex, Hertfordshire, Cambridgeshire, Huntingdonshire, Norfolk and Suffolk. The location of Templar property in eastern England is shown on Map 3.1.

In the Middle Ages this was one of the most well-developed and densely populated areas of the country. New settlements were only possible by using the marginal areas of the fens or marshes, or by clearing woodland, and the Templars had to look to existing landholders to give them estates here. The Templars were astute in attracting the attention of the crown, and some of their most important early estates were the gift of King Stephen and his Queen, Matilda. The best-known of these gifts was the estate at Cressing in Essex, and it is the great barns at Cressing Temple that symbolise the power of the Templars in the countryside and provide a link between the present and the past.

Cressing was given to the Templars by Matilda, Queen of England and Countess of Bolougne in 1137 for the benefit of the soul of her father, her husband and herself. Her husband added the nearby town of Witham to the grant, making this one of the largest Templar holdings in the country – about 1,400 acres. The 1185 inquest treats Witham and Cressing together, showing that there were 85 tenants farming the land in small plots, of which the

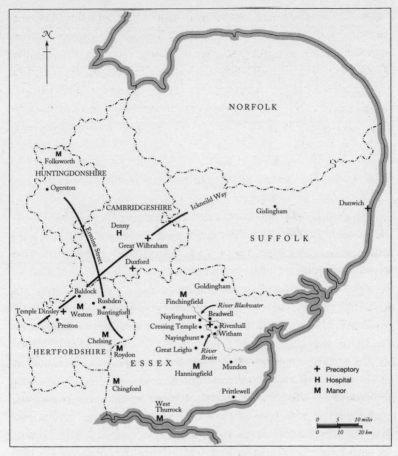

Map 3.1 Templar properties in Eastern England

largest was two virgates, for rents of between 10 and 15s per virgate plus boon works (labour service with food) of ploughing, reaping, mowing, carrying goods to the market at Maldon and to London, and driving pigs to and from the Templars' estate at West Hanning-field. Surnames of the tenants, probably those from the more ur-banised Witham, indicate that this was not an entirely agricultural

Table 3.1 Distribution of names on Templar estates in Essex, 1185

Place	Locative Name (%)	Trade Name (%)	Son/Daughter of (%)	Single Name (%)	Other Name (%)
Cressing/Witham	23	23	19	16	19
Rivenhall	0	14	57	0	29
Finchingfield	15	6	3	58	18

community but included a mason, Goldin the merchant, as well as rural craftsmen such as a smith and thatcher, and a door-keeper for the Templars' preceptory.

Apart from their names, little is known about the medieval peasant as an individual, but the names can tell us about where their family might have come from, what trade they followed and even whether they had a distinguishing feature such as a Redhead or Whiteleg. For a discussion on name evidence and its uses, see p. viii. The twelfth and thirteenth centuries saw the start of the use of surnames by commoners. The 1185 Inquest shows variations in this across the country, and it also shows that in areas such as the Danelaw that Scandinavian names were very much in evidence (Table 3.1). The place-names being used as surnames at Cressing all come from Essex. Some refer to places within the manor, such as Kingswood, others from nearby estates, including Terling and Rivenhall, suggesting that the Templars were moving their tenants around their estates in a similar way as the organisation of settlements in France described by Duby.

The numerous, fairly small holdings on the Cressing/Witham estate suggest that this was being farmed on an open-field system, probably on a three-field rotation with one lying fallow each year. But this is an area of early enclosure. R. Britnell describes small, compact holdings around Witham, and it is probable that the two virgates held by Adam of Cressing in Ravenstock field were enclosed and were the same two virgates described in 1428 as a croft.[9]

The Templars built their preceptory at Cressing away from the existing village, and set out their field system using existing tracks and boundaries to create a well-organised demesne. Back projection using the nineteenth-century tithe map, which shows the Templars' land as still exempted from tithes, and a series of sale particulars have enabled P. Ryan to show that the demesne was clustered about the preceptory in a central block with outlying woods to the north.[10]

The preceptory of such a large and extensive estate should reflect this in its buildings, but extensive excavations have only revealed six Templar structures so far, including the two standing barns. The 1308 inventory shows that on the site there was a capital messuage or large house and its necessaries, a garden, a dovecote, and a chapel dedicated to the Blessed Virgin Mary with a cemetery and sepulchre for the brothers, and those who died on the manor. There was also a windmill and a water mill. The house had a hall containing a table, two forms, and an ewer and bowl. There were two separate chambers, probably in a wing of the hall, and a chapel that contained service books, but only brass and pewter vessels rather than the gold and silver found in other chapels. The household offices included a buttery, kitchen, larder and pantry and a separate bake-house that contained a bread oven. On the site were a cider mill and press, and a smithy.

Livestock and crops at Cressing Temple, 1313
25 bullocks
18 draught oxen
9 cows, 4 heifers, 5 calves
572 sheep
1 boar, 4 sows, 17 other pigs, 36 piglets
6 old geese, 8 goslings, 1 rooster, 6 hens, 2 peacocks, 7 peahens, 1 hive of bees
601 arable acres of which:
252 sown with wheat

16 sown with beans
80 sown with peas
25 sown with drage
75 sown with oats
53 fallow
In a storehouse, 300 wooden tiles, old carts and harness
The granary is empty

This can be compared with the crops and livestock on the manor of Borley in 1308 and the Writtle manor in 1328.

Livestock and crops at Borley, 1308
4 draught oxen
4 horses
500 acres of demesne on a three-field rotation of wheat, peas and
   oats

Crops at Writtle, 1328
248 acres of wheat
32 acres of maslin
32 acres of barley
211 acres of oats
17 acres of peas
28 acres of peas and beans
9 acres of drage[11]

This shows the more intensive and mixed nature of the farming at Cressing, with most of the produce being sent to London or the Templars' market at Witham, or being stored in the great barns at Cressing.

Cressing Temple Barns

The great barns at Cressing are two of the few standing remains on a Templar site in the British Isles. The barley barn (Plate 3.1) is the

Plate 3.1 The barley barn at Cressing Temple

oldest structure. Tree ring dating of the oldest timbers gives a felling date of *c.* 1205–35; those of the wheat barn (Plate 3.2) a felling date of *c.* 1257–80. But the felling date is not necessarily the date that the timbers were used in their present context. Timber was a valuable commodity in the medieval and early modern period, and was re-used whenever possible. The timbers could have been used elsewhere and brought to Cressing when the original building was demolished.

Another way of dating a wooden structure is on the structural evidence and the carpentry. Cecil Hewitt, whose work on historic carpentry opened a new avenue of historical enquiry, used joints as the criteria for dating the barns. He observed that the barley barn was constructed on a less sophisticated system than the wheat barn, containing few mortice and tenon joints, but mainly held together by lap joints. The wheat barn was constructed to the highest standard of excellence, using more advanced building

Plate 3.2 The wheat barn at Cressing Temple

techniques. The design of the barley barn is based on a box frame and the lap joints dated it to about 1150–1200; whilst the notched joints and arcade sections of the wheat barn dated it to *c.* 1275. Both barns had been repaired and altered in the following centuries, and that accounts for the brick noggin infill and the brick plinth, as bricks were not in common use in the British Isles until the fifteenth and sixteenth centuries.[12]

Although, using this method, it is possible to estimate the introduction of a specific technique, it is more difficult to date when it went out of use. Local traditions and builders often went on using out-of-date ways of construction long after they had been discontinued elsewhere. It is difficult to question the dedicated expertise of Hewitt, but the documentary evidence needs to be taken into account as well. No great barns appear in the 1308 or 1313 inventories. Possibly these were where the timber tiles and the old carts and harness mentioned in the inventories were stored, and the livestock were housed, but the inventories do not state this. Added to this, the *Anonimalle Chronicle* notes that the site was attacked during the Peasants' Revolt in 1381 and burnt to the ground. So far no burnt layer seems to have been found in the excavations, but a timber barn would have been a tempting and combustible target. Possibly the barns were built by the Hospitallers after the 1381 revolt, but the first documentary evidence for the 'great barns' is in 1656 when the site was known as Temple Farm and included a dwelling house, two great barns, stables and a malt house.[13] The *Royal Commission on Historical Monuments, Inventory of Essex*, published in 1922, dates the barns to the sixteenth century.

The house that would have been the Templars' hall was still there in 1659 when the diarist John Evelyn stayed in it, and it is included in the 1673 *Hearth Tax Return*, but it disappears in the eighteenth century when the house and chapel were demolished.

The site is undoubtedly the Templar site and, whether or not the barns were built by them, they do constitute a magnificent memorial to past occupants of the farm.

Witham and town planning

In Witham we encounter the Templars not as farmers but as urban developers. The manor and half-hundred of Witham were given to the Order by King Stephen in 1147–48. By that date Witham was already an ancient settlement site, with occupation dating from the Neolithic period. Its popularity as a settlement was due to its situation within the confluence of the Rivers Brain and Blackwater. At Witham the Templars built a manor house on a spur of land lying within an Iron Age fort, on a site that later became known as Temple Farm. The fort helped to form a defensive enclosure set within a small town that was already a Saxon burgh and had a market and streets around it. The Templars were to change this, altering the focus of the town, founding their own market and planting their own town around it. This became the nucleus of modern Witham. Britnell suggests that part of the reason for this expansion was that the existing Witham market only served a local area. The Templars wanted to attract trade from a wider area and create a regional market that they controlled, and at which produce from their extensive Essex holdings could be sold to London dealers.[14]

Many new towns and markets were founded in the late twelfth and early thirteenth centuries. The Templars were following a trend set by the crown and other large landowners who perceived that a market and a planted town would bring in a good annual income from the market fines and tolls, and the rents of town houses. It would also create a new landless population dependent on the produce brought in from the rural estates. It took the Templars two tries to identify the perfect place for their market. A market set up in 1199 was abandoned in 1212 and supplanted by the new town and another market where the London road crossed the River Brain. The new town was laid out on either side of the river in plots of about half an acre each and a triangular market place. The development took a number of years to complete and was probably built in five stages. As late as 1258 some plots still did not have buildings on them.[15] Britnell suggests that the new market and planned settlement at Witham changed the 'kind of community' the Templars had on their Essex manors of Cressing and Witham. More tenants were landless or had only smallholdings, offering instead trades, crafts and commodities. The tenants of the new market were artisans and tradesmen and, as well as including the expected trades of butcher, baker and carpenter, also included a seller of grease and two packmen or travelling salesmen. A fulling mill that was derelict by 1307 suggests that at one time there had been a textile industry in the town, probably encouraged by the Templars.[16]

The new town of Witham was a success. Its inhabitants made more than a good living, and it was to flourish. Its site today is identifiable as the Newlands.

Essex estates and values

The 1185 Inquest shows that the Templars had a considerable amount of land in Essex, including holdings at Bradwell, Finchingfield, Rivenhall and Terling. There is indirect evidence through the transport of pigs that West Hanningfield was also theirs by 1185. Here they were to build a small manor house consisting of a hall, kitchen and brewhouse. This manor specialised in raising livestock, especially sheep, with its main income coming from the sale of fleeces, and in 1308 its staff included a shepherd and a herdsman who were each paid 3s a year.

Grants of land in Essex continued in the thirteenth century – a tribute to the high public profile the Order managed to maintain, and to the west's continued preoccupation with events in the Holy Land. A manor in Roydon near Harlow was given to the Order by Robert Fitzwalter in 1205. Like so many Templar properties, this is still identifiable as Temple Farm. Its land lay beside the River Lea and included water meadows and a fishery, as well as woodlands which were cleared and enclosed. Land in Sutton was given to the Templars by Constance Partridge in 1245. A grant that consisted of strips in the open fields of Little Sutton and 88 acres in Great Sutton and pasture on the marshes. The 1309 Inquest included Templar lands on Foulness, Havengrove Island, Prittlewell, Rochford and Chingford.

Sutton in 1309

1 messuage	6s 8d
Fruit and herbage from the garden	13s 4d
1 dovecote	5s 4d

Arable land 360 acres in demesne

180 acres value per acre 12d	£9
180 acres value per acre 8d	£6

On the marshes

130 acres on three marshes value per acre 12d	£6 10s
Pasture for 440 sheep	£9 3s 4d
15 acres of mowing meadow value per acre 2s	30s
1 windmill	20s
4 woods without pasture and underwood	20s
Perquisites of the court	2s
Rents	£6 7s 1d and 1 pound of pepper
Total	£42 10s 9d[17]

Chingford in 1309

Manor house and garden produce	6s 8d
In demesne	
310 acres value per acre 4d	£5 3s
34 acres of mowing meadow	£6 8s
23 acres of pasture	£3 9s
100 acres of wood	
Water mill and pond	
Total	£15 7s 8d

The totals indicate receipts only, not the final profits from the estates.

Comparing the values of estates across time in the medieval period is difficult. Domesday, which is the major source for the eleventh century, gives geldable values rather than receipts, although in some cases there is a remarkable similarity between the geldable value in 1086 and the receipts of 1308–9. In places a relative estimate of changing values can be obtained (Table 3.2).

Some of the differences in values between 1086 and 1185 at Finchingfield and Rivenhall can be accounted for as the Templars

Table 3.2 Values of Templar estates in Essex, 1066–1338

Estate	1066	1086	1185	1308–9	1338
Chingford	£6 10s	£7 10s	N/A	£36 11s	N/A
Cressing	N/A	N/A	£11	£43 16s 9d	£46 0s 6d
Finchingfield	£17 16s	£31 16s	£8 9s	N/A	N/A
Hanningfield	£15 16s	£25 12s	N/A	£15 6s 8d	£4
Rivenhall	£6	£5	10s 2d	N/A	£3
Witham	£13 18s	£15	£11	£40 10s 11d	£46

held only a portion of land at these places and not the entire parish or manor. Both Cressing and Witham show that the efforts the Order put into planning these estates meant that profits increased and overall there is good evidence that the Templars were careful husbanders of their land in Essex.

HERTFORDSHIRE

The most important preceptory in the British Isles outside London was that of Temple Dinsley in Hertfordshire, and this is the one that we know least about. However, this is being remedied by the Temple Dinsley Archaeological Project that has been working on the site since June 2000. Further information on this can be found in the Gazetteer. It was at Dinsley that the provincial chapters were often held. Many of those entering the Order in the second half of the fourteenth century were received at Dinsley, and many of the agreements made between servants and pensioners were made there. Both Jacques de Molay, the last Grand Master, and Himbert Peraut, the last Visitor, stayed at Dinsley, as did Henry III.

Dinsley lies a few miles south-west of Hitchin in what is still a densely wooded and isolated area, which raises the question as to why Dinsley was chosen for such an important preceptory. It is on no major route, and although it could be reached from London with some ease, it was a difficult journey for knights and servants from other preceptories. But there is documentary evidence from the trial of the Templars and from the inquest on the corrodians to show that they made this journey at least once a year, usually in June at the feast of St Barnabas. Was the site chosen because of its seclusion? The inquisitors at the trial liked to think so.

Visitors to Temple Dinsley in 1290
Master Robert De Torvile
Thomas de Bray, chaplain
Robert Daken, preceptor of Scotland
Thomas de la Fenne from Bisham
Robert le Scrop from Sandford
Robert de Barrington from York
Roger de Cranford from Bruer
Robert de Gloucester, preceptor of Ireland
Thomas of Toulouse, preceptor of London

Even the Templars acquisition of Dinsley is in some dispute. Was it the land granted to them by King Stephen in 1142, or was it part of the four carucates in Preston given to them by Bernard Balliol and Oliver Malvoir, or was it the 15 librates of land called Wedelee, part of Balliol's manor of Hitchin, given to them before 1147 when Stephen confirmed that this land belonged to them? The charter evidence is as follows:

1. 1142   King Stephen granted the Templars rights and privileges (but not land) on their holding of Dinsley. Dated at Ipswich.
2. 1142   King Stephen confirmed a grant of an acre in Dinsley, given to the Templars by John Chamberlain, called Smith Holes. Dated at York.
3. *c.* 26 September–December 1142   King Stephen granted 40s worth of land in the manor of Dinsley to God and the Brother

Knights of the Temple of Jerusalem and Hugh d'Argentine, and two mills and the men of the land. Dated at Oxford.

4. 27 April 1147 At Paris, in the presence of Pope Eugenius II, the King of France, the Archbishops of Sens, Bordeaux, Rouen, and Tours, and knights of the Order clad in white robes, Bernard Balliol granted the Templars 15 librates of land called Wedelee in his manor of Hitchin.

5. April 1147–48 Confirmation by King Stephen of a gift of waste in Dinsley. Dated at Oxford.[18]

It is clear from this that the Templars had some land in Dinsley prior to 1142, and it is probable that this was given to them by Stephen as Dinsley is a royal manor in Domesday that contained the two mills the Templars were to hold. The Balliol grant confuses the issue. Its date and the distinguished personnel present when it was made have led to the assumption that this must refer to the Templars' most important preceptory of Temple Dinsley. *Domesday Book* refers to a now lost place of Welei next to the Hitchin entry. Dr Round's essay, in *The Victoria County History of England and Wales, Hertfordshire* (1971), suggests that this is probably the Wedelee of the Balliol grant. But this is not necessarily the same as Dinsley. Both Welei and Wedelee could be represented by the modern place-name of Well Head which is less than a mile from 'Temple End' on the road between Hitchin and Great Offley. The 1185 Inquest adds to the confusion about Dinsley by failing to mention it at all. It must be part of the entry for Preston as it lies within that parish boundary.

The date of the Balliol charter and its illustrious witnesses is probably related to the gathering of troops preparing to leave for the Second Crusade, and is a good example of events connected to the Holy Land affecting the fortunes of the Order elsewhere.

It is not clear whether Dinsley was intended to become the site of a preceptory at all, as the baillie in which it lies is named after

Weston to the north-east of Hitchin, given to the Templars by Gilbert, styling himself Earl of Weston before 1138.

It should have been expected that a site of major importance, such as Dinsley, would have had a large complex of buildings, but little is known about these at present. The inventory shows that it had a chapel, hall, bake-house and smithy. In the chapel were sacred vessels, service books, a carpet and four banners. It is the latter, not found elsewhere except in London, that gives some clue to the site's importance.[19]

After the Hospitallers were suppressed in 1543 the site passed to Sir Ralph Sadler, who built a mansion and park on it. The Templars' graveyard became the kitchen yard where human remains were found in the nineteenth century. One was accompanied by a pewter chalice and covered by a gravestone with a foliated cross on it. A broken stone effigy, known since 1728 and now in Hitchin parish church, is supposed to have come from Dinsley, and in 1885 feet that matched the Hitchin figure were found at Dinsley. Like the effigies in the New Temple church, this was a crossed-legged knight, probably an associate of the Order, and may even have been Bernard Balliol himself. Rumours about Temple Dinsley having a complex of underground passages and buried treasure were current in the fourteenth century, and Edward III sent a commission to dig there to see if they could find the alleged Templar fortune.

The Templar lands were exempt from tithes, and their goods were exempt from market tolls. Perhaps it was these economic inequalities that made them unpopular locally. Even though they paid to have the rood loft in Hitchin church painted, unfavourable comments were written about them. Hildebrand of Hitchin, a monk allegedly writing between 1297 and 1305, reported that they were arrogant and licentious, and 'in their evening feast it is credibly confirmed their carousing can be heard in the town'. This was clearly impossible. Dinsley was three miles from Hitchin and, by the time Hildebrand was writing, housed only a few elderly brothers. This is evidence of the growing body of lies and misinformation building up against the Order in the late thirteenth century.

Suppositions about Temple Dinsley continued down the centuries. In the early twentieth century descriptions of the area included word pictures of files of knights travelling fully armed down the local footpaths, and the field named Pageant field in Dinsley was thought to be where the Templars held their tournaments.[20] Pageant field did not get this name until 1729 when it was enclosed from a larger field, and holding tournaments would have been against the Order's Rule as encouraging competition and pride. The image of the Templar Knight at the lists comes from Sir Walter Scott's *Ivanhoe*.

The privileges given to the Templars at Dinsley included fishing rights on the River Hiz, free warren in the demesne of Dinsley, Stagenhoe, Preston, Chelsing, Walden and Hitchin, and the right to erect a gallows. They used this at least three times, hanging a man in Baldock in 1277, and in 1286 they hung Gerle de Clifton and John de Tickhill for stealing a silver chalice and four silver spoons from the priest at Dinsley, and Peter son of Adam for taking and torturing a woman. The theft from the priest at Dinsley suggests that the precincts were not as secure or as secret as suggested in the trial proceedings.

Templars arrested at Dinsley, 1308	Length of service
Henry Paul	4 years
Richard Peitvyn	42 years
Henry de Wicklow	16 years
Robert de la Wold	18 years

As well as the brothers there was a resident bailiff at Dinsley, a carter, four ploughmen, four labourers, a cook and a gardener, as well as six pensioners. When the manor was held by the king's commissioners, it was used for pasturing 142 royal horses cared for by two grooms who received 6d each a day for their sustenance and 1s 5d each for the horses. Receipts from the manor in 1311–12 amounted to £82 19s 9d three farthings, but when it passed to the Hospitallers they rented it out for £18 a year when it comprised one manor, three carucates of land and 40 acres of wood.[21] The site of the preceptory is now the Princess Helena College.

Preceptors of Dinsley

Richard Fitz-John   *c.* 1255
Ralph de Malton   *c.* 1301
Robert de Torvile   1308

Baldock New Town

Just as in Essex, the Templars added a new town to their possessions in Hertfordshire, but, unlike Witham, Baldock was a new development, there being no Domesday entry for Baldock. It was built on land given to them by Gilbert de Clare in 1148. The 1185 inquest shows it to be a fully developed town by that date, although it was not to get its market charter until 1199.

The name Baldock has given rise to speculation that it is a corruption of the French word for Baghdad, and was chosen by the Templars to remind them of their role in the east. This assumption was accepted by Ekwall and published in the place-name bible, *The Concise Oxford Dictionary of English Place-Names*. The link between the Templars and Baghdad is tenuous. If they were going to call it after their eastern possessions, surely Jerusalem or Gaza would have been more relevant. Dissent on the origin of the name appeared in the 1940 volume of the *East Herts Society Transactions* when H.C. Anders suggested that it was more likely to derive from Bald–oak, or a dead oak. This seems a more likely explanation, and the debate on the name shows how a connection with the Knights Templar can even seduce a distinguished linguist into fantasy.

The 1185 inquest shows Baldock to be a fully developed borough with holdings set out as burgage tenures for freeman, surrounded by open fields divided into units of one-and-half-acre plots let for 1s per half-acre to 117 tenants. The market was held down the wide main streets of the town with the boundaries of the medieval town marked by the High Street, White Horse Street, Hitchin and North Streets.

The site was ideally positioned for a market, being on the main road from London going north, and the Icknield Way, connecting the eastern and western parts of the country. Bearing in mind that there was no pre-existing settlement on this site, we have to ask where did the Templars' tenants come from, and how did they attract them to their new town? When the king founded a new town, the new inhabitants were encouraged to settle with grants of land and favourable tax concessions. The Templars could offer freedom from market tolls across the country and, at Baldock, an excellent trading position. The list of surnames in the 1185 Inquest has 17 that show the place of origin. One each came from London and Essex and two from Cambridgeshire. The rest came from Hertfordshire but not from the Templars' other estates in that county. The surnames show an impressive list of trades and services in the town. These include a goldsmith, vintner and a mercer, suggesting that luxury items were available in the town, as well as the expected range of trades, such as five smiths, a tanner, a mason, a carter and six textile workers (Table 3.3).

Table 3.3 Distribution of names on Templar estates in Hertfordshire, 1185

Place	Locative Name (%)	Trade Name (%)	Son/Daughter of (%)	Single Name (%)	Other Name (%)
Baldock	15	47	9	17	13
Preston	10	18	33	18	22
Weston	5	21	17	26	31

Rents from the market stalls and shops at Baldock amounted to £6 1s 9d, but this does not take into account the tolls and fines from the market and infringements of weights and measures. When the king's commissioners tried to take these over in 1308 they provoked a riot. The 1185 Inquest includes Weston, the village that gave the Hertfordshire baillie its name. It was worth £1 4s 6d in cash, but the majority of tenants rendered service rather than paid rent. There were also small parcels of land at Buckland and Preston and a larger holding at Preston next to Dinsley.

All of these vills were farmed on the open-field system with the villagers having strips in each field. At Weston there is evidence of a three-field system, but at Preston, where the holdings are larger and there was at least one enclosure by 1185, we can see the start of engrossing and the formation of an enclosed rather than an open landscape. This is an example of pragmatic farming tailored towards the topography. Preston is in a wooded area that is suited to small, enclosed fields, Weston lies on a chalk ridge where large open fields were normal. The Templar manor at Weston has been identified as Lannock Manor. The amount of the land held there in demesne was 37.5 per cent, compared with 27 per cent at Preston. Other land was added to the baillie of Weston in the thirteenth century – Temple Chelsing, north of Hertford, in 1253 and a low-lying manor on the River Rib in Bengeo.

The way in which the Templars managed their Hertfordshire estates can be compared with those of the other great Hertfordshire landowner, St Albans Abbey. The abbey's manor of Codicote lies only a few miles to the south of Dinsley and Preston. Here the monks founded a market and a fair with at least ten shops. The manor was farmed on a three-field system but, like Preston, there is evidence of enclosures being made in the thirteenth century, although Codicote's tenants had much smaller holdings than those at Preston. They also were liable for much harsher services. This was because the abbey kept much more land in demesne than did the Templars and, as the 1308 Inquest shows, the Templars were using hired labour to run their farm at Dinsley. Codicote was never as successful a market as Baldock, owing to its position off the beaten track. Baldock was another success for the Templars and one of its most lucrative holdings.[22]

The riddle of Royston Cave

Nine miles to the north of Baldock is Royston. Royston is also on a major north–south, east–west crossroad. At this crossroad an underground, man-made chamber was discovered with its walls decorated with what appear to be religious carvings. Speculation as to its date and origin have fascinated antiquarians and historians since it was discovered in the eighteenth century, and with the Templars known to have been in the area, naturally the cave has been attributed to them.

The cave and its carvings have been analysed by Sylvia Beamon, who suggests that there is a strong link between the cave and the Templars. Its vertical bell shape is similar to structures found in Palestine and Czechoslovakia, whilst its round interior is similar to the Templars' round churches. The shallow carvings scratched in the chalk include a crowned lady, John the Baptist, a Templar cross, a man with a sword, St Lawrence and his grid-iron, and other figures and symbols, including a heart and a sun disk. Beamon makes a convincing argument that the Templars stored goods here for sale at Royston market, and presents evidence that the Templars claimed free stallage at Royston Wednesday market, as well as holding property in Royston. The *Curia Regis Roll* records at least two disputes between the Prior of Royston and the Templars in the early 13th century. The relationship between the Templars and Royston Cave although not conclusively proved, is a possibility.

CAMBRIDGESHIRE

The Templars had only three estates in Cambridgeshire, but the one at Denny is important. It is one of the few sites that was occupied by three different religious orders without a break and is a rare example of standing Templar structures.

Denny is a gravel island on the fens, surrounded by water and channels edged with willows, reeds and sedge. When the waters withdrew in summer, verdant pasture and good hay meadows were left behind, and abundant fish and wild fowl meant additional resources. It was occupied first by a cell of Benedictine monks from Ely, followed by the Templars, and lastly by the Minoresses or Poor Clares. Each of these orders adapted the buildings on the site for their own use, but excavations have managed to reveal the different phases on the site. The Templars moved on to the site by 1176, as in that year they came to an agreement with the Prior of Ely over a dispute concerning Denny's lands. But none of the Cambridgeshire land is in the 1185 Inquest. This means we do not have a list of tenants for that date, which is frustrating as we do have one for 1297.

Denny and the other hospital at Eagle in Lincolnshire give us an insight into the life of the brothers, and give us some indirect evidence that British knights served abroad but retired home when they were sick, elderly or infirm. The majority of those arrested at Denny were elderly, and one was described as insane. They represent the largest single group of Templars outside London, and as Eagle is the third largest group, this reinforces the idea that British knights returned to end their days in their own country. Eileen Gooder suggests that some of those arrested at Denny and Eagle would have been servants looking after the sick, but there is no evidence to prove this, and elsewhere servants were not arrested.[23] The preceptor at Denny had previously been the preceptor at Eagle so may have been skilled in working with the sick and elderly. He must have been elderly himself as he had been received into the

Order at Dinsley 42 years before. Four of the knights arrested at Denny had been in the Order for less than ten years, the rest had service of 26 years upwards. At least two died before coming to trial and no attempt was made to interrogate the brother described as insane. Only five of those arrested at Denny ever gave evidence.

Templars arrested at Denny	Length of service
William de la Ford, preceptor	42 years
John de Moun, preceptor of Duxford	38 years
William de Chesterton, infirm	30 years
Alexander de Bolbeck	30 years
William de Scotho	28 years
William de Welles	26 years
Robert the Scot	26 years
John de Newent	8 years
William de Thorp	7 years
William Raven	5 years
Roger Dalton	4 years
William de Marringe, died in Cambridge Castle	
Roger de Ludlow, died before testifying	
John de Hanville, died before testifying	
John de Hauteville, insane[24]	

Robert the Scot's life history is some of the only evidence we have available about a knight's career. He had gone to the Holy Land as a secular knight and had joined the Order in Syria, but left it again within two years. This broke the Rule and made him apostate. Wishing to rejoin, he took a penitentiary journey to Rome and was absolved by the Pope. He rejoined the Order in Cyprus in 1291. It is probable that the other elderly and infirm knights could have told a similar story.

There were three pensioners at Denny. Ralph Bonnet had food for life at the sergeant's table following an agreement made between him and Jacques de Molay in 1293. William de Sutton had a stipend and food for life in return for a toft of land he gave to the Templars in 1302 and a promise that he would bequeath his goods to the Order when he died. James of Gislingham had a pension as a reward for his loyal service.

The provisions of the agreements made with corrodians show that the Templars were well aware of the indignities of old age. Written into the agreements was a clause that promised that when the pensioner was too old or infirm to eat at table he would be served with the same food in his room.[25] The 1308 inventory from Denny shows that each brother had a bed, a tunic and a clothes bag. As the Rule decreed, they slept in a dormitory where 11 beds were found and 2s of money. The preceptor had his own room where four mazers and six silver spoons worth 20s were found. The brothers ate in the hall at two long trestle tables and washed their hands in basins on side tables situated against the wall as they entered. The buildings on the site included a kitchen and a bake-house. The most valuable items were in the chapel and these can be compared with the scant possessions found in the chapel at Cressing.

Items in the chapel at Denny, 1308

3 silver chalices	4 choir copes
2 gilt chalices	4 silk tunicles
2 cruets	6 complete sets of vestments
2 basins	2 missals for the Templars' use
1 thurible and a silver pyx	2 volumes of a legendary
2 surplices	A glossed psalter
2 rockets	2 other psalters
1 silk altar cloth	2 antiphonals
A thurible and an old silk hanging	2 manuals
2 graduals	2 old tropes[26]

Table 3.4 Distribution of names on the Templar estate of Denny, Cambridgeshire, 1297

Place	Locative Name (%)	Trade Name (%)	Son/Daughter of (%)	Single Name (%)	Other Name (%)
Denny	15	23	17	0	45

As no priest was arrested at Denny, it is assumed that one came in from outside. The 1297 Hundred Roll records that the Templars at Denny had three hides at Elmney, another fenland island, with meadows and marshes and two fisheries. There were 52 tenants at this time, most with smallholdings of a toft, a croft and a few acres of land, but paying high rents for these – an average of 4s for a house and a toft – as well as performing labour services and supplying hens. It was possible to survive with only a small amount of land on the fen because of the other natural resources available. There is evidence that the Templars were reclaiming land from the fen and enclosing this. Field-names and tithe maps show a number of small, enclosed as well as three open fields. In 1310, eight to ten ploughmen were needed to work this land, as well as three herdsmen for cows, pigs and sheep.

In the thirteenth century the Templars were involved in an unusual investment. They purchased dairy cows and then leased them out to their tenants. By the time of the arrests, they were loan-leasing about 45 cows out on this scheme. There is also evidence that they were increasing their flocks of sheep, a practice continued by the Poor Clares who had 600 sheep on the fen by 1400.

Denny is below sea level and easily flooded. To prevent this, earthworks surround the site with the buildings in the middle. The buildings were re-modelled by the nuns, but the remains of the Templar buildings have been plotted by excavations. These show that the Benedictines planned, but did not finish, a cruciform church. The rest of their buildings were probably made of wood and have left no trace. The Templars' church was also cruciform with a two-bay nave and a square-ended chancel. The nuns added an upper floor to the church and used it as a lodging. The church windows show a transition from the round-headed Norman arches to the pointed early English style. The Templars built a two-storey rectangular building to the south-west of the church which was probably their hall and dormitory. The remains of a glass urinal were found on this part of the site (remember these were elderly knights), and there was evidence that the windows may have been glazed, a rare luxury in thirteenth-century Britain and essential to keep out the east wind blowing across the Fens. The floors may have been tiled with yellow tiles with patterns of trefoils, scrolls and flowers, but these may have been an innovation by the nuns.[27]

A number of Templar burials were also discovered at Denny. All had degenerative diseases of the joints and bones. The most interesting burial lay outside the west door of the Templars' church. This was a male with a mortuary cross and a circular lead plate on his abdomen with three concentric rings on it forming a cross.

The other land the Templars held in Cambridgeshire was at Duxford, alias Dokesworth, Wendy and Great Wilbraham. A small preceptory was built at Duxford on land given to the Order by the Colville family, amounting to four hides, with a water mill. The Hundred Roll shows that the Templars had 508 acres of demesne at Duxford. In order to work this, their tenants ploughed, harrowed and reaped six to eight acres of corn each and did three days work a week at Michaelmas and two days hoeing and mowing. At the time of their arrest the Templars employed a carter, six ploughmen, a shepherd, a cowman and his boy, a reap-ward, stackers and a cook to feed the harvesters. The possessions at Duxford were worth £4 13s 4d, but this does not include John Mohun's (the preceptor's) possessions which he took into Cambridge Castle. He was arrested at Denny and was accused of having spoken contemptuously of God and of denying the immortality of the soul.

An Austin Friar from Cambridge claimed that he had heard a brother from Duxford, whose name he knew not but he thought it was the preceptor, say that no man had a soul after death, no more than a dog.[28]

In Great Wilbraham the Templar lands were on the north-east of the village, an area still bearing the name Temple End. This was worth about £15 a year and was 150 acres in extent. In 1279 the land was held by 12 free tenants and nine crofters. Great Wilbraham was famous for its wool and fleeces, which were worth £15 3s 4d and were sold to the king in 1279. Although there was no preceptory at Great Wilbraham, two knights were arrested there. They were probably living in a small manor house with a chapel attached. The inventory of Great Wilbraham shows that, as well as wool, cheese was made on the manor, probably ewes' milk cheese.

HUNTINGDONSHIRE, NORFOLK AND SUFFOLK

In Cambridgeshire the problem facing the Templars was repelling the floods; in Huntingdonshire there was the additional problem of clearing thickly forested land. In the 1185 Inquest Huntingdonshire and Northamptonshire were bracketed together for administrative purposes in the baillie of Ogerston. Ogerston is now a deserted village, partly in Huntingdonshire and partly in Northamptonshire. It lies in the north-east corner of a field by the Billings Brook in the parish of Washingley. In 1926 the *Royal Commission on Historical Monuments* reported it to be in poor condition with the village earthworks barely visible. In 1185 the Templars held nine acres of heavy clay soil and wood here. Clearance of this was under way by 1187 when the Templars owed 3d to the king for assarts in Ogerston.

One of the Templars' benefactors in Huntingdonshire was David, Earl of Huntingdon, the brother of William the Lion of Scotland. He is assumed to be the model for Sir Kenneth, the Scottish crusader in Sir Walter Scott's novel, *The Talisman*, but the accounts of his exploits in the Holy Land are largely mythical. The crusading 'myth' starts in 1165, before he was given the earldom by Henry II in 1170, and he was probably too young to go on a crusading campaign. He is also supposed to have accompanied Richard I on the Third Crusade. The adventures attributed to him by *Boece* amount to an odyssey of epic proportions. On the way home the earl was blown on to the coast of Egypt and taken prisoner by the Saracens. Liberated by Venetian merchants, he crossed Europe and found a ship at Sluys, but another tempest drove him towards Norway and he was only saved from drowning by promising God that he would found a church in Dundee and an abbey at Lindores. There are elements borrowed from the life of St Louis in this account, and the facts are that Richard I sailed on 7 August 1190 but David was married in England to Matilda, the daughter of Hugh of Chester, on 26 August 1190. He probably never visited the Holy Land, but the chroniclers wished to suggest this to raise his status in the eyes of the Church. His main importance in the web of history is that the three final claimants to the Scottish throne in 1291 – John Balliol, Robert Bruce and John Hastings – were all his descendants.

More profitable than Ogerstone was Folkesworth. The two virgates the Templars had in 1185 were added to in 1201, and by 1279 they had 12 acres in demesne and the rest leased to free tenants. This was good arable land but, lying beside the River Nene, was liable to flood. As there are records for 1185 and 1279, we can see that the value of the land increased by 8.5 per cent in that hundred years, and that rents had increased from 1s for a virgate in 1185 to 6s in 1279. There is evidence of the hunger for land in the thirteenth century as the population increased, affecting an isolated manor far away from any urban complex.

The most easterly counties of Norfolk and Suffolk are the least well recorded of the Templar holdings. They had a small estate at Hadiscoe in Norfolk, within the cloth-making area where the Templars owned a fulling mill. They had 100 acres of pasture in

Table 3.5 Distribution of names on Templar estates in
Huntingdonshire, 1185

Place	Locative Name (%)	Trade Name (%)	Son/Daughter of (%)	Single Name (%)	Other Name (%)
Folkesworth	26	0	21	0	53
Stebbington	40	10	10	0	40

Gislingham, Suffolk, land at Hadstock on the Suffolk/Essex
border, and a chapel, a mill, a hall with two solars, a fish pond and
waste at Dunwich. The chapel contained three bells and an organ,
and there were six containers of wine in the manor house.[29]

As Dunwich was still a viable port at this time, the wine was
probably brought in direct from Gascony, and this isolated eastern
port would have made a useful exit point had any Templars wished
to leave the country secretly in 1308. There is no record of any
having done so.

CHAPTER FOUR

THE TEMPLARS IN THE COUNTRYSIDE: NORTH-EASTERN ENGLAND

On their northern English estates the Templars held land in what had once been the Danelaw. In the counties of Lincolnshire and Yorkshire, where a large number of Templar properties lay, this is reflected in place-names, the personal names of the Templars' tenants and the landholding patterns. The Templars also encountered a wide range of different landscapes in the north, from remote moorland heights to the low-lying Lincolnshire fenland.

The wide geographical range of the Templars' lands can be seen as the analogy of the baronial honour; for example, the Leicester honour, which had lands across the length and breadth of England and was managed from a central estate. The number of professionals needed to do this, in the form of treasurers and stewards at the centre, reeves and bailiffs on the estates, and specialists such as shepherds and dairymen, was considerable. As far as the Templars were concerned, they needed these professionals to help them cope with the different conditions they found on their estates. Unlike their brethren in the Holy Land, they were not fighting the infidel but the elements and a hostile environment, but fighting these with the common aim of ridding the Holy Land of the infidel and maintaining it under Christian rule. In order to do this they had to maximise the profits from their land, tame what was often inhospitable land and put this into production. As latecomers to the landed scene in England, this was often marginal land that had to be won from the forest, moor or fen, filled with people and cultivated. In Yorkshire, following William the Conqueror's scorched-earth policy known as the 'harrying of the north', much of the land was still depopulated and waste in the early twelfth century. The Templars and the Cistercians were given land in these desolate areas and helped to revive the local population and economy. In Lincolnshire, which had borne the brunt of much of the fighting between Stephen and Matilda, and where the Templars land was often in small parcels scattered across the county, they consolidated these into coherent estates based on their Lincolnshire preceptories.

LINCOLNSHIRE

The Lincolnshire estates were based around the preceptories of Aslackby, Cabourn, Eagle, Mere, South Witham, Temple Bruer and Willoughton. Map 4.1 shows the distribution of the Templars' property in Lincolnshire. These were at the head of baillies that reflected the geographical and administrative divisions of the county, encompassing Lincoln city, Kesteven, Lindsey, the Soke of Bolingbroke, Holland and the Isle of Axholme. One baillie could hold several preceptorics, although one central preceptory received the monies to be sent to the New Temple in London. These are what Professor Riley-Smith refers to as 'a pragmantic response to a situation in which hard-pressed administrations in the east were faced with the prospect of receiving and managing scattered endowments'.[1]

The Templars were given grants of land early in their stay in England from some illustrious patrons who may have been anxious to imitate, or at least to be seen as being as pious as, King Stephen and his queen. Roger Mowbray, born in 1118, had demesne estates on the Isle of Axholme. He had a special relationship with the Templars, being a crusader himself. The son of Nigel

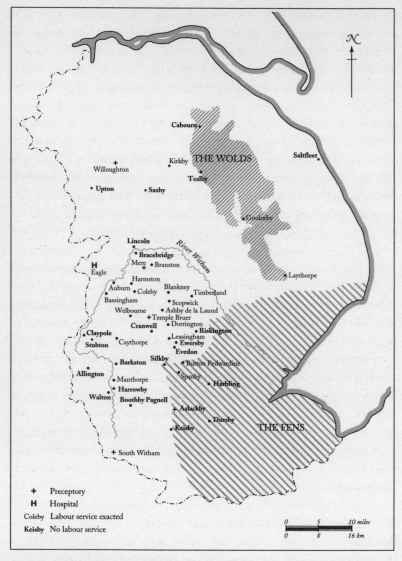

N

Cabourn

Kirkby   THE WOLDS
                                      Saltfleet
Willoughton
Tealby
Upton   Saxby
                    Goulceby

Lincoln
Bracebridge   River Witham
Mere Branston
H
Eagle   Harmston
Auburn   Coleby   Blankney   Timberland   Laythorpe
Bassingham   Scopwick
Welbourne   Ashby de la Laund
            Temple Bruer
Cranwell   Dorrington
            Leasingham   Riskington
Claypole   Caythorpe   Ewersby
Stubton   Evedon
Barkston   Silkby
                   Burton Pedwardine
Allington   Manthorpe   Spanby   Harbling
Harrowby
Walton   Boothby Pagnell
            Aslackby
            Keisby   Dunsby   THE FENS

South Witham

+   Preceptory
H   Hospital
Coleby   Labour service exacted
Keisby   No labour service

| 0 | 5 | 10 miles |
| 0 | 8 | 16 km |

Map 4.1 Templar properties in Lincolnshire

d'Aubigny, he took over the honour of Mowbray and its name at the age of nine. At the age of 18 he fought with the victorious English against the Scots at the Battle of the Standard. As a supporter of King Stephen, he was taken captive with him after the Battle of Lincoln and was forced to cede some of his lands to his captors, Ranulf, Earl of Chester, and William Romaine. Perhaps because of this setback, he departed to serve in the Second Crusade. On his return he sought to regain his lost lands. The honour of Mowbray was restored to him, but his feudal power was limited and in 1174 he was involved in an unsuccessful revolt against Henry II that was backed by the Scottish king. The result of this ill-judged affair was the loss of more lands and castles. Two years later, aged nearly 60, he departed for the Holy Land again, this time as a pilgrim seeking absolution. He returned from this expedition only to leave again at the age of 65. He fought at the disastrous Battle of Hattin, where he was captured by the Saracens, but the military orders, recognising his munificence to them, ransomed him. He died shortly after his release and was buried in the Holy Land.

Mowbray's career is an example of the interweaving of events in the Holy Land with feudal life in the west. Absolution from his sins was the main aim of his enlisting in the crusades, but adventure and a love of action might also have been in his mind as he was known by his contemporaries as a great warrior.[2] His piety is demonstrated by the generosity of his gifts to religious foundations that included St Mary's Abbey, York, Kenilworth Priory, and Rievaulx Abbey as well as the Knights Templar and Hospitaller.

Roger Mowbray's gifts to the Templars

Brimham, North Yorkshire, half a carucate

Hampton in Arden, Warwickshire, advowson of the church

Timber from the forests of Nidderdale, Malzeard and Masham, Yorkshire, to build houses at Penhill, Cowton and Stanghoe

Balsall, Warwickshire, tenements
Bagby, Yorkshire, arable and pasture
Thorp, Yorkshire, 2 bovates
Weedley, Yorkshire, demesne and a carucate
Althorpe and Burnham, Lincolnshire, rents and the advowson of
    the church and chapel
Beltoft, Lincolnshire, services of tenants
Keadby, Lincolnshire, all land and wood

Other benefactors in Lincolnshire included Roger Mowbray's
captors, Earl Ranulf and his half-brother William Romaine. Ranulf,
who was described by Henry of Huntingdon as ruthless and ready
to rush into war, held the tenurial rights of the Soke of Bolingbroke,
and his brother was the chief lord of Lindsey.

The 1185 Inquest shows that the Order held the advowsons
of 21 churches that were worth £22 15s 2d a year, and 24 and
one-sixth of a mill that was worth £8 10s a year, as well as land in
over 100 vills in the country. With the rents, services and profits
from produce, Lincolnshire was one of the Order's most profitable
counties.

These profits often had to be won from the waste. Temple
Bruer, which was to become one of the most important preceptories,
playing host not only to the general chapter but also to Henry III
and Edward I, was carved out of the heathland lying between
Sleaford and Lincoln. The original grant of land was from William
of Ashby before 1169. The site was situated on the crossroads
of the road from Lincoln to Sleaford and that from Stamford to
Lincoln, on a high, sandy ridge part of a barren heath that was best
used for rough grazing. This may be the reason for 12 of the 36
tenants in 1185 having only a toft and no other land, as the heath
could supply the other resources they needed – grazing for animals,
furze for fuel, bracken for fodder and bedding, and wild fowl and
game for the pot.

We can see a parallel here with Denny, where tenants had small-holdings, supplementing these from the natural resources available locally. But there was obviously some arable at Bruer as six tenants held two bovates each and a further 12 tenants a toft and a bovate. As the original grant had been for 'all his waste', it can be assumed that in the 20-odd years that had elapsed between the grant and the inquest some heathland had been cleared and put into production, and that an unknown, but probably large amount was in demesne as all tenants, regardless of the size of their holding, owed four days' service on the land, as well as cash rents and hen rent of four hens a year.[3]

At least a generation had passed between 1185 and the founding of the vill. Nine tenants in 1185 had locative surnames, indicating an origin from elsewhere (Table 4.1). All of these were from Lincolnshire and all came from vills where the Templars had other property. This could indicate that the Templars were moving tenants from one estate to another, perhaps by coercion or perhaps by promises of more land and lower rents.

Table 4.1 Distribution of names on Templar estates in Lincolnshire, 1185

Place	Locative Name (%)	Trade Name (%)	Son/Daughter of (%)	Single Name (%)	Other Name (%)
Allerthorpe	3	15	11	53	15
Bracebridge	0	57	14	28	0
Bruer	25	11	19	33	11
Lincoln	21	14	35	21	7
Mere	7	7	14	43	28
Rauceby	5	19	5	43	28
S. Witham	12	12	6	50	18
Weedley	31	12	12	37	18
Willoughton	16	8	4	58	12

The great heath at Bruer was best suited to sheep grazing and one of the 1185 tenants was a shepherd. By 1246 the Templars had a flock of 300–400 sheep at Bruer and 100 pigs rooting in the woods at Aslackby. In 1298 the Patent Rolls show the king's agents purchased 14 sacks of wool from the Templars in Lincolnshire for £134 15s 7d, of which nine came from Bruer, and six of these were of the highest quality.

Its site on a crossroads made Bruer an ideal place for a market and fair. It is possible that Henry II granted them these in the twelfth century but it was not until 1259 that they became operational. Then the original market day of a Thursday was changed to a Wednesday and an annual fair held was held on 24–26 July.[4] The preceptory at Temple Bruer is now incorporated into Temple Farm, and its tower is still visible today. In the 1530s John Leland, travelling from Stamford to Lincoln, went past Temple Bruer:

From Ancaster to Temple Bruer all by Champaign of Ancaster Heath 4 miles. There be greate old vast buildings but rude at this place, and the east end of the temple is made in a circular fashion. The heath is good for sheep.[5]

In Leland's day there must have been enough of the church still visible to show that it was circular, and an eighteenth-century print shows part of a standing circular wall. This had disappeared by the nineteenth century (Plate 4.1).

The preceptory itself was set within a walled enclosure that may have been intended for defence as well as creating a conventual enclosure. Further defensive measures were taken in 1306 when the Patent Rolls show that the Templars were given a licence to crenellate the great gatehouse at Bruer. The plan of Temple Bruer can be seen in Figure 4.1.

Two excavations, nearly a hundred years apart, have taken place at Bruer. The first shows how myths about the Templars survived into the nineteenth century and helped to influence the interpretation

Plate 4.1 Temple Bruer. Thomas Hearn, watercolour
Reproduced by permission of Lincolnshire County Council: Usher
Gallery, Lincoln

of an archaeological site. Comparing the two reports shows how
archaeologists in different centuries can interpret the same site in
different ways. The Reverend Dr Oliver was the first excavator of
the site in 1837. He published his conclusions as an addition to his
History of the Holy Trinity Guild of Sleaford (1838). His most exciting
finds came when his workmen discovered a vault and an underground passage covered with plaster that led to a labyrinth of rooms.
In these, Oliver claimed to have found the skeleton of a man in a
sitting position, the skeleton of an elderly male with only one tooth,
a body thrown down, with two holes in the front of its skull, and
evidence of burnt and charred bones, as well as many other human
skeletons, including a child and an adult surrounded by burnt
material. Oliver interpreted this space, which lay between the church
and the tower, as a vestry where the postulant knight waited to

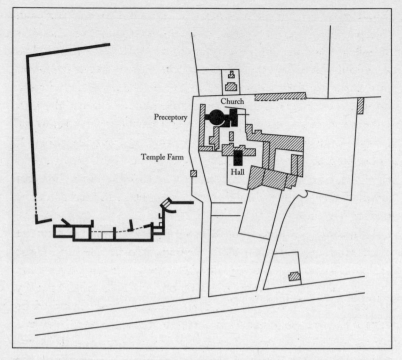

Figure 4.1 Plan of Temple Bruer (Adapted from St John Hope, 1908)

enter the chapter through a trapdoor. The remains, he concluded, were human sacrifices made at the time of the Templars!

The site was re-excavated in 1908 by W. St John Hope, who specifically wanted to find the chamber with the human remains. He found the trapdoor, but the stairs down to the vault had been removed. However, he could see a small rectangular chamber and an oven. There were no human remains. In his report he wrote: 'As Dr Oliver does not describe his "dreadful chamber" but merely says one was found he was probably putting something on record that he had been told, which his horror of the Templars and all their works caused him to imagine a reality.'[6] Had Dr Oliver allowed his imagination to run away with him and made up his report? It should be noted that the underground, plastered passage and vault have parallels with the vaulted chamber found beneath the New Temple in London. The secret vault could have been Bruer's treasury, and it was obviously earlier than the church, but if the bones existed outside Oliver's imagination, where had they come from and where did they go? Hope found internments cut into the rock to the north of the church in what might have been the Templars' graveyard, but this was not in the position that Oliver described. It is possible that Oliver had stumbled on to an Iron Age or earlier burial site, or even a Roman cemetery, as Ermine Street runs past Temple Bruer making it an ideal site for either a Roman fortlet or an Iron Age farm.

Excavations show that the church itself was 52 feet in diameter with a roof supported on eight columns, but by the time Hope excavated it only the foundations remained in an open farm yard. The Templars had another round church in the area at Aslackby that was visible in the seventeenth century and was described by William Camden in *Britannia* as a round church, now rebuilt as a farmhouse called Temple. This fell down in 1891. The defensive towers, walled enclosures and strengthened gatehouses, which are a characteristic of many Templar sites, are reminiscent of their small forts guarding the roads in Palestine. The defences did not keep the sheriff and his men out in 1308 and four brothers were arrested at Bruer – John of Eagle, Richard of Bisham, Alexander of Halton and their chaplain, Ralph of Evesham. As well as the brothers there were nine corrodians at Bruer. One, Walter, son of Ralph of Calverthorpe, a loyal servant of the preceptory, had a room in the west gate and a place in the stable for his horse. In all there were 19 pensioners in Lincolnshire, compared with only two in Yorkshire, and five of the Lincolnshire corrodians were retired servants.[7] In 1185 the income from Bruer was £4 14s 3d. In 1338 Bruer and its subsidiary holdings were worth £106 13s 1d after expenses were paid.[8]

The preceptory complex that we know most about is South Witham in Lincolnshire. This was a small preceptory but excavations showed that it had been re-modelled at least three times during its occupation by the Templars. South Witham shows the dual characteristics of a monastic precinct and a fortified farm. It was entered through a gatehouse with a room on the first floor, with the guesthouse immediately opposite to this inside the gate. The hall lay in the centre of the site. This had started as an open hall, without a ceiling and with the hearth at its centre, but was later divided into two with a solar or private room at the east end. The chapel stood to the south of the hall and was reached by a passage from the hall and set within its own garden court. The chapel was rectangular and made of good-quality masonry. Domestic offices, including the kitchen with five ovens, stood separate from the hall, with a workshop where some iron working was carried on. Like Bruer, it had a defensive tower, which was strongly made with a central wall dividing it in half and with no internal access between the two halves.

The farm buildings included animal houses, barns and a smithy. The barns remind us of Cressing as one was an aisled barn and the other a 'great' barn. Apple seeds recovered from the floor of the barns show that fruit was stored there, grain was stored in a third aisled barn, which had a threshing floor outside it. Two well-built pig sties lay outside the gatehouse. There were fish ponds to the north of the site, and the River Witham, on its old course, had been damned to form a mill race. This mill was kept in hand rather than leasing it out.

The archaeologists identified at least three main building phases on the site, with some buildings being re-modelled up to seven times. Usually the chapel was the first building to be constructed, but at South Witham evidence suggested that the chapel was later than a hall, part of which lay beneath the chapel foundations. A second aisled hall was built around 1164, and the chapel itself was deemed to be early thirteenth century, and this was followed by the construction of a larger hall, the tower buildings, the kitchens and workshops and at least one barn. The mill appears in the 1185 Inquest so was built by 1184. In the final stages the chapel and hall were reconstructed and the buildings were enclosed within a wall. Cobbled and paved paths crossed the enclosure so that occupants could move about the site dry shod.[9]

The only other Templar hospital in the British Isles was at Eagle in Lincolnshire. This lay eight miles outside Lincoln and was probably a royal grant from King Stephen, with Henry II adding the church and the mill. Like the hospital at Denny, there were more brothers at Eagle than elsewhere in the county, and most of them were elderly. Of the eight arrested at Eagle and taken to Lincoln Castle, three died in prison and two were too elderly and infirm to testify.

Templars arrested at Eagle, 1308	Length of service
Simon Streche, preceptor	8 years
Robert de Barnwell, priest	
Robert de Halton, died in prison	
Geoffrey de Joliffe, died in prison	
John de Vale, died in prison	
John de la Wold, chaplain, did not testify	
John de Waddon, priest	20 years
Henry de la Wold	30 years[10]

The hospital stood on the site of Eagle Hall, and its only visible evidence is a series of banks and ditches.

Other preceptories in Lincolnshire included Willoughton, just off Ermine Street to the north of Lincoln, Aslackby on the fen edge and Mere. The Templars also held property in Lincoln itself, including a number of houses, one of which was leased to Aaron the Jew for 3s a year. The Jews of Lincoln were to be notorious for the alleged murder in 1255 of the boy who became Little St Hugh of Lincoln. It was alleged that Koppin the Jew enticed the boy into his house and kept him for a month from July to August during which time he was scourged, crowned with thorns and finally, on 27 August, crucified. Koppin and 18 other Jews were supposed to have confessed to the crime and were executed. The cult of Little St Hugh was seriously anti-Semitic and its propaganda was to lead to the expulsion of the Jews from England. Aaron the Jew of Lincoln may have lived in the Jews House on Steep Hill, Lincoln, but his claim to immortality is his role as one of the chief financiers of twelfth-century England. He established a system of financial agents across the country, and his clients included Henry II, who owed him £616 12s 8d, the Archbishop of Canterbury and the Templars themselves. Aaron financed many church and cathedral building projects that would have been impossible without his loans. When he died in 1186 all his possessions, including his debts, were appropriated by the king. It was found that his credit network was so complex that a special branch of the exchequer had to be set up to collect the outstanding debts. In 1193 there were still at least 430 debts outstanding, amounting to over £15,000. The Templars were not only connected to the Jews of medieval England as landlords, but it was to the New Temple that the tax on the Jews was taken after collection.

In all, by 1185 the Templars held 11,460 acres and 188 tofts in Lincolnshire in 182 separate vills. Lees suggests that these were held mainly by money rents rather than service, and that this was made possible because Lincolnshire lay in the Danelaw which lacked the heavy service requirements of the south.[11] Other evidence, indeed the 1185 Inquest itself, shows that in some areas of the county heavy services were exacted. Graham Platts gives examples of this from non-Templar manors at Market Stainton, West Rasen, Little Bythorne and Couthorpe in the thirteenth century. At Market Stainton, Roger de Colville's tenants had to render three days' service at harvest. At the Templars manor of Gouceby, which neighbours Stainton, the tenants paid a cash rent, four hens and did four days' service on a manor where most tenants appeared to be unfree and held only a toft. The labour obligation was higher at Aslackby, including six days work, carting, and mowing one bovate of land.[12]

Had the Templars wished to commute service into cash they could have started with their new settlement at Bruer, but even at Bruer tenants were obliged to render four days' service, regardless of the size of their holding. Overall, there was an equal division between Templars land where the tenants owed service and that where they did not, suggesting that there was no clear administrative policy on this, and that the local custom was regarded. Property shown in bold on Map 4.1 (see page 92) shows where there was no labour service.

Using the 1279 Hundred Rolls, Platts estimated that the average annual income from a manor on the fen edge was £7 and on the wolds £8. Unfortunately there are not comparable figures that can be used from the Templar manors in Lincolnshire for this date. Aslackby, a fenedge site, had an annual income below £7. Platts shows that the part of that vill held by John Marshall in 1283 had 112 acres of arable and 40 of meadow. On other manors in the area Platts found that there was a change in farming practice at the end of the thirteenth century from sheep grazing to arable. He attributes this to the climatic change and wetter conditions that badly affected low-lying fenland and vills on clay. The search for more land that could be cultivated meant higher land prices and the clearing of woodland.[13]

Remarkably, as land prices rose in the 1280s the Patent Rolls show the Templars starting to purchase land and other property in Lincolnshire and Yorkshire to extend their estates. Between 1286 and 1305 they purchased 394 acres, 100 acres of wood, houses in Lincoln and Grantham, tofts and rents. Most of these were in places where they already had land and it would seem that they were trying to consolidate their estates in vills such as Eagle and Cranwell. Land was in short supply at this period, and prices high, but so were the returns from the land as a rising population struggled to feed itself from less and less resources, and this may have encouraged the Templars to invest in land. Even so, this meant that there was less surplus cash available to send to their brethren in the east. However, this period coincides with the withdrawal of the Templars from the Holy Land, which may have led to a movement to increase and improve estates in the west and, as we saw at Bruer, to strengthen their fortifications. Once the *raison d'être* for the Templars' presence in the countryside had been removed, other landowners would begin to cast greedy eyes at their possessions, and any resentment the local community might have felt about the Templars' economic privileges could come into the open. As the arrests in 1308 revealed, the Templars themselves were hardly in a position to defend themselves, and the land purchases in Lincolnshire might have been a last desperate attempt to ensure economic security in the British Isles in the face of a rising tide of opposition.

YORKSHIRE

Roger Mowbray, whose life was intimately tied up with the defence of the Holy Land, gave the Templars property on his Yorkshire estates as well as in Lincolnshire. One of his most lucrative gifts was the castle mill, two tofts and seven acres of land in York. These were leased out to 11 tenants in 1185 paying £11 7s 4d in rent a year. By 1308 a chantry chapel for the soul of William Appleby had been added to the site. In 1308 the chapel contained sacred vessels, service books, vestments worth £5 13s 4d and a chalice that the assessors were unable to value. A dwelling had been attached to the mill, and it was here the Templars stayed when they had business in York.

Evidence from the trial, charters made by the Templars and the inquest on the corrodians shows that members of the Order travelled between preceptories frequently, and that brothers had often

held office at more than one preceptory in their career. The surnames of brothers often coincides either with the location of a
preceptory or a Templar manor, which might mean that they had
been recruited from the local population, or that that was their
point of contact within the Order. Most brothers assembled at the
general chapter once a year, and would have been familiar with
each other. In each baillie or region the profits from each estate
were collected at a central point before being sent to the New
Temple at London for shipment overseas, but there is little surviving evidence of this, and no manorial or court accounts remain for
Templar holdings. Eileen Gooder, in her in-depth survey of Temple Balsall,[14] shows that once the Templars' property was in the
keeper's hands in 1308 there was movement of livestock and goods
between Templar manors and preceptories. We do not know
whether this was the usual practice, although the 1185 Inquest
shows that pigs were moved between estates in Essex. The castle
mills at York played host to servants from Temple Newsam and
Copmanthorpe as a pan belonging to Newsam and a great jar from
Copmanthorpe were found in the mill's kitchen in 1308, and in
the final days of the Templars the preceptor of Copmanthorpe
managed the York properties.[15]

Yorkshire preceptories
Copmanthorpe
Cowton, by 1185
Faxfleet, by 1185
Foulbridge
Hirst, by 1155
Newsam, by 1185
Penhill, by 1185
Ribston
Westerdale
Wetherby[16]

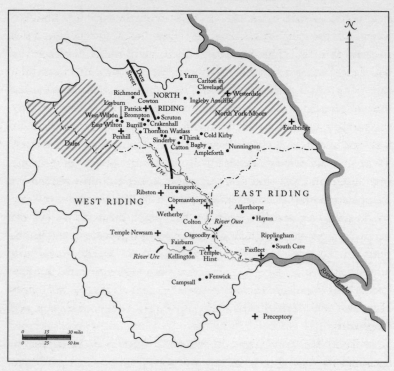

Map 4.2 Templar properties in Yorkshire

Templar property in Yorkshire can be seen on Map 4.2.

The Templar holdings cluster around the Rivers Swale and Ure on the North York Moors, and along the River Aire. Once more they took over marginal land, either waste or land with poor soil, such as Cold Kirby on cold, heavy clay. Of the five preceptories founded before 1185, four are in vills that are in Domesday. Of the remaining five, none are in Domesday, meaning that once more the Templars had to develop the wasteland, just as their brethren had done in Judaea as described by Theoderic 1169–74.

Temple Hirst, on the low-lying land along the eastern flood plain of the Aire, appears only as a total sum in the 1185 Inquest with no details of its tenants. Three different grants made between 1155 and 1174 comprised the Templars' lands, situated on both sides of the Aire. These were added to in the thirteenth century with land in East Hirst and the entire vill of Osmanthorpe, which was given to the Templars by Robert de Stapelhurst in order that they might establish a chantry chapel for his soul.[17] The 1308 inventory shows the usual complement of buildings, including a hall, dormitory, kitchen, bake-house, brewhouse, dairy and chapel. There appears to have been a cellar under the hall where a chest was found, and a pewter salt and some tankards. In the dormitory there were two chests and one clothes bag. The goods in entirety were worth £9 3s 3d. The evidence from the inventory of the farm stock showed mixed farming but with a concentration on sheep. There was some arable land, and two barns at Potterlaw and Kellington where plough oxen, wheat, barley, oats and rye were found.[18] In the 1880s the south door of the preceptory at Temple Hirst was still visible, and a tall white tower set within a paved courtyard.

At Temple Hirst, Temple Newsam and other northern preceptories livestock and carts had been collected to send to Scotland for the king's war. Thirteen cows were waiting at Hirst and sheep and carts at Newsam and Copmanthorpe. The inventories stated that these did not belong to the Templars but had been sent there by the king who was using the preceptories as staging-posts for provisions for the Scottish Wars.

The Templars and the Scottish Wars

The Templar Rule forbade the spilling of Christian blood, and the Templars owed obedience only to the Pope and not to any secular ruler. As an international organisation with brethren scattered across western Europe it was essential that they did not become involved in local wars because not only would this have led to them spilling Christian blood, but it might also have set Templar against Templar. Although in England and Scotland they were involved in government as advisers, office-holders and treasurers, they were not obliged to swear fealty to either crown until 1296 when Edward I demanded that Brian de Jay, the Master of the Templars in Scotland, swear fealty to him at Edinburgh. Subsequently, as Master of the Templars in England de Jay was to bear arms against the Scots, and was killed at the Battle of Falkirk in 1298. Evidence suggests that de Jay was an unusual member of the Order – hot-headed, unscrupulous and cruel. His decision to accept Edward as his overlord may have been personal rather than involving the whole Order, but it left the Templars in England in an invidious position. If they refused to obey a commission of *oyer* and *terminer* calling them to arms against Scotland or France, they could be accused of treason for disobeying their overlord, but if they obeyed, they broke one of the important precepts of the Templar Rule. Furthermore, in 1300 Pope Boniface VIII ordered Edward to cease hostilities against Scotland, which was under his protection, and the Pope was the spiritual and temporal overlord of the Templars.

There is no evidence that any Templar apart from Brian de Jay and perhaps one other who accompanied him on Edward I's Scottish campaign was actively involved in the war, but the network of Templar preceptories across the country provided the king with a tempting series of staging-posts where provisions for the war could be collected. However, it was not until after the arrests that Templar goods and livestock were re-routed into the war effort. On 19 June 1308 Edward II optimistically requested that John Wogan, the Irish justiciary, provide the following provisions from the Templar estates in Ireland:

1,000 quarters of wheat
1,000 quarters of oats

200 quarters of peas and beans
200 quarters of salt
300 tuns of wine
  3 tuns of honey
1,000 stockfish

From the Templars' estates in Cambridgeshire and Huntingdonshire he demanded:

1,000 quarters of oats
  500 quarters of wheat
  500 quarters of malt

Any deficiency was to be made up out of the estates of the Bishops of Coventry and Lichfield.[19] Edward's shopping list gives us some idea of the resources needed to keep a fourteenth-century army in the field when commodities on the ground were going to be in short supply. In his work on medieval diets, Professor Dyer has estimated that a quarter of corn would produce about 420lbs of coarse bread. So 1,000 quarters should produce 42,000lbs of bread and, as Dyer also suggests that a labouring man would consume about 26lbs of bread a week, this would keep 16,153 men going for a week, or about 2,000 men in the field for about five months. Dyer also estimated that it would take 300 acres of well-drained land to produce 200 quarters of grain, meaning that the Templar lands in Ireland had to exceed 3,000 acres of arable to produce the required amount and about the same in Cambridgeshire and Huntingdonshire.[20] Their land in these two counties amounted to about two-thirds of this, and Edward's demands were typically unrealistic.

Temple Newsam and other Yorkshire preceptories

Another important preceptory in Yorkshire was Temple Newsam near Leeds, which now lies at junction 46 of the M1. The Templars purchased this land from William de Villiers. Here there were

16 tenants, mostly holding land in units of one bovate at a rent of 2s a year plus two cocks and 20 eggs each, and four days' service. In the autumn the tenants were to provide one man to plough, and in the spring to sow, and they were to repair the banks of the pond, and wash and shear sheep. In 1308 there were 335 muttons on the farm and 247 lambs, but Newsam was not solely a sheep farm. It was divided between livestock and arable, with wheat, rye and oats grown on the demesne. In 1308 the buildings consisted of the usual chapel, hall, kitchen, buttery, bake-house and a barn.

No trace of the Templars' buildings survive today, but on 14 February 1903 a farmer ploughing a field south of Temple Thorpe farm hit a stone that proved to be a coffin lid. A subsequent excavation revealed the Templars' chapel foundations, indicating a rectangular structure about 55 feet long and 30 feet broad. The farmer said that probing the field with an iron bar revealed a considerable area of stone foundations. This probably indicated a complex of buildings similar to those at South Witham.

The area was known in the eighteenth century as the Old Temple, and the tithe map shows Templar lands exempted from tithes lying near a small brook that crosses the site. Bones from the site were examined in the early twentieth century. It was suggested at that time that some were female as they were of small size, but these could equally well have been the remains of a young male. Another skeleton was described as a 'very big man – even a giant'. Dental evidence suggested that this was a male aged between 25 and 30 when he died, whilst the smaller skeleton was aged about 17. Other bones were found, but could not be made to form a complete skeleton.[21] Undoubtedly the site of the preceptory had been found, and the burials were either those of Templars, associates or their servants. No brothers were arrested at Newsam or at Copmanthorpe in the Vale of York.

Further north and lying just off Dere Street near Scotch Corner was Temple Cowton. This was also a useful staging-post for material going to Scotland, and the area had seen military action at the Battle of the Standard in 1138. Edward I stayed at this preceptory on his way to Scotland in 1300, and the 1308 inventory shows that a chest of documents belonging to English and Scottish estates were found here. As well as the usual service books, vessels and vestments in the chapel, there were two hanging bells and two hand-bells. One of the hanging bells was probably the sacristy bell, rung as the priest raised the host. The other may have been to call the brethren to prayer and to mark the passing hours, as well as serving as a warning of a Scottish advance, and perhaps calling in the cows that gave the preceptory its name.[22]

At Ribston the documents found by the assessors in 1308 remained in the area, and eventually became part of the Ribston Hall muniments. Ribston was given to the Templars by Robert de Ros in 1217. Like Roger de Mowbray, he fought in the Holy Land, and the fifteenth-century effigy in the New Temple is thought to be a later member of his family, although how the effigy came to rest in the Temple Church is not known. Ribston lies on the bank of the River Nidd close to another gift of Robert de Ros at Wetherby. He also gave them the church at Walshford and the whole vill of Hunsingore – in all, about 3,600 acres – creating a compact block of land. In the thirteenth century the banks of the Nidd were wooded but by 1230 were being cleared and illegally enclosed. In 1231 there was a dispute between the Templars and Matthew of Cantilupe. The Templars accused him of enclosing the common pasture, and he accused them of enclosing a spring in Ribston churchyard and building a chapel there. The dispute was settled amicably. The Templars agreed that they would not allow Matthew's parishioners to enter their chapel, nor bury any of them in their graveyard, but they were allowed to keep their chapel. In return, they allowed Matthew to keep 12 acres of the enclosed land and released the spring from their enclosure. They also agreed that the land next to Matthew's court could be enclosed by boundaries agreed between them.[23]

These disputes represent an interesting debate on privilege. The Templars were exercising their right to have their own chapel and priest, but were compromising with regard to burials as they could have claimed that privilege as well. Matthew was establishing an enclosure that would become glebe land by removing this land from the common, and thereby setting up another privilege. The chapel was dedicated to St Andrew and it was given donations of land to support it and maintain its lights.

There were other disputes over privileges in Yorkshire, and in 1274 the juries called to the Hundred courts accused the Templars of reducing the crown's revenues, ignoring the royal court, appropriating land without documentary evidence of legal possession and oppressing people by abusing their liberties. How far this represented what was happening on the Templar estates and how far it was the evidence of those wishing to appease the crown, or from those who had grudges against the Templars is not clear. It could be seen as the start of a smear campaign against them, and an attempt to whittle away their privileges. For example, in Leeds Templar houses were marked with a cross to show they were exempt from tax. This was clearly against the spirit, if not the letter, of the papal privileges to the Order, and the rights and liberties granted and confirmed by English kings, which in general did not extend to tenants.

The Templars also had preceptories in the Yorkshire Dales. Penhill in Wensleydale lay on the north slope of the hill overlooking the River Ure near Jervaulx Abbey. In the early twentieth century the preceptory remains were still visible in the land above Temple Farm, and in 1840 the mound thought to be the site of the chapel was investigated. Several stone coffins were found, and the pedestal of high altar. Penhill was the gift of Roger Mowbray. At the same time he gave the Templars timber to build three houses at Penhill.[24]

At Foulbridge there are visible Templar remains where the preceptory has been incorporated into a farmhouse. The Royal

Commission report shows that the preceptory hall was a three-bay aisled hall with thick walls and a cross-wing to the east. The roof was a sophisticated tie post design that is thought to represent the work of craftsmen brought in from elsewhere rather than living locally. Dendrochronology from the roof gave a felling date of about 1288, so it was built, or at least used in this context, late in the Templars' occupation and probably hides the foundations of an earlier building. The 1308 inventory shows that this was a large building containing five tables, with a chamber which was probably in the cross-wing and separate domestic offices and a chapel.[25]

The Royal Commission Report describes the North York moors as having arable farming in the valleys and grazing in the moors. In the medieval period it was an isolated and wild area granted to ecclesiastical landlords such as the Cistercians and the Templars, who reclaimed the land and improved it so that its taxable value increased and, by the thirteenth century, was higher than that for the Vale of York.[26] Work on rural Yorkshire in the medieval period has demonstrated the contrasts between the upland areas, where the rivers rise to flow to the North Sea, and the lowland area of the Vale of York. It also emphasises that much of the settlement in the county was promoted by the great monastic houses. The Benedictines were the first on the scene, claiming the best land and most favourable positions, whilst the later foundations, such as by the Cistercians, were left to colonise the more remote areas, reclaim villages from the waste and put land back into production. The role of the religious houses in the development of the county's agriculture and economy was crucial. The monastic estates were organised around a mother house with a network of tracks and roads spreading across the country to cells and granges that would send produce, livestock and fleeces back to the centre of the estate. We can only assume that the Templars organised their estates in much the same way, but that during the thirteenth century some rationalisation took place and the smaller preceptories became manorial farms as only four preceptors were arrested in Yorkshire from Cowton, Faxfleet, Hirst and Newsam. Other brothers bore local surnames showing that they were recruited in the area and had probably never served abroad.

Yorkshire Templars arrested in 1308
Geoffrey des Arches, Knight, preceptor of Temple Newsam
Ivo de Etton, preceptor of Temple Hirst
William de la Fenne, preceptor of Faxfleet
John de Walpole, preceptor of Cowton

Others:
Thomas de Betterby, Penhill
Adam Creyte, Temple Hirst, porter
Henry de Kereton, Cowton
Roger de Sheffield, Cowton
Stephen de Radenage, Westerdale, priest

Preceptory origin not known:
Henry Craven
William de Herdwick
Robert de Langton
Henry de Rochester
Ralph de Roston, priest
Patrick de Ripon
Richard de Ripon
Thomas de Stanford
Henry de Suggind[27]

In all, the Templars had land in over 70 vills in Yorkshire worth in total in 1308 £1,460 18s 11d, compared with the value of Lincoln-shire of £934 9s 8d. The annual value of all the English and Welsh Templar holdings in 1308 came to £4,720 so between them Lin-colnshire and Yorkshire accounted for half of this. A breakdown of the inventories suggests that although the goods found had a

Table 4.2 Valuation of Templar property, 1308

	Temple Newsam	Temple Hirst	Copmanthorpe
Livestock	£95 17s 2d	£70 4s 5d	£15 1s 9d
Crops	£57 15s 6d	£68 10s 6d	£15 9s 6d
Goods	£10 14s 8d	£9 3s 3d	£10 11s
Total	£164 7s 4d	£146 18s 2d	£41 1s 6d

higher value than those in other houses in the country, the Templars were not living in luxury (Table 4.2).

For the king's war effort
Temple Newsam	13 sheep, 6 carts
Temple Hirst	12 cows
Copmanthorpe	10 sheep

BORDERLANDS

In 1308 writs for the Templars' arrests were sent to all county sheriffs, but this was probably a matter of form as, so far as can be ascertained, there is no evidence of Templar establishments in the two Palatine counties of Durham and Cheshire, little evidence of land in Lancashire, and only one or two scattered holdings in Cumberland and Westmoreland, but they had one preceptory in Northumberland. This was at Thornton in the parish of Hartburn, seven miles west of Morpeth and in an excellent strategic position on a high ridge with clear views in all directions. Essential to a site lying in the no man's land beyond Hadrian's Wall, it was surrounded by thick walls, and in 1827 the Reverend Hodgson noted that many of the walls in the area contained worked stone that he presumed came from the Templars' preceptory, and that grass grown lines in the stack-yard of a farm indicated where Temple Thornton once stood.[28]

The Templars were in a vulnerable position at Thornton. Technically and morally unable to defend themselves against invaders from the north, but with the ancient secret track known as the Devil's Causeway connecting the English and Scottish borders running through their land. Here the defensive towers and crenellations seen further south were an essential feature of the landscape, and perhaps this is why an above average establishment was found at Thornton. In 1308 four brothers were arrested there.

Templars arrested at Thornton, 1308
Michael de Sowerby, preceptor and priest
Robert de Canville
Walter de Gaddesby
Geoffey de Welton[29]

The 1308 inventory shows that the neighbourhood lived in constant fear of the Scots for as soon as the king's keepers took over they sold £24 15s 6d worth of wheat, barley and oats immediately 'for fear of the coming of the Scots'. Property at Thornton included a mill and a brewery that might have been a commercial operation as it was leased out for 10s a year. Travellers on the Devil's Causeway needed refreshment on their journey, and not all the traffic between Scotland and England was unfriendly. Packmen, merchants and monks would have passed peaceably between the two kingdoms, and the area was not continually one of surprise raids and reprisals.

The agriculture at Thornton was mixed, mainly sheep and arable, but there is evidence from the accounts of the keepers that the Thornton flocks had been hit by a murrain in 1308 as the keepers found 69 fleeces of ewes, muttons and shear hogs that had died in the murrain, and the expenses for the manor include the purchase of ointment for the sheep. It has been suggested that this was foot rot, but it could have been scab or even foot and mouth disease. Wages for employees on the estate included 3s 9d to a man

for keeping 68 sheep and eight lambs, and 3s 11d for milk purchased for the lambs, showing that these were being reared by
hand. The same man washed and sheared a further 192 sheep.

Wages of £4 6s 11d were paid to others for weeding, carrying
hay, and reaping and binding corn. This was far in excess of 5s 11d,
the cost of the commutation of labour services owed by the tenants.[30] In this case the commutation of labour service for cash
looks like bad economics, but there are variables that we do not
know. Did the Templars always have to buy in labour at crucial
times of the farming year, and was it their usual practice to commute service for cash on this manor? The 1308 accounts record the
farm management of the king's keepers and not the Templars.

The wages bill for 1308 included 40s a year for six carters, one
cowherd, one shepherd and a cook who kept house for the manor
and made the porridge for the servants. The porridge would have
been eaten with salt as two bushels of salt were purchased expressly for the servants' porridge. Once the four resident Templars
were arrested the manor became liable for their expenses whilst
they were imprisoned in the castle at Newcastle. This was 4d a day
for each Templar for 315 days, making a total of £21, and the
manor had to bear the further expenses of eight horsemen and
10 footmen who formed the escort when the Templars were
conveyed to York for their trial. The journey from Newcastle to
York took three days and cost 40s.

Expenditure and receipts, Thornton, 1310

Expenses	£80	10s	6d
Receipts	£94	2s	7d
Value of manor	£13	2s	1d

The inventory shows the usual modest collection of goods, cook-
ing pots, farm implements, but also four sealed chests and two
barrels with all the charters and deeds of brother Michael, the late
keeper of the manor. These sealed containers must have held the

manorial accounts for Thornton and had they survived would have been valuable evidence of the way in which the Templars managed the manor. Given the number of containers, it is possible that these contained deeds and accounts from other manors as well. In the chapel was a chalice, a black vestment and three service books that Roger de Fawdon took away and would not hand over to the king's keeper and custodian of the lands.

The Scottish Wars had a profound effect on Thornton. In 1338 the Knights Hospitaller claimed that in peace the land at Thornton was worth 6d an acre, but since the war only 3d an acre. They also reported that the house at Thornton had been torn down by the surrounding lords, and the goods carried away. Rents which in the Templars' time had been worth £30 a year were only worth £12, and in 1338 they had received nothing because of the Scottish Wars. This emphasises the front-line position of Thornton, its isolation, and the power of the border lords who could do what they wanted in their own territory without the fear of the king's justice and could appropriate what they wanted once the Templars were removed. Four brothers and their servants would not have been a match for a determined warlord, whether English or Scottish. But when they worked the manor it was profitable and their success in turning the waste of the Yorkshire moors, the heaths of Lincolnshire and the debateable lands of Northumberland into going concerns was a tribute to their determination.

CHAPTER FIVE

THE TEMPLARS IN THE COUNTRYSIDE: THE MIDLANDS, THE CHILTERNS AND OXFORDSHIRE

In the Middle Ages most of the Midlands was an area of villages surrounded by open-field agriculture. It was densely populated by the twelfth century and it is not surprising that the Templars, coming relatively late on to the scene, had few estates in this area. In the North Midlands their lands in Derbyshire, Nottinghamshire and Rutland were managed from one of the Lincolnshire precept- ories. Rents from Nottinghamshire included five marks for the mill at Girton, which was specifically set aside for sick and infirm brothers. Other property in Nottinghamshire included tenements in Newark and Nottingham and small parcels of land. In Derby- shire they held two tenements in Derby worth 4s a year and a close worth 1s 10d, and another two tenements in Chesterfield leased in 1185 to William the baker and the wife of Richard the Tanner. There were no Templar preceptories in these northern Midland counties, and it was the Knights Hospitaller who were prominent in Derbyshire.

In the neighbouring county of Leicestershire the Templars were to build a preceptory, but evidence from 1308 suggests that this was more likely to be linked to estates in Warwickshire than with those of its northern and eastern neighbours. Eileen Gooder shows that in 1308–9 livestock, crops and food were transferred between Rothley in Leicestershire and Temple Balsall in Warwickshire.[1] What is not clear, however, is whether this was for the convenience of the king's keepers of the estates, or followed the Templars' usual practice. The locations of the Templars' estates in the Midlands are identified on Map 5.1.

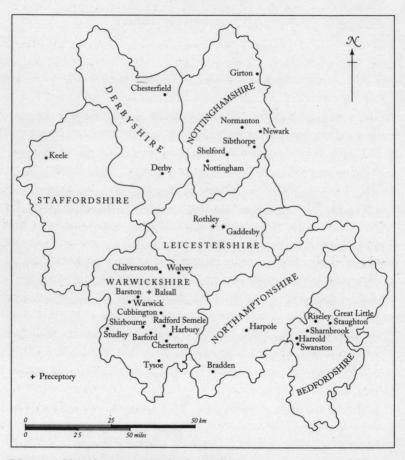

Map 5.1 Templar properties in the Midlands

THE PRECEPTORY AND ESTATE OF ROTHLEY,
LEICESTERSHIRE

There is some dispute among historians as to when the Templars acquired Rothley, and how much land they possessed there. *The Victoria County History* suggests that John de Harcourt gave them the land in 1203. Earlier writers, such as John Nichols, suggest the grant was later, in about 1218, but that the grant did not include the whole manor, which was granted to them by Henry III in 1231. It was at this point that the preceptory and church were built, and this is confirmed by a document in which the Abbot of Croxton claims 22s rent from the Templars for an assart made in 1231 when the king granted them the manor.[2]

As well as being a manor Rothley was also a soke with jurisdiction and privileges over a number of other manors. It is not clear whether the Templars were granted the fees from the soke or merely part of it. The 1240 *Testa de Neville* treats the soke as Templar property, but this was contested in the 1274 Hundred Rolls, although it would appear that by 1285 they were receiving the perquisites from the soke, and also had a weekly market and an annual fair in July.

Rothley lies on a brook which runs into the River Soar on the west of the road from Leicester to Loughborough. As the suffix 'ley' implies, this was a heavily wooded area and woodland clearance was required to make the land profitable. Assarting and clearance probably accounts for the structure of the estate at Rothley, with Rothley at the centre of a number of small, dispersed hamlets and granges, served by chapelries of the mother church at Rothley.

The profits from Rothley were to go directly to the Holy Land as aid for the Templars at Acre. This may have been the wish of the original donor, John Harcourt, who had been on crusade, and it reminds us that the prime function of the Templars in the British Isles was to provide resources for the fight against the infidel. Rothley was a valuable property with profits of about £40 a year. A further £4 5s came from the hamlets. The land was leased in units of a virgate with each virgater paying 3s a year in 1274, and about 70 acres were held in demesne. Profits must have increased because in 1338 the manor was worth £66 13s 4d.[3]

The preceptory was described by T.H. Fosbrooke as 'typically monastic, lying low amid pastures of vivid green through which the Rothley brook winds its course to Charnwood'. Very much in the mould of Bruer and South Witham, the buildings included a tower and a chapel within an enclosed court. The 1308 inventory confirms the similarity, describing a hall, kitchen, pantry, brewhouse and buttery as well as farm buildings and the chapel. The chapel contained vestments, service books, a chalice worth 10s and two silver vials that Ralph the Chaplain had taken into custody. The hall contained trestles and a wash-basin, but there is no mention of a place where the brothers could sleep, which suggests that Thomas of Walkington the preceptor of Temple Balsall arrested at Rothley was merely visiting, and that by 1308, the estate was run by lay labour. The high number of livestock listed show that several herdsmen were needed and probably ploughmen as well. Livestock included 24 plough oxen, 550 sheep, pigs and draught horses. Wheat, rye, drage, beans, peas and oats were stored in the barns, and other livestock and crops were found at Gaddesby and Babgrave.

Assets found at Rothley, 1308

Goods   £6 11s 1d
Crops   £45 6s 10d
Livestock £36 11s 4d[4]

As at other preceptories the goods and chattels only amounted to a small proportion of the value, and half of the total was made up of the goods in the chapel. Unless a considerable amount of goods were taken into prison with the brothers, or looting went on after the arrests, it points to an austere life-style – there was no evidence of the luxuries or wealth that the Templars were accused of possessing. The buildings, including the rectangular chapel, are still visible at Rothley, having been incorporated into a private dwelling, now a hotel.

Preceptors at Rothley
Stephen of Todmarsh
John Feversham
William of Ewerighwith
William of Wold
Alexander Blund
William of Colewell, *c.* 1271

WARWICKSHIRE

Warwickshire was felt to be important enough to have a baillie in its own right. It was worth £70 17s 4d in 1185, and was added to in the thirteenth century. Its central estate was Temple Balsall, another gift from Roger Mowbray. Mowbray also divided the nearby manor of Barston into two, giving half to the Hospitallers and half to the Templars. Gooder suggests that Barston was an older settlement than Balsall, but a higher percentage of locative names in Barston in 1185 suggests an influx of newcomers to settle on the Templars' lands (Table 5.1). This tells us that compared with other areas there was a fairly mobile population on the Templars' estates in Warwickshire, locative names showing movement from one vill to another, usually within a short area, although one householder occupying a Templars' tenement in Warwick came from Kent, and a tenant in Hardwick from France. A high proportion of names describe tradesmen. As well as the expected range of rural craftsmen, there are three masons listed as tenants at Tysoe indicating building activity there.

The Temple Balsall entry in the 1185 inquest presents a problem as it mentions that some land was put aside to form a park. In

Table 5.1 Distribution of names on Templar estates in
Warwickshire, 1185

Place	Locative Name (%)	Trade Name (%)	Son/Daughter of (%)	Single Name (%)	Other Name (%)
Balsall	12	5	7	66	10
Barston	20	9	6	56	9
Flechamstead	0	18	0	72	10
Harbury	9	18	9	27	37
Hardwick	9	0	0	72	19
Newbold	37	0	63	0	0
Shirebourne	13	21	17	35	13
Tysoe	11	22	5	22	40
Warwick	7	28	0	31	34

twelfth-century England this usually meant a deer park where the
animals were reserved for the lord to hunt. The Rule forbade hunting and no deer were found in 1308, but the park could mean a
paddock for the brothers' palfreys. The 1185 Inquest suggests that
the demesne was leased out at this time. Gooder takes this to
indicate that the preceptory was not yet built, and points out that
the first evidence of a preceptory at Balsall is in about 1220 when
Brother Arnoulf de Osnaville, 'preceptor of Balsall', witnessed a
charter.

Preceptors of Temple Balsall

Arnoulf de Osnaville	*c.* 1220
Robert English	*c.* 1229–48
Alan de Hayton	1259–60
Thomas de Walkington	1308

Gooder's in-depth analysis of Temple Balsall shows that during
the Templars' occupation the manor supported about 31 persons
who ate in the hall. From the inventory and subsequent keepers'

accounts she concludes that they were fed on a high cholesterol diet of cheese, bacon, ham and beans with a supply of dried fish for Fridays and Lent.[5]

As the corrodies mention different tables within preceptories, this implies that a different meal might have been served at each. At the high table where the knights dined they probably consumed beef, ham and bacon, whilst the servants were more likely to get pottage – a savoury oatmeal porridge – as their staple diet. However, accounts for the hospital at Eagle, drawn up in 1308, show that £8 13s 4d was spent on bread and £10 4s on flesh and fish, and a further £10 on beer. At Chingford the food provided for customary tenants undertaking labour service was bread, cheese and ale in the morning, and bread with two cooked dishes in the evening, whilst boon workers were given a dish of meat and fish with milk or cheese in the morning and a loaf and two herrings or cheese in the evening. Work on diet in the Middle Ages by Professor Dyer shows that the diet of the aristocrat was likely to be based on protein from meat and fish, that of priests more on bread with dairy produce, whilst the foundation of the peasant diet was bread and pottage, but with a growth in the consumption of meat after 1350.[6] By these standards the Templars' tenants and servants had a good, if not healthy, diet. The hens and eggs that formed part of the rent on many Templar manors would also have added to the diet, and the dovecote found on every manor would have provided a good source of protein. The inventories show that all preceptories included gardens and most had orchards, providing another valuable addition to the diet. Salt was an essential commodity in the Middle Ages. It helped to make the food more palatable, but was also needed to conserve food. The Templars had their own salt pans in coastal areas, and some rents were paid in pepper or cumin which would add spice to otherwise bland fare.

The contents of the inventory of Balsall show that this was a moderately well-appointed preceptory. But when the value of goods is compared with other inventories taken in the fourteenth century it can be seen that the Templars' goods are on the same scale as those found in peasant inventories, rather than what might be expected from a manorial household. The modest array of furniture, pots and pans are similar to those owned by the poorer peasant. At Balsall the assessors noted that some food and drink that should have been present was missing, indicating that some had helped themselves.

The preceptory is now known as the Old Hall and stands by the parish church of Balsall. The more modern exterior masks the aisled hall of the Templars. Dendrochronology shows the timbers used were felled between 1176 and 1221. The 1308 inventory describes a hall, chamber and chapel, and the whole was probably set within its own enclosure.[7] The value of the manor had risen from £10 5s 7d a year in 1185 to £69 17s 5d in 1308.

Values of Templar estates in Warwickshire and Oxfordshire, 1185

Warwickshire			Oxfordshire		
Balsall	£10	5s 7d	Cowley	£14	4s 10d
Harbury	£2	10s	Hensington	£5	3s
Hardwick	£2		Merton	£5	11s
Newbold		18s 6d	Oxford	£2	1s 6d
Shirebourne	£10	6s 9d			
Tysoe	£3	6s 4d			
Warwick	£2	19s 4d			

At Balsall the buildings and mills were in disrepair in 1308, and when the keeper took over the manors they were over-manned. Servants were dismissed, the manor was cleared of sheep and the cows leased out to tenants. Gooder sees this as an attempt to put what had become a ramshackle and unwieldy estate back into profitable production, and she suggests that the state of the manor was evidence of the Templars' 'negligence and apathy'.[8] It must also have been connected to the lack of recruits, and the loss of the prime reason for making sure that estates were well managed and profitable – the defence of the Holy Land. In the face of this disappointment the brothers struggled to maintain their grip on their estates and to keep this viable. Aggressive landownership disappeared and decay was the result. Prior to the first decade of the fourteenth century we catch glimpses of the Templars defending their rights over land in the king's court, and making sure that their neighbours did not encroach on these.

KEELE

The only preceptory in Staffordshire is unusual as it appears in the 1185 inquest as a gift from Henry II worth eight marks. At this point there was no preceptory or manor house where Templars were residing, and in 1206 the manor was leased to William de Edinton for 10 years at a rent of 10 marks. Christopher Harrison, in his *Essay on the History of Keele*, suggests that the land was being administered from Dinsley in Hertfordshire, but this is a misunderstanding of the way in which the Templars operated, as the lease was made at Dinsley with the agreement of the general chapter.[9]

The estate had been taken back in hand and a preceptory built by 1255 when the first documentary evidence for this appears. Harrison suggests that foundation of the preceptory resulted in an influx of tenants eager to take advantage of the Templars' privileges, and he recounts the story of Templar houses being marked with a cross to show exemption from local taxes. A considerable amount of labour would have been needed as part of the manor was still waste. The Templars' tenants cleared some of this and created four common fields. Nevertheless there was still 30 acres of waste in 1308. Once more there is a picture of decay in the preceptory, with the hall and the dovecote needing repairs, and no mention of a chapel. The whole estate was worth £20 4s 9d. This shows a steady rise in the value of the estate thanks to the efforts of the Templars and their tenants.

But the Templars had another source of income at Keele. Today Keele is noted for the eponymous university and its position astride the M6, a major route. In the Middle Ages Keele was also on a major route, with laden packhorses coming from the north-west on their way to London. The Templars were allowed to charge 4d for each laden packhorse passing through their lands at Keele, helping to increase their profits from the estate.[10]

BEDFORDSHIRE

There were no preceptories in Bedfordshire, but the Templars possessed some sizeable estates in that county at Great and Little Staughton on the Huntingdonshire border – Harrold, Langford, Melchbourne, Riseley, Sandy and Sharnbrook – all of which appear in the 1185 inquest. Placenames indicate the type of land the Templars were trying to farm. Sharnbrook and Langford were on the Great Ouse and liable to flood. Melchbourne was on a stream that only appeared in exceptionally wet weather. The area was densely wooded. The Ordnance Survey map shows that even today there is a belt of woodland from Harrold in the south to Melchbourne in the north. This meant that woodland had to be cleared before cultivation could start.

The Bedfordshire preceptories were managed from Hertfordshire and, like much of the Hertfordshire land, came into the Templars' hands soon after their arrival in the British Isles. The estates at Sharnbrook and Langford were confirmed as belonging to the Order in 1142, and a grant of a virgate in Sandy followed in 1154. The estate at Sharnbrook was the result of several small gifts that, put together, made a good-sized block of land, but one which was complicated to manage as the labour service requirements on the land given by each donor was different.

Labour service obligations at Sharnbrook

Donor	Service requirement
Alice de Claremont	2 autumn ploughs
De Bray land	All service
Odell land	Mowing hay, ploughing and a gift at Christmas[11]

Much of the land at Sharnbrook had to be cleared from woodland. In 1185 the Pipe Roll shows that the Templars had illegally assarted 25s worth of land, and in 1189 they were pardoned for the illegal possession of 200 acres of assarts. Temple Wood and Temple Spinney still exist in the village today. Land clearance and the need to find tenants to work the newly cleared areas may account for the large proportion of locative names among the Templars' tenants in Sharnbrook (Table 5.2).

Locative names at Sharnbrook included a family from Edworth, Bedfordshire, and Rushden, Northamptonshire, and those living on newly reclaimed land such as the Newhay. There is also evidence that Sharnbrook was developing some urban features with a merchant living there, as well as rural craftsmen such as smiths. At Melchbourne there were two plasterers who were involved in putting the daub infill into the wattle and daub panels of timber-framed

Table 5.2 Distribution of names on Templar estates in Bedfordshire, 1185

Place	Locative Name (%)	Trade Name (%)	Son/Daughter of (%)	Single Name (%)	Other Name (%)
Langford	22	33	44	0	0
Melchbourne	28	29	14	29	0
Sharnbrook	33	10	29	10	14

houses. These individuals only represent those occupying the Templars' property and not the whole village. Record linkage shows that in the case of Sharnbrook there may have been some stability of family members with a smith and a merchant still occupying Templar premises in 1279.[12] Unfortunately there is no proof that these were from the same family or whether they occupied premises suitable for these trades. A dispute over title to land in 1247 provides another link to the preceding generations. Matilda, the widow of Alexander son of Osbert, sued Stephen Turner for the restitution of lands held from the Templars that she claimed as her jointure from her late husband. In 1185 Osbert, son of Azor, had held one virgate from the Templars. This could refer to the same virgate being claimed by Matilda. It could also be the same virgate on the Templars' land held by William Alexander in 1279.[13] If these names are linked and this is not coincidence, these show the same family holding Templar land through three generations. The sequence also shows the rise in rents between 1185 and 1279.

Rent per virgate on the Templars' estate at Sharnbrook, 1185–1279

1185	4s
1247	7s
1279	14s

Value of Swanton Manor, Harrold, 1308

Goods	£1 1s 10d
Grain	£43 15s
Livestock	£49 15s
Total	£110 17s 10d

In Harrold the Templars had to establish a foothold in a vill that already had two strong landlords, Harrold Priory and Ralph Morin.

They also had to cope with frequent floods that inundated their land. In 1240 Ralph Morin claimed that the Templars had taken one acre of meadow in Crescroft where he used to make hay and graze his beasts. Brother Richard of Dinsley, representing the Templars as their bailiff, said that he and Ralph had reached an agreement that each would graze their beasts on the common land, but the jurors from the vill said the land was Ralph's and the Templars should not put their beasts on it. A little later the Templars claimed that Morin had diverted a stream that had flooded their land and washed away the earth. The jurors again declared for Ralph. The next time Ralph and the Templars came into court the Templars complained that Ralph had broken an agreement and had driven his beasts and horses beyond the dykes that enclosed the Templars' land and had devastated crops and pastures. Ralph said that the beasts had got in because the enclosure was faulty. The problems continued. In May 1244 the Templars summonsed Ralph for putting his sheep and other beasts in their common pasture. Eventually Ralph agreed that the Templars could graze 140 sheep on the common pasture of the vill, providing they did not damage his crops or stray on to his demesne. In return, the Templars granted him half of the common pasture between Cakesbrook and the road to Harrold.[14]

These disputes over land, enclosures, trespass and damage appear in great numbers in the thirteenth century as cases heard by the Justices of the Eyre. Small local squabbles that should have been settled locally were taking advantage of the king's justice. In the later Middle Ages undoubtedly these arguments would have erupted into violence, and it is a tribute to both parties that an agreement was reached without this happening. It is also noticeable that as the disputes escalate the Templars mobilise their most important figure, the Master and his agents.

The Master was also involved in a dispute with the Prior of Chicksands over the common pasture in Little Staughton. It was to this vill that Hugh le Prest, felon and outlaw in Lincolnshire and murderer in Huntingdonshire, fled when pursued by the sheriffs and the hue and cry of these counties on 18 June 1271. Hugh took refuge in the house of Roger, one of the Templars' servants, but was discovered, dragged out and slain. His horse was later discovered grazing on the Templars' land and was deemed to be the property of the whole vill.

Possibly Hugh was hoping that the Templars' privilege of offering sanctuary would protect him. This was a privilege which often brought the Order into conflict with its neighbours and the officers of justice, who frequently violated sanctuaries in order to get their hands on the wrongdoers, and their goods.

THE CHILTERNS AND BERKSHIRE

On the Chilterns the Templars had a manor at Radnage, and another at Wycombe, as well as land in Calverton, Chalfont St Peter, Hedgerley and Stony Stratford in Buckinghamshire. Where the Thames formed a boundary between Buckinghamshire and Berkshire they founded a preceptory on the Berkshire side at Bistlesham, or Bisham as it became known. The site was given to them in about 1145 with 40 acres of assarted land. This was a richly wooded area lying on a mixture of clay and chalk, ideal for mixed farming. Its proximity to the river meant there was easy access from London and Bisham was to become an important preceptory, playing host to the general chapter. The 1308 inventory shows the site included a forge and had a total value of £132 12s 1d.[15]

Other manors in Berkshire lay on the Berkshire downs at Inkpen, Kintbury and Sparsholt. These were administered from the Oxfordshire preceptories rather than Bisham, and because of this appear in the Sandford Cartulary. For a map of the Templar properties on the Chilterns, Berkshire and Oxfordshire see Map 5.2.

Map 5.2 Templar properties in the Chilterns, Berkshire and Oxfordshire

The Sandford Cartulary

The Sandford Cartulary was compiled in the second half of the thirteenth century at the instigation of Robert le Escroppe, preceptor of Sandford in 1265. It contains details of all the land and manors administered from Sandford. These were widespread, including not only properties in Oxfordshire but in Wiltshire, Hampshire and the Isle of Wight as well as Berkshire. It is evidence for the efficient organisation of the Templars' network of holdings, and of the many documents referring to this that are now lost. The 1308 inventories show that most preceptories had chests and barrels containing their muniments, but only those copied into a book at Sandford survived. The Cartulary is now in the Bodleian Library. It was transcribed by Agnes Leys in 1938 and published by the Oxfordshire Record Society.[16]

OXFORDSHIRE

The first preceptory built in Oxfordshire was at Cowley, now part of the city of Oxford. This was erected on four hides of land given to the Templars by King Stephen's queen, Matilda, in 1139, with other grants of land following in the first half of the thirteenth century. The preceptory was on the north side of the road to Dorchester, on the Thames just below the bridge, with open fields to the south and the east of the vill. In 1185 a quarter of the land was in demesne, about 120 acres.[17] The rest was let to 16 tenants in blocks of half virgates for 3s a year, and to 16 cottagers paying between 3s and 9d a year. All tenants owed heavy labour services: half virgaters had to work at least two days a week throughout the year, ploughing, sowing and harrowing in spring, and provide four men each for a day's boon work in the autumn, and carry produce to market on a Saturday. The cottars owed 1–2 days work a week and, as well as paying a cash rent, had to supply four hens a year.

Temple Cowley was densely populated, but the land was added to by subsequent grants and by assarts that created large pastures. By the mid-fourteenth century it included a sheepfold, two mills, a fishery and the church, and the Templars had started to enclose the arable land. A charter of *c.* 1180 shows a special relationship between the Templars at Cowley and Osney Abbey. The abbot promised to have a special service in the abbey for all the dead Templars, to make a special obit for the Master of the Temple, and every three years to make an ovation for all Templars alive or dead.[18] This is an unusual charter, as other religious institutions viewed the Templars' colonisation of the British countryside with suspicion.

Not to be outdone by her rivals in 1141, the Empress Matilda gave Temple Cowley rights of pasture in Shotover Forest, and lest anyone forget that she was the rightful occupier of the throne of England, this was for the soul of her father, Henry I. Shotover Forest was surrounded by vills, of which Cowley was one. A survey taken in about 1298 which shows the forest boundaries gives the Templars' holding as Akemere wood, which lay just beyond the forest in the vill of Horsepath and was granted to the Templars in 1225 by Bernard Malet.[19] Horsepath included land on the slopes of Otmoor described in 1823 as 'dreary and extensive'.[20] Nevertheless, this was a large holding of at least 880 acres as well as woods and common pasture on the moor. 120 acres was in demesne, but this does not seem to have produced the heavy service load found at Cowley. However, the returns from the manor were not commensurate with the amount of land in it, and this could be the result of hiring labour to work the demesne.

Value of Horsepath 1194–1338

1194	£3 14s
1195	£6
1308	£6 9s 2d
1312	£6 4s 5d
1338	£7[21]

After Thomas de Sandford gave the Templars Sandford on Thames in 1239 the preceptory at Cowley was deserted and a new one built at Sandford. The original grant gave the property to the Templars at Bisham, and they may have intended the new preceptory as a rival to Cowley and a base for them in Oxfordshire. Good sense prevailed and Cowley was abandoned in favour of Sandford. Much of the Sandford land was pasture on islands and eyots in the Thames and in order to take advantage of this livestock were ferried across in flat-bottomed punts.

Merton, near Bicester, was an important manor which was given to the Templars in 1152–53 by Simon, Earl of Northampton, for the soul of himself and his wife, and confirmed by Malcolm King of Scotland in his capacity as Earl of Huntingdon and Simon's overlord. Although in an isolated spot, it had 25 tenants in 1185, most holding either one or half a virgate, and was worth £4 12s 8d a year. Much effort was put into clearing woodland at Merton, as well as in the construction of a water mill, a mill leet and a bridge. By the end of the thirteenth century the land had been extended to seven hides and the number of tenants to 49, of whom 37 were virgaters and 12 cottars.

Value of Merton, 1185–1338

Date	Number of tenants	Value
1185	25	£4 12s 8d
1279	49	£7 10s 9d
1308	31	£6 5s 10d
1338	N/A	£5 12s 6d[22]

Services were estimated to be worth 57s 9d in 1311, but no information on this was given in 1185.

In 1311, whilst the manor was under the care of the king's keeper, it was mainly arable, with some sheep (Table 5.3), but this does not really give the entire picture of the resources of the manor as this was rich dairy land, and in 1311 there were 165 cheeses and 19 gallons of butter in stock.

Table 5.3 Land use in Oxfordshire on the Templar demesne, 1308[23]

Estate	Arable Acres	Pasture Acres
Cowley	300	28
Horsepath	280	9
Merton	224	40
Sandford	300	28
Sibford	200	6

Although Table 5.3 emphasises the dominance of arable farming in 1308, this is not reflected in the value of the land (Table 5.4).

Table 5.4 Land value on Templar estates in Oxfordshire, 1308[24]

Estate	Arable (per acre)	Pasture (per acre)
Cowley	6d	3s
Horsepath	6d	2s
Merton	10d	3s
Sandford	6d	3s
Sibford	6d	2s

The difference in value between arable and pasture and the greater amount of arable land, even on manors like Merton which was on heavy clay or Sandford which was liable to flood, are an indication of the difficulty in feeding an ever-increasing population since every acre of cultivatable land was at a premium.

As well as country estates the Templars had 11 tenements in Oxford which were occupied by craftsmen such as a goldsmith, a cordwainer and a smith.

Like the Bedfordshire manors, name evidence reveals a relatively high percentage of trades and craftsmen. However, evidence from the 1308 inventories for Oxfordshire includes lists of tenants and these show that simple surnames have disappeared and there is

Table 5.5 Distribution of names on Templar estates in
Oxfordshire, 1185

Place	Locative Name (%)	Trade Name (%)	Son/Daughter of (%)	Single Name (%)	Other Name (%)
Broadwell	4	8	0	82	0
Cowley	12	12	0	63	12
Merton	9	12	12	52	16
Oxford	0	36	9	55	0

Table 5.6 Distribution of names on Templar estates in
Oxfordshire, 1308

Place	Locative Name (%)	Trade Name (%)	Son/Daughter of (%)	Single Name (%)	Other Name (%)
Essendon	0	30	0	0	70
Horsepath	42	15	0	0	23
Littlemore	54	4	0	0	42
Merton	15	15	0	0	70
Sandford	18	36	0	0	45

an increase of locative and trade names, indicating more spatial
mobility on the Oxfordshire estates, and an increase in number
of trades. Unfortunately, later comparative material does not exist
for Bedfordshire. In 1308 the simple surnames have disappeared
and there is an increase in locative and trade names (Tables 5.5
and 5.6).

Farming for the market?

Were Oxfordshire estates being farmed for the market? David
Postles asked this question about seigneurial demesnes in order
to see how Oxfordshire estates responded to the growing

commercialisation of society between the late twelfth and early fourteenth centuries. One key to this was, he felt, the effort to use labour more intensively. An example of this would be the continuation of heavy labour service obligations, as seen at Cowley. Another key was the size of the demesne. Compared with the manors Postles looked at, the Templars had a smaller ratio of demesne on their manors, which suggests that they were relying on rents rather than produce to make a profit. However, at Cowley a quarter of the land was in demesne, and part of the service obligation was to carry produce to market. This manor, it would seem, was being farmed for a market economy.

The manorial accounts used by Postles do not exist for the Templars' manors so comparison is difficult, but one feature that emerges from Postles's study and the Templars' manors is the density of population in Oxfordshire. All the Templars' manors had a large number of tenants. Even in 1185 the rents were high, and Postles suggests they had been since Domesday. This was a land already feeling the pinch of scarcity.[25]

HOW DID THE TEMPLARS FIT IN WITH THE REST OF SOCIETY?

One factor that is easily forgotten when discussing the Templars in the west is that it is the conventual side of their life that was most important, and this meant living within an enclosed community dedicated to the worship of God. Although in popular imagination, fuelled by Sir Walter Scott, Templar knights thunder about the countryside fully armed on war horses, this was not the case. In the west the members of the Order were monks adhering to their vows of chastity, poverty and obedience, observing silence within the preceptory precincts, and hearing the offices throughout the day and night. But there is no evidence that they undertook manual work, and they were not confined to the cloister. They attended the general chapter, and there was movement of brothers between preceptories. There is no evidence in the 1308 inventories of any intellectual or literary activity. The only books found were the service books, and no writing materials were discovered, although it is possible that they took these into prison with them. It is also possible that some theological dispute went on within the preceptory walls, but it is more likely that, as Jacques de Molay suggested, these were simple and unlettered men with strong religious ideals and a burning ambition to reclaim the Holy Land for Christ. It has been assumed that recruits came from the knightly rather than the aristocratic class, and all recruits had to declare themselves free men when they were initiated into the Order. However, we do not really know who these men were. We have some names, but many of the surnames are the same as Templar preceptories or manors, and this could be the location of where they entered the Order rather than where they came from.

Thus, to answer the question how did the Templars fit in with the rest of society, we have to piece together the evidence from what little we have. They were manorial landlords and held manorial courts, just as any other lord of the manor. They collected rents and demanded labour service and gifts from their tenants, just as any other manor did, and they employed professionals and servants to look after their livestock. Other landholders did the same. They were often involved in disputes with their neighbours about trespass, damage and illegal enclosure, but this was normal in the medieval countryside.

Moving about the countryside the Templar would have been instantly recognisable, with cropped hair, a long beard and the Templars' white or brown mantle. Any who met them would have known who they were. They were also part of the establishment. In their early years in the British Isles they probably spoke Norman French or Latin rather than English, which would have set them apart. They helped to collect taxes and tithes but did not pay these themselves, making them unpopular and objects of suspicion, and the papal bulls threatening excommunication to those who pulled Templars from their horses or otherwise harmed them suggests that they were liable to be assaulted by their neighbours.

The Templars were also visible in public life, acting as crown officers, envoys and treasurers. Those carrying out these tasks were a handful of high-ranking Templars, who were usually stationed in London or at one of the urban preceptories such as Bristol. There would seem to be a wide gap between them and the ordinary brother or sergeant in a small, isolated rural preceptory, worshipping God and overseeing the daily life on the manor.

CHAPTER SIX

THE TEMPLARS IN THE COUNTRYSIDE: THE WELSH MARCHES, WALES, THE WEST AND SOUTHERN ENGLAND

THE MARCHES AND WALES

In the Middle Ages the Welsh Marches were a frontier zone between people who spoke different languages, had different cultures, and lived by a different legal system. This was a lawless and violent area where the Marcher lords fought their private wars and the king of England's justice did not go. The Marcher lord had the liberty to build castles, hear all pleas, collect fines and ransoms, operate prisons and gallows, authorise and run markets and fairs, issue coins, and control weights and measures. All roads and rivers and any seaboard in his territory belonged to the Marcher lord who was the representative of a powerful group in local society.

Those living in the Marches went in fear of warfare, sudden death, kidnap and robbery. This was a military landscape with stone castles looming over the countryside at all strategic points, and a broad band of waste (uncultivated land) marking where the frontier land lay. Woodland was cleared in the Marches not only to make the land productive, but to give the occupants a clear view of anyone who might be approaching them, and to protect them from wolves. In 1281 Peter Corbet was given a writ to take and destroy all wolves he could find in the forests and parks of the Marcher counties and Staffordshire.[1]

This was a secular landscape where, apart from a few exceptions such as Haughmond Abbey, the majority of the lordships in the hands of warriors. Perhaps it was appropriate that both the military orders should have houses in the Marches. The Templars had two preceptories in Herefordshire and one in Shropshire, as well as scattered holdings in these two counties, and in Worcestershire. See Map 6.1 for Templar properties in Wales and on the Marches.

The documentary evidence for one of the preceptories shows the fluidity of the frontier. The earliest references to Garway in Herefordshire are to Llangarewi, showing it to be in a Welsh-speaking area. Llangarewi was granted to the Templars by Henry II, along with the right to assart 2,000 acres of wood. The Templars' possession of this land was confirmed by Richard I in 1189 for the sake of his father's soul, and later John was to add rights in the royal forest of Aconbury to the holding. By this time it was known as Garway and was in an English-speaking area.

The county of Hereford was on the major north–south route along the border with Wales. Garway lay in the south-west of the county, 11 miles south-west of Hereford on the south bank of the River Monmow, facing the Black Mountains and sandwiched between two castles. John Webb described the situation in 1844 as 'a remote and romantic spot above a dingle that descends towards the river Monmow. No place, indeed could have been better suited to the tranquillity enforced by the role of these monastic soldiers, to whom silence and devotional exercises were enjoined as preparation and accompaniment to the hard-ship and self possession of the religious life.'[2] Garway lies in a belt of nucleated villages, and the preceptory lay in the centre of the village by the church. Although this was the parish church dedicated to St Michael, it was redesigned by the Templars. In the last quarter of the twelfth century they added a round nave, which was connected to the chancel by a magnificent Norman arch (Figure 6.1).

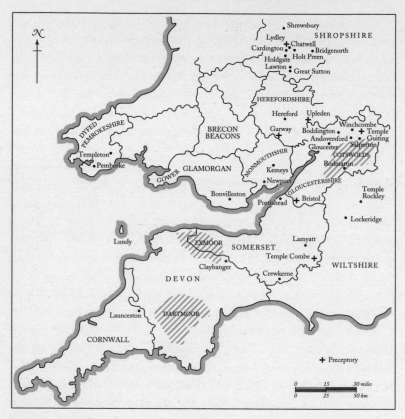

Map 6.1 Templar properties in Wales, the Marches and the West of England

Garway Church is good evidence that the round-naved churches associated with the Templars are in fact frozen in time, and that given the opportunity and resources the Templars re-modelled their churches as building techniques and architectural taste changed. In the late thirteenth century the round nave was rebuilt on a rectangular plan, the apsoidal eastern end of the chancel was squared off and a freestanding tower was built. The foundations of the

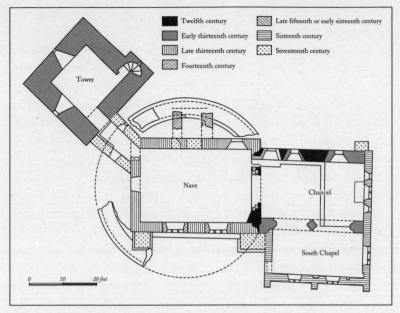

Figure 6.1 Plan of Garway Church (Based on the RCHME report, 1931)

round nave were discovered in 1927 and found to be of massive proportions. Inside the church are a number of coffin lids with foliated crosses on them, and in the south chapel a series of incised lines that appear to represent a chalice, a holy wafer, a fish and a serpent. It is not clear whether these and two other reliefs of a crucifixion and a head date from the Templars' time. These could even pre-date the Templars as the name Llangarewi indicates that there was a church on the site before it was given to the Templars, and the fish was an early Christian symbol. Nevertheless, these have been interpreted as being part of the Templars' mystical rituals.

As was shown at Temple Bruer, legends about the Templars' activities have become associated with their preceptories. During a visit to Garway in the early twentieth century by the Cambrian Archaeological Association the then vicar, the Reverend E.F. Powys, suggested that the tower had been used as a place of confinement for refractory Templars and that it was still known locally as the prison. He also pointed out that the east and west windows of the church were abnormally high and this was so that outsiders would not be able to observe the Templars' initiation ceremonies. He claimed that his predecessor had found an old chest under the floor of the chancel that had contained the deeds and other documents belonging to the Order (now of course long disappeared).

In 1308 Garway consisted of a manor, a water mill and a chapel that might have been the south chapel in the church. There were 200 acres in demesne, lying in open fields. A number of other estates were managed from Garway, including those in Wales. This needed a large establishment. It included a baker, and cook, and other servants, as well as three corrodians. Perhaps because of its proximity to the border with Wales, and the visits that its brethren had to make into what was still sometimes hostile country, the Templars arrested at Garway in 1308 were younger than elsewhere. Philip de Mewes, the preceptor, had been in the Order for five years, and William de Pocklington for three.

Wales was really the Hospitallers' territory and the Templars had only a few scattered manors in Gower, Glamorgan, the Lordship of Newport and a mill at the Pembroke Castle bridge. In the Gower peninsula the Templars held Llanmadoc manor and church, which were given to them by Margaret, Countess of Warwick. Llanmadoc lies on the western tip of the peninsula on a road that goes nowhere else, close to the Bristol Channel and overlooking extensive sand dunes. Here the land was divided into strips in the manor's open fields. The Templars had 123 acres in demesne, but by 1308 had leased all but eight of these to tenants at an annual rent of 6d per acre. Eleven villeins shared another 63 acres between them, and although they owed labour service for these as well as cash rents, this had been commuted to cash.

Commutation of labour service to cash, Llanmadoc manor, 1308

2 days harrowing a year or 2 days ploughing	2d
Week work and weeding	1d
2 days hay-making	1d
4 days boon work	4d
Total cash per year from the commutation of demesne rents	£4 14s 8d

Also on the manor were four cottars paying 24s rent between them[3]

Llanmadoc is one of the best examples on the Templars' estates of a decision to decrease the amount of land in demesne in order to commute labour services into cash. This may not have been a purely economic decision but one of expediency as managing the manor from far-distant Garway would have been difficult, and the only Templar servant found on the manor in 1308 was a stockman who looked after the plough oxen and draught horses. Llanmadoc was seized in 1308 by the Sheriff of Carmarthenshire, who, with an escort of 12 men, took a leisurely three days to ride from Carmarthen to Llanmadoc, charging the crown 1s a day for his expenses and 6d each for his men – nearly as much as the manor was worth a year.[4]

One of the features of the Gower and Dyfed landscapes is the number of Anglicised place-names that consist of a personal name plus 'ton', the Anglo-Saxon word denoting a village, for example Reynoldston in Gower, or Wiston in Dyfed. These were sites where the Normans encouraged settlement by outsiders, offering redemption from taxes for a given period and free land. This gave them enclaves of friendly populations living in villages that are characterised by regular patterns of streets and village green. The Templars founded a village like this a few miles from Narbeth in Dyfed that became known as Templeton. Another Welsh manor managed from Garway was Pencarn on the coastal road from Newport to Cardiff. The Templars also had 12 acres of land at Bonvilleston, which was given to them by William the Harper in 1203, plus a further 30 acres from John de Bonville in 1205. This land was leased to Margam Abbey which was closer and in a better position to oversee the organisation of the tenants on this land.

The Templars' presence in Wales was not strong, and they appear to have had little influence on the local population. No Templars arrested in 1308 had Welsh surnames or bore the names of Welsh places.

Wales, Ireland and Scotland were not the only alien states that the Templars entered via grants from a conquering power. There is an analogy with the Templars in Aragon who were granted land in areas that had been previously under Muslim domination during the *reconquista*. Here they needed to encourage the Muslim population to stay as their tenants rather than departing to Moorish Spain, and they also needed to attract new settlers into the area as well.[5] Inducement was in the form of special privileges, and the exemption from labour services.

How far were the Templars who were in charge of the farms and manors aware of what was going on in other provinces? There is good evidence that the Grand Master visited different provinces frequently, and the Master of the English Templars and other brothers travelled backwards and forwards between England and the continent. Letters passed between provinces, and orders and requests for aid from the east were part of the Templar's everyday life. We can be reasonably sure that the Templars were aware of what was happening in other provinces, and there may have been a central policy on how to manage the colonisation of land in hostile or frontier situations. As the central records of the Order have not survived, we can only reconstruct what might have happened from local records. There is evidence in Aragon that the Templars sub-let their estates to other religious bodies when these were at a distance from the nearest preceptory. This happened at Bonvilleston, and the village of Templeton was to be assimilated into the Lordship of Narbeth. Forey points out that sub-infeudation meant higher rents in the short term, but did not enable the Templars to work their demesne and maximise the profits from this when market prices were high. In Aragon it often made it difficult for them to collect the dues and services owed to them as overlords of the property.[6]

The Welsh estates lay at the end of a chain of authority that started in Jerusalem and was administered through a provincial government, of which Garway was its last management post. This made Wales, lacking any preceptory of its own, difficult to manage, and it is significant that when the Hospitallers took over Garway and its estates, the Welsh estates were immediately leased out.

Two other frontier preceptories lay in the Welsh Marches: Upleden (Upleaden) at Bosbury in Herefordshire and Lydley in Shropshire. Upleden had no Welsh estates attached to it. Lydley was given to the Order by representatives of the great Marcher families of the Fitz-Alans and the Costellos. William Fitz-Alan also added the whole townships of Cardington and Enchmarsh. The preceptory at Lydley stood on the site of what is now Penkridge Hall in an isolated position close to Botwood Forest and the open common of Lawley. Cardington and Enchmarsh lie at the foot of Caer Caradoc between Wenlock Edge and the Long Mynd. This is an upland region and was heavily wooded in the Middle Ages. The Templars were quick to realise the economic potential of their Lydley estates and by 1185 had cleared over 170 acres of the forest, built a mill and had 45 tenants in the vills of Cardington, Enchmarsh and Chatwell paying £6 15s 7d in rent a year. None of these tenants owed labour service, but instead their heirs had to pay one-third of their goods at their death. This points to the newly cleared land being

Table 6.1 Distribution of names on Templar estates in Shropshire, 1185

Place	Locative Name (%)	Trade Name (%)	Son/Daughter of (%)	Single Name (%)	Other Name (%)
Cardington	16	14	10	37	23
Chatwell	0	20	10	50	20
Enchmarsh	0	10	20	50	20

freehold or customary land. The lack of labour service may account for the large numbers of staff resident at Lydley in 1308 with 16 farm servants, eight ploughmen, and a shepherd for 280 sheep. The relatively high proportion of surnames associated with trades at Chatwell and Cardington show these to be well-developed villages, providing services for the surrounding countryside (Table 6.1).

Lydley is an area of upland pastoral farming with arable in the valleys, and Gaydon suggests that the Templars at Lydley practised a strong and aggressive lordship that brought them into conflict with their neighbours.[7] This is reflected in the lease in 1263 of Castle Holegate, a valuable arable manor. Most of this land was kept in demesne, and the Templars' success in farming soon made them the envy of their neighbours. In 1274 this envy erupted into violence when Sir John Giffard and his men ambushed the Temple servants as they took oats to Ludlow market, stealing the grain and harrowing it into the ground using the horses stolen from the Templars' carts. The convoy appeared to have been travelling without an armed guard, and the Templars did not resort to violence, as was often the case in the Marches, but took Giffard to law.

In 1308 the Lydley estates were worth £44 and Upleden £32 4s 4d a year.[8] Two brothers were at Lydley. Henry de Halton, who was described as the warden, and Stephen de Stapelbrugge, who escaped, threw off his robe and fled to Salisbury where he was eventually arrested. His evidence was to help condemn the Templars in the British Isles.

Preceptors of Lydley

John de Houton	1261
Richard Lovel	1273
Stephen	1292
Henry of Halton, 'warden'	1308

THE WEST — THE TEMPLARS AND SHEEP FARMING

The three western preceptories of Temple Guiting in the Cotswolds, Temple Combe in the Blackmore Vale of Somerset and Temple Rockley on the Marlborough Downs in Wiltshire were all in sheep-farming country. Temple Guiting was the gift of Gilbert de Lacy. It consisted of 1,460 acres, including sheep walks on the wolds, and there is archaeological evidence for sheep-cotes on the hills above Guiting, probably put there by the Templars. These are boat-shaped, banked enclosures that contained shelter for the animals, a fodder store, a lambing shed, and residential accommodation for the shepherd, and are a universal feature of the Cotswold landscape. R.C. Baldwyn and H. O'Neill, who excavated the Guiting cotes, think that these indicated that there was a coordinated organisation of the Templar estates in Gloucestershire, with sheep being brought to the high pastures from manors in the lowland.[9] As the Templars also had a fulling mill at Bereton it is probable that woollen cloth was being made on their Gloucestershire manors and being sold in Bristol and Gloucester, and this is reflected in the high proportion of trade surnames in the area (Table 6.2).

Temple Combe lies in the lush Vale of Blackmore. It was the centre of an estate that included land in 14 vills. In some of these mixed farming of livestock and arable in open fields was carried on, but there was a great deal of cloth-making in this area, and all the villages on the Mendips had common pasture on the hills that was open, unfenced sheep walks. To increase their share of this the Templars purchased 20 acres of land in West Harptree that became

Table 6.2 Distribution of names on Templar estates in Gloucestershire, 1185

Place	Locative Name (%)	Trade Name (%)	Son/Daughter of (%)	Single Name (%)	Other Name (%)
Aniford	16	16	0	0	68
Guiting	0	23	0	46	31
Kineton	0	18	9	18	36

known as Temple Hydon. With this 20 acres went the right to pasture 1,000 sheep and 60 other beasts on the Mendips.

It was in a cottage in the village that the Temple Combe head was found. This head, which may or may not be associated with the Templars, is a medieval painting on wood of a bearded head that may represent Christ, and is now in Temple Combe church.

Templars arrested in 1308

Temple Guiting	**Length of service**
John de Coningham	36 years
William de Crawcumbe	3 years

Temple Combe	**Length of service**
William Burton	4 years
John de Ivel	
Walter de Rockley	
Roger de Wyle	

Temple Rockley on the chalk of the Marlborough Downs was another sheep-farming manor. It was given to the Templars in 1155 by John Marshall and his family added another two hides of land at Lockeridge in 1185. Evidence for the importance of sheep in this area comes from the service requirements for Lockeridge which stated that each five-acre holder was to find one woman to milk the ewes and make cheese, and one man to wash and shear the sheep. Between Rockley and Lockeridge the Templars had pasture for 1,200 sheep on the Downs.

Work on monastic estates has shown that sheep were the most numerous livestock, and that on secular estates there was an increase in the numbers of sheep kept in the thirteenth century. But sheep farming by the tenants was on a small scale. The huge flocks on the Downs belonged to the landlords who recognised the value of sheep to their economy. These sheep were not being farmed for their meat, although mutton was an essential feature of the monastic diet, but for their wool which was a valuable cash crop, either as fleeces or when made into cloth. The Templars' licence was for the export of wool rather than cloth so it is possible that the cloth made at Combe and Guiting was for their own use, to make the white mantles for the knights and the brown for the sergeants.

BRISTOL – THE TEMPLARS, TRADE AND SHIPPING

In the late thirteenth and early fourteenth centuries Bristol was the largest city after London with a population of more than 10,000. It was a prime commercial centre and, after London, the most important point of entry from Gascony and its wine trade. It developed into a trading centre in the ninth century as a convenient crossing-point on the Avon, and by 1200 was a walled city with a royal castle. It began to extend beyond the walls in the twelfth century, with the parish of St Mary Redcliffe in existence by 1158. This settlement was in the Berkeley fee and it was intended to become a trading rival to Bristol.[10] It was in Redcliffe that the Templars were given land by Robert, Earl of Gloucester, sometime before 1147. This became known as the Temple Fee, and its location exists today as Temple Meads where Isambard Kingdom Brunel built his Great Western Railway Station.

By 1185 the Templars had 27 tenants on their fee paying between 6d and 4s a year rent. Even at this time this was an industrial

Table 6.3 Distribution of names in the Temple Fee, Bristol, 1185

Place	Locative Name (%)	Trade Name (%)	Son/Daughter of (%)	Single Name (%)	Other Name (%)
Bristol	18	22	11	22	26

area with three skinners among the Templars' tenants, suggesting a tannery, and a little later it became known for its textile industry – and the weavers' gild was to have its gild chapel in the Templar church (see Table 6.3).

Redcliffe and Bristol were taxed separately and it was not until the two realised that working together in a common interest would be more profitable that they were united. Joint efforts between Bristol, Redcliffe and the Temple Fee included the construction of a new wall south of the river that helped to include this area within the city of Bristol and enclosing a marsh so that the Avon was diverted and made more accessible for shipping. The Templars also constructed a stone bridge built over the Avon. From the Bristol preceptory the Templars administered an inland estate that stretched as far as Cornwall. The chapel survives but in ruins, having been badly bombed in 1940.

One reason for the Templars' interest in helping with projects on the Avon was to improve access to the port for shipping. The Templars were ship owners with a fleet at La Rochelle and another at Marseilles. Although the sources on their maritime activities are scarce, it is possible to reconstruct these from state papers and other accounts. They needed shipping for three purposes: (1) the transport of men, horses, pilgrims and goods to the Holy Land; (2) transporting goods, pilgrims, money and resources in the west; and (3) for use in battle.

Transporting men and horses was done in two types of vessel: galleys that had holds which could be used for merchandise or horses and were powered by sail, with oars used in shallow water, and landing barges for taking the horses ashore, powered by oars. The difficulty of transporting horses by sea led to many crusaders taking an overland route that took considerably longer. The journey from London to Italy took about four months, with the final stage on northern Italian galleys. William of Tyre describes how the Byzantine fleet had specially adapted vessels for the transport of horses, with large openings in the stern with ramps for the horses to be led down. These had to be powered by oar to enable them to be manoeuvred backwards on to a beach, which would have been impossible under sail. These vessels were known as busses and could carry 40 war horses and 40 men at arms as well as the crew. It was this type of boat that Richard I used to take him from Marseilles to Cyprus and from Cyprus to Acre. The manpower needed to propel one of these was considerable, and most of it came from slave labour.[11] Muslim slaves were one of the commodities transported in the Templars' fleet. The Templars would have needed a large fleet of this type of vessel during a crusade in order to transport their recruits to the Holy Land. They also had a war fleet that was seen in action at the Siege of Damietta. This too included busses or other ships of small draught as they were operating in a river, but there were larger galleys and other ships present.[12]

The Templars' pilgrim fleet was based at Marseilles. In 1233 they were granted the right to dock their ships there and carry pilgrims to the Holy Land, but after protests by local ship owners this was restricted to two ships a year, leaving for Easter and in August. They were allowed to carry 1,500 pilgrims in these, and to keep one ship in the port for their own use.[13]

Their main fleet was at La Rochelle, and it was this fleet, berthed away from the theatre of war, that was part of the maritime network linking the Order in the British Isles with the continent. We know the class and names of at least two of the ships plying between La Rochelle and the south coast. In 1230 Henry III issued a licence to the Templars' ship *La Templere* from La Rochelle to land, bringing wine and victuals for the brothers. A little later another licence was given to the Master and the brothers of the Temple for the vessel called *La Buzard* to come into port.[14] The first of these was probably a galley, the second a merchant ship – 'buzzard' was the technical word for such a vessel, which was usually square sailed and powered by a combination of sail and oars. These ships brought in wine and other produce from France and left laden with wool and bullion for the brethren on the continent to forward to the east. Licences to export wool were granted to the Templars by Henry III and Edward I. Edward I's licence mentions export from Dover, and it was to this port that Templar personnel left when going on a mission for the king. When on official business the Patent Rolls show that the constable of Dover Castle was ordered to provide a ship for the Templars.

The Templars had licences to land in the ports of Rye, Winchelsea and Portsmouth. In 1231 Richard the Templar from Southampton was given permission to bring his ship into Portsmouth. The Templars had houses at other ports, including Dunwich in Suffolk and Shoreham in Sussex, but Bristol and Dover were the main points of entry for the Gascon wine and victuals sent to them from the French preceptories. The indications from the Patent Rolls is that this was for their own use and not for resale.

A galley could take 40 weeks to build at a cost of over £200, and it was cheaper to buy a second-hand ship. In 1214 King John purchased a ship from the Templars in Spain that cost him £133. He was to pay this money to the Templars in London who would repay it should the ship prove unsound. In the mid-1220s a Templar, Brother Thomas, was in charge of outfitting the royal fleet and oversaw the building of a 'great ship' at Portsmouth, evidence of his expertise as a shipwright. He received 10 marks for ropes, cables and anchors to repair ships at Fowey, and regular payments for wages and sustenance for carpenters and others working on the great ship. The constable of Portchester Castle was ordered to send ballistas and other armaments for the ship, and in 1226 Thomas organised a muster of 200 ships for the king. He also had charge of imports of wine for the king in Portsmouth, inspecting and sealing the casks on board ship before these were taken ashore. In 1227 he was accused of taking the king's wine for himself, was arrested by the bailiffs but released soon after, and on 21 September 1227 he organised another muster of the fleet at Portsmouth.[15]

The inventory for Cooley in Louth, Ireland, shows that the Templars owned a small boat there worth half a mark, and they must have had similar craft for use on rivers and sea-fishing elsewhere that escaped being listed by the commissioners. Other features of the Templars' coastal properties were their saltpans. For example, at Shoreham in Sussex Alan Trenchmere gave the Templars a saltpan near to the land where the Templars' chapel lay. Salt was not only a valuable addition to the diet, but also essential for preserving food, and some rents on the south coast were paid in salt rather than cash or services.

SOUTHERN ENGLAND – SURREY AND SUSSEX

Shoreham, where the Templars had their saltpans, was one of the small ports on a river lining the south coast. But its position made it vulnerable to raids from the sea by pirates or the French. Behind it, on the Downs, was a line of castles, each protecting the access routes through the South Downs formed by the river valleys. Arundel Castle guarded the Arun gap, Bramber the Adur gap and Lewes the Ouse gap. The Templars had two preceptories above the south coast. Shipley was situated between the Rivers Adur and Arun, and Saddlescombe was in a valley in the Downs, about where the modern town of Brighton is located (see Map 6.2).

Shipley was given to them by Philip de Harcourt when he became Dean of Lincoln in about 1139. His charter quotes from the Bible, pointing out that one should render unto Caesar what is Caesar's

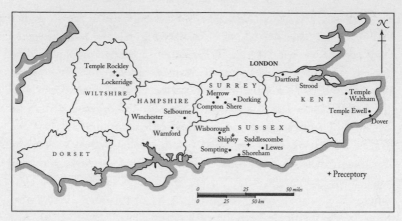

Map 6.2 Templar properties in the South of England

and unto the Lord what is the Lord's, and therefore he is giving to God the land that his brother Richard gave to him. Richard de Harcourt was a Templar so this was an appropriate gift. He is probably the Richard de Harcourt who became the preceptor of Renneville in France in 1150. Saddlescombe was the gift of Geoffrey de Say in 1228.

The 1185 Inquest contains no Sussex material. Evidence for their holdings in this county must be taken from the 1308 inventories, the minister's accounts for 1308–12 and the Hospitallers' Cartuluary BL Ms Cotton Nero E VI. Shipley lies on rising ground above the River Adur, with a fair part of the manor lying on the heavy Wealden clay. There is strong evidence for seasonal transhumance in this area, with flocks and their guardians coming down the drove roads from the north to find summer pasture on the Weald. Usually the summer camps set up by the shepherds and herdsmen were situated on outlying portions of manors to the north, but in the Templars' case they could accommodate them on their Sussex manors and did not need temporary camps. If the Templars followed the usual practice in southern England, it is probable that flocks were sent from the Surrey and London manors to summer pastures at Shipley. Throughout Surrey, Sussex and Kent there are markedly contrasting landscapes, with large open fields and sheep walks on the Downs, and a patchwork of small fields edged with thick belts of woodland in the Weald. At Saddlescombe, although there were 650 sheep on the manor in 1308, the arable crops from the open fields surrounding the settlement were worth more.

Value of the Templars preceptories in Sussex, 1308
Saddlescombe
Goods	£5	11s	6d
Arable	£14	15s	
Livestock	£4	16s	

Shipley
Goods	£4	8s	1d
Arable	£18	0s	2d
Livestock	£9	3s	6d

Value per acre for arable
Compton	12d
Saddlescombe	6d
Shipley	4d[16]

This can be compared with the extents taken of two similar Sussex manors in 1292.

Laughton manor
Arable	£3	5s	2d
Meadow	£8	11s	6d
Pasture	£4	19s	6d

Willingdon manor
Arable	£5	7s	6d
Meadow	£20	0s	2d
Pasture	£4	11s	

At Laughton the winter and summer pasture was differentiated, and the manor included foresters to manage its woodland. Reed beds gave an additional income at Willingdon.[17]

Although the numbers of livestock are not given for these two manors, the value of the meadow and pasture indicate that this was extensive and would have been used for grazing and winter fodder for large herds and flocks. On these manors the production of arable crops was small when compared with that on the Templars' manors. At Laughton and Willingdon it was grown for home consumption, on the Templars' manors it was more likely produced as a market crop, and by the first decade of the fourteenth century, with resources becoming scarce because of failed harvests and a rising population, this would have been a more economic use of their ground.

The Sussex preceptories also managed land and manors in Surrey and Hampshire. The latter included an assart at Selbourne, and the former land and manors near Guildford, including the manor of Merrow and land at Shere. Surrey was the most wooded county in the country and the Templars' rents included payment for woodland pasture and pannage. There were 216 acres of arable at Merrow worth between 4d and 7d an acre in 1308.

The difference between the names listed in Table 6.4 and earlier lists of names is dramatic. By 1308 everyone had a distinctive surname and was no longer distinguished as being the son or daughter of another tenant, or known simply by his or her first name. The growth in the number of locative names shows that not only was the population more mobile, but there were those in a village who were known by the location of the house in the village, such as At

Table 6.4 Distribution of names on Templar estates in Sussex, 1308[18]

Place	Locative Name (%)	Trade Name (%)	Son/Daughter of (%)	Single Name (%)	Other Name (%)
Compton	75	0	0	0	25
Saddlescombe	50	10	0	0	40
Shipley	56	21	0	0	17

Wood, suggesting that their family had been there long enough to have fused with their dwelling place. The names comprising 'other' still included those that described a physical feature of the family, such as Long, Brown or Redhead, but by 1308 also included compound surnames such as Simmonds or Rowlandson, which formerly would have been given as the son of Simon or the son of Rowland. In his analysis of Sussex surnames Richard McKinley suggests that the latter example was rare in Sussex and that names were more likely to be either a single name such as Godwin or with the 's' added. He sees the change of this type of surname as occurring in Sussex in the late thirteenth century and being common from 1300 onwards.[19] Table 6.4 confirms this trend. These male appellations applied equally to the daughters of the families. Occasionally the surname Dauter appears, but not in any great numbers. This reflects the legal position of married women in society who became their husband's property, and of course took his name, whilst the unmarried woman or girl bore her father's name. This was an accepted aspect of a male-dominated society of which the Templars were part.

THE TEMPLARS AND WOMEN

It was to Saddlescombe that Azo, Archbishop of Canterbury, sent a request at the end of the twelfth century asking for permission for Joan, the elderly wife of Richard Chalfield, knight, to spend her final days there – not as a corrodian but as a member of the Order. It added that as she is an aged woman no sinister suspicion can arise on either side, and she is vowed to observe chastity.[20] This and a few other similar instances raise the question of the place of women in the Order. The Rule forbade Templars from having any contact with women on pain of expulsion, but women were admitted to preceptories with their husbands as corrodians, and women gave the Order generous gifts of rents and land. Some notable examples of this are Stephen's queen, Matilda, and his rival the Empress Matilda, as well as other aristocratic ladies.

Helen Nicholson thinks that in some cases the Templars allowed women to become members of the Order and to dwell within the preceptory walls. She quotes from the example of a grant in 1178 by Eudes de Pichange to the Templars' house at Langes in France where his mother had been a sister of the order; and cites other scattered evidence for women joining the Templars. On this evidence Nicholson and Alan Forey conclude that the Templars were willing to admit women to the Order, but Forey adds that this may have been before the Rule was codified.[21]

Archbishop Azo's letter, however, shows that the Templars were aware of the scandal that might occur from admitting women to their cloisters and that this was to be avoided. This may have been even to the extent of having only male servants in the precinct. Although Forey suggests that slave women worked in the Aragonese precincts no women appear among the Templar personnel in the English preceptories, although they often appear as tenants in their own right.

Apart from the elderly wives of knights and those who wished to have care and maintenance in their last years and renounced their goods, what other women might have wanted to enter the Order? This was a masculine order and it had no sister houses as some monastic foundations had, and, unlike the Hospitallers, it had no obvious role for women to undertake and no possibility of advancement within it. The Templars themselves saw women as temptresses who would entice them into sin, encourage them to break their vows and endanger their souls. This attitude is not surprising as the Church taught that women were tainted through the perfidy of Eve, who corrupted Adam and engineered mankind's fall from grace. Women were dangerous. But on the other hand, civil law placed widows and wards under the protection of the Church, and the Templars were members of this Church. On the whole the evidence for the admittance of women into the Order is slight, and we do not have the reply from Saddlescombe about the Archbishop's request for the admission of Joan Chalfield to the Order. They might have refused, and in this were within their right, as the Archbishop had no jurisdiction over them.

What we do have are rumours and gossip about the Templars and women that surfaced during the trials. In Cyprus, for example, a woman came forward to say that she had slept with a Templar, in France there was a popular saying that a girl did not become a woman until she had slept with a Templar, and when charged with sodomy some Templars denied it saying they could have a pretty woman any time they wanted.

Part of the twenty-first-century obsession with the relationship between the Templars and sex is caused by a failure to understand that a vow of chastity meant exactly that in the Middle Ages, and although there may have been those who broke this vow, they risked expulsion from their Order, excommunication and eternal damnation. We should not judge the Templars or other religious orders by twenty-first-century sexual codes, or the treatment of women in the Middle Ages outside the context of their period.

KENT

Finally in this tour around the Templars' English estates we reach Kent, the entry point for travellers from the continent and the exit for those Templars going on the king's business. The Templars' possessions in Kent combined to form a block that stretched from the River Medway to the Channel at Dover, where the Templars had a chapel on the western heights (see Map 6.2). The baillie of Kent was concentrated on three manors. Strood on the Medway, Temple Waltham near Chilham, south-west of Canterbury with woodland in Kingswood, and Temple Ewell behind Dover where there was a preceptory. Strood was the gift of Henry II, Waltham came from the Archbishop of Canterbury, and Ewell was the joint grant of Henry II's brother William and his distant cousin William Peverel. All of these grants were made before 1185 and amounted to about 1,000 acres plus tenements and other property.

Kent is an unusual county as the inheritance system in part of it was based on 'gavelkind' that divided the land between all sons rather than the eldest inheriting it (primogeniture) or the youngest (borough English). The effect of gavelkind was the development of smaller and smaller holdings. This can be seen happening on the Templars' manors of Strood and Ewell, but not at Waltham which was formerly the property of the Archbishopric of Canterbury. All the Canterbury manors were tightly controlled from the centre, and the subsistence agriculture produced by gavelkind was discouraged. At Waltham there were some very large holdings that included arable, meadow and wood as part of the tenancy, whilst a high proportion of locative names on the manor suggests that the Templars took over a manor that had been peopled by those from outside (Table 6.5).

Gavelkind has an effect on the landscape and settlement patterns, and as holdings grew so small they were no longer viable so the tenants moved away to find other land. It is possible that the incoming tenants at Waltham were refugees from gavelkind. The fragmentary nature of the gavelkind holdings produced dispersed villages with small farms surrounded by their few fields away from the villages. This pattern can be seen at Ewell, and at Strood and

Table 6.5 Distribution of names on Templar estates in Kent, 1185

Place	Locative Name (%)	Trade Name (%)	Son/Daughter of (%)	Single Name (%)	Other Name (%)
Ewell	10	13	10	52	15
Strood	12	12	5	54	17
Waltham	43	0	16	23	16

Ewell the fields were sub-divided and often held jointly by two or three relatives. These partitioned holdings led to service obligations being allocated collectively between groups of tenants rather than on a single tenant.

Service obligation on the Templars' manor of Temple Ewell in Kent, 1185

At Temple Ewell service was owed collectively, with no weekly works. Tasks included ploughing, harrowing and stacking wheat as well as thatching and repairing barns and houses, fencing and enclosing land, malting in spring, salting, drying and packing herrings, carrying and fetching withies from Ospringe to string the herrings, collecting seed for sowing, taking surplus grain to market and returning with loads of salt, and wheels and yokes, from Canterbury, and delivering corn to Dover Castle.

The Templars would supply the materials for repairing the buildings, and the labourers were allowed to take away the old material. A professional thatcher was to be appointed to undertake the work, and he was to be chosen by the whole manor court, and the tenants were to find him lodgings and food, and to give him an assistant. Five men were to stack the demesne corn at harvest and were to receive three meals each a day. The maltsters and the herring salters were to be given the fuel and raw materials for this. The carriers were to have food and maintenance for themselves and their horses, and were not obliged to travel after sunset. Men were also to be appointed to take care of the sheepfolds, to carry these from one place to another, and to go to the hall mote on the Weald.

In all there were 61 tenants at Ewell in 1185, and the manor was a hive of activity, with the by-employments such as salting herrings suggesting activity on an industrial scale. Many of the tenants had only a few acres, or only a messuage and a garden, and the surnames suggest that their incomes were supplemented by domestic industry such as weaving, and a fulling mill reinforces this. Like many other manors in this area, there was a detached portion on the Weald where the livestock was taken in the summer.

Service obligation at Strood, 1185

The manor at Strood was divided into a rural and an urban portion. The holders of messuages in the urban part of the manor paid hen rent, attended the manor court, and were obliged to provide men for carting, mowing, hay-making, reaping and ploughing on the demesne. Each five-acre holder in the rural part of the manor was required to do weekly boon works, but this could be commuted to 1d an acre. Most of the rural tenants held only a few acres, whilst the urban tenants followed trades. They included a vintner, a baker and a cook.

Service obligation at Temple Waltham, 1185

No services were required at Waltham, only cash rents and hens. There is no evidence of any by-employment or domestic industry here, and most of the holdings were large enough to feed an average family and to leave a surplus for market.

Rentable value of the Templars' estates in Kent, 1185

Ewell   £8 15s 3d
Strood   £11 18s
Waltham   £7 11s 3d

The rentable values of Ewell, Strood and Waltham indicate that the best profits from rents in this area were to be had from the urban areas, as a high proportion of the rents from Strood came from the urban part of the manor.

It would have been possible for the Templars to disgavel their land in Kent, but there is no evidence that they did this. Neither is there much evidence that they took advantage of the fluid land market that gavelkind produced as heirs to partitioned land sold this. The Feet of Fine for Kent show that the Templars purchased about 100 acres during the thirteenth century, but there is no evidence that this was gavelkind land.

Nothing remains of the preceptory at Ewell, but it has been excavated and was probably a substantial site as it was used as a royal residence at times. Its buildings included a hall and a massive chamber block, and a single-celled chapel. The manor house at Strood stood on the west bank of the Medway. It had no pretensions of being a preceptory, but its complex of buildings followed the model of preceptories, including a hall, buttery, kitchen and chapel, and one brother was resident there in 1308.

In 1308 a number of eminent members of the Order, including the English Master, William de la More, were arrested at Temple Ewell. Were they gathered there prior to an escape overseas or were they leaving openly and in defiance of the king? Had they wished to effect an escape it would have been better made from one of their more isolated coastal houses such as Shoreham or Dunwich, but the traditional route for the Master to take on his way to the continent was through Dover. This was an act of open defiance.

THE TEMPLARS IN THE ENGLISH COUNTRYSIDE: CONCLUSIONS

Throughout this examination of the Templars in the English countryside we have visited their land, met their tenants and what remains of their preceptories and houses. We have followed them through woodland, marshes, over moorland and open fields. In all the English counties except Cheshire there was a Templar presence,[22] either as absentee landlords, the sole brother in charge of a manor, or as a group of brothers in a preceptory. They lived simply in walled enclosures containing a hall where they could eat, a chamber to sleep in, a chapel for worship and a graveyard. Farm buildings in the precinct showed that these were agricultural as well as religious enclaves.

They suffered the occasional squabble with their neighbours over the enclosure of land, the rights to graze livestock on common pasture and the privileges of the Church, but on the whole, compared with other religious houses, these were minimal. Their everyday life was conducted in keeping with their Rule and that of a religious order – they were dedicated to prayer, observed the offices during the day and night, and offered obits for dead brothers. They ate at the table designated for their rank in the Order – knights, sergeants, chaplains or free servants – in the company of pensioners who were either loyal servants or had given property in return for board and lodging for life, and a dignified burial. All of this was probably set within a fairly elderly community, as the younger brethren should have been overseas fighting for the cross.

The inventories taken in 1308 show they lived a frugal life. Unless many goods had been looted when the Templars were arrested, the inventories show that the brothers had few possessions or comforts. Their halls usually contained a table, trestles and a wash-basin by the door. The chamber had a bed for each brother and a clothes bag. Attention has been drawn to the number of silver spoons found in 1308, suggesting wealth and a luxurious lifestyle. Exactly the same feature was noted in the inventories taken after the Dissolution of the Monasteries. At Denny in Cambridgeshire, for example, each nun had her own silver spoon. Six silver spoons were found at Denny in 1308 and in all 53 were listed.[23] This amounted to one spoon between every two brothers who were arrested. Only the New Temple in London possessed goods that might have given rise to the rumour that the Templars owned a fabulous treasure, and most of the wealth in the New Temple was concentrated in the church. Does this mean that, as suspected by eager treasure hunters, the Templars spirited away their wealth before their arrests and hid it in some yet to be discovered hiding place? The gap between the arrests in France and any action being taken against the British Templars would have given time for provisions of this sort to be made. But where did it go? The papal edict to the secular princes ordering them to arrest all Templars at large and seize their goods was sent to all the rulers of western European countries. The treasure had to be taken somewhere isolated and far away from the view of the secular or ecclesiastical authority. It has been suggested that the highlands and islands of Scotland could provide a hiding place, or remote caves or even graveyards hide the Templar treasure.

This is all speculation. There is no evidence for the existence of any treasure. But if this is the case, why were there persistent rumours about the Order's fabulous wealth? This was probably due to a misunderstanding about the Templars' treasuries in London and Paris that did indeed contain large sums of money, jewels and plate. However, this did not belong to the Templars but was held by them as trustees for others, including the King of England. The citizens of London would have seen the carts laden with taxes taken into the New Temple, and drawn the conclusion that this was going into the Templars' coffers.

Poverty was one of the vows taken by the Templars and the surviving evidence from the goods and small amount of cash found in the preceptories and manors in 1308 shows that in the British Isles at least they kept this vow. Nevertheless they were major landholders. Did their fabled wealth come from the revenues of their estates, and were they managing these to the best effect? Between the 1185 Inquest and the 1308 inventories the Templars increased the value of their estates by over 50 per cent. This included land brought into production from the waste, as at Temple Bruer, and the foundation of new towns such as Baldock in Hertfordshire. The rents on their estates doubled from 1185 to 1308, but so did the number of tenants. The Templars were landlords at a critical time in the history of the English population as it rose to an unprecedented level, straining resources to their uppermost. This resulted in the division of land into smaller and smaller holdings until these were no longer viable for subsistence and food had to be purchased in the market, sending up prices. Both of these trends would have benefited landlords.

On some Templar manors, for example Hackney, there is evidence that the amount of land in demesne was reduced in the thirteenth century, showing that the Templars preferred the assured annual rent from this manor rather than the fluctuations of market prices. But on other manors, such as those in Oxfordshire, a large amount of land continued to be reserved for the demesne and heavy service obligations continued to be exacted from the tenants.

Information from the requirements regarding the cartage of produce to market shows that the Templars were using local markets, or London if that was within easy reach. There is no evidence that grain or livestock were shipped overseas for brothers in the east and this would clearly have been impracticable. Export licences granted to them are for the shipment of wool, and the Templars were taking advantage of the demand for English wool on the continent. There were large sheep runs on manors such as Guiting, Bruer, Rockley and Newsam, and the occasional mention of a fulling mill such as at Ewell or Witham suggests that some of the wool was processed on the manor. 'Irish' cloth was being produced on some of the Templars' manors in Ireland. The only other evidence for industrial activity are the forges found within Templar preceptories, surely only for their own use, and the herring salting at Ewell. All the preceptories were concerned with agriculture and even the New Temple in London was raising livestock within its enclosure.

Map 6.3 shows the total value of the Templar estates in each county in 1308. It indicates that Yorkshire and Lincolnshire were

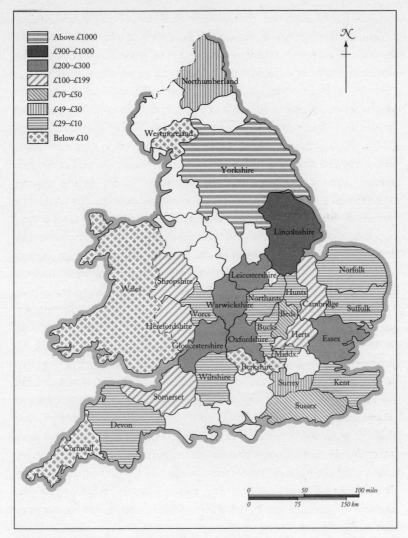

Map 6.3 Cumulative county value of Templar estates, 1308

the most valuable, but these were also the counties where the Templars had the largest number of holdings. If this is reconfigured to show the most productive counties in terms of the size and number of holdings (shown on Map 6.4), we can see that the estate centred on Rothley in Leicestershire was the most valuable. The profits from Rothley were sent directly to the Holy Land to aid the brothers in Acre and this may have been an incentive to make this into a super-efficient estate. The 1308 estate shows this to have been a mixed farm but with a flock of 550 sheep. Similarly, the second most profitable estate at Temple Guiting was predominantly dedicated to sheep farming. The two preceptories in Hereford, the third most productive area, had a large amount of demesne in open fields, and were exploiting cleared woodland and putting in tenants to farm it. In Cambridgeshire wool was a good cash crop at Great Wilbraham and innovative farming at Denny led to the leasing out of cows to their tenants.

Unfortunately the information we have on the Templars' farming practices comes from two fixed points in 1185 and 1308, and we lack the sources that show us how they responded to short-term events and whether the amount of demesne and the way the land was farmed changed to take account of these. But we must not ignore the external influence peculiar to the management of estates belonging to the military orders – that is events in the east.

Did events in the east influence life in rural England? One simple measure of this might be in the number of charters granting land to the Templars, and when. Figure 6.2 shows the figures for charters giving property to the Templars. It is possible that the increase of grants in the 1150s was connected to the Fall of Ascalon and the Templars taking responsibility for the city of Gaza. These would have been high-profile events that the Templars would have publicised. The increase in the 1220s is probably connected to the Fifth Crusade. But most of the grants were given to the Templars for the soul of the donor and his or her family, and not specifically

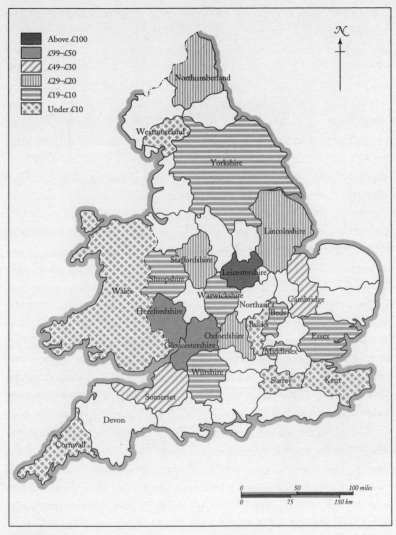

Map 6.4 Average value of Templar manors, 1308

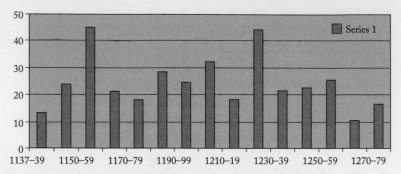

Figure 6.2 Number of charters granting land to the Templars (by decade)

for aid in the Holy Land, and it is probable that these have no connection with events in the east at all. Forey's analysis of the Templars in Aragon shows that grants of land decreased after 1220. In England the decrease was much later, starting in the 1260s, and in the closing years of the thirteenth and early fourteenth centuries the Templars started to purchase land as it came on the market. Georges Duby noted a similar trend in rural France and suggested that this is connected to the change from arable to pastoral farming and the acquisition of the great flocks of sheep.[24] As some of the Templars' purchases were around Temple Bruer, where they already had large flocks, this would seem to be the case in England as well.

The crusades meant that land came on to the market as knights struggled to equip themselves. Simon Lloyd suggests that this altered the tenurial structure and patterns of local and regional power. An example he gives of this is Hugh Fitz Henry who joined the Templars and sold his estates in Berkshire, Oxfordshire and Buckinghamshire to go on crusade.[25] Although the Templars were not the beneficiaries of these lands, it is rare evidence of a knight joining the Order expressly to go on crusade, and it reinforces their role in the countryside as a recruiting body for the war against the infidel.

Table 6.6 Distribution of names on Templar estates in England, 1185

Place	Locative Name (%)	Trade Name (%)	Son/Daughter of (%)	Single Name (%)	Other Name (%)
Bedfordshire	28	24	29	13	5
Bristol	18	22	11	22	25
Cambridgeshire	15	23	17	0	45
Essex	13	14	26	24	22
Herefordshire	5	15	13	45	21
Hertfordshire	10	28	20	20	22
Huntingdonshire	33	5	16	0	47
Kent	22	8	10	43	16
Lincolnshire	13	17	13	41	15
Oxfordshire	6	17	6	63	8
Shropshire	5	15	13	45	22
Warwickshire	13	13	13	39	22
Yorkshire	18	9	14	39	20

There were three types of tenant on the Templars' estates: free-men who were in the minority; villeins who had holdings ranging from a few acres to one or two virgates and paid cash rent as well as performing labour service; and cottars who had a house and a small piece of land, and must have worked for the villeins and freemen, probably performing their service for them. These tenants appear to us only as names in the inquisitions, but these names can tell us something about them, where they came from and what they did, and the trends of naming patterns show us something of regional diversities in England (Table 6.6).

The most mobile of the Templars' tenants are in Huntingdonshire and Bedfordshire, both counties, it should be noted, on one of the major road systems in the country known as the Great North Road. Perhaps it is not surprising that the least mobile are those tenants on the Welsh Marches in Herefordshire and Shropshire, who were well off the beaten track and also in a dangerous frontier zone. The new town of Baldock is represented in the proportion of trades shown for Hertfordshire, with Huntingdonshire and Kent being the least endowed with trades. However, in the case of Kent the result is skewed by the large agrarian manor of Waltham that the Templars acquired from Canterbury. Strood and Ewell had a good variety of trades among their tenants. In 1297 Cambridge-shire and Huntingdonshire show the most developed move to-wards tenants being identified by a name other than their own. This is significant in showing that tenants were beginning to have roots in the holding, and could be recognised as a previous tenant's son. This was well on the way to the situation seen in Sussex in 1308 where all the tenants had a surname.

These tenants and their holdings are part of our link to the Templars' activities in the countryside. Their names and the land they farmed help to build up a picture of this. These are the people who dealt with the Templars on a daily basis, whose toil and sweat helped to maintain their rents and revenues, whose service kept the demesne in production and the preceptories in good order, and indirectly they were affected by events outside their own little worlds as much as the knights themselves.

CHAPTER SEVEN

THE KNIGHTS TEMPLAR IN IRELAND AND SCOTLAND

Ireland and Scotland were part of the Templar province of England, and although there were separate Masters for these countries they appear to have been chosen in the English general chapter from among the English brethren. Although not part of the Anglo-Norman conquest of Ireland and its colonisation, the Templars have been perceived as part of this, and there was some misunderstanding among nineteenthcentury Irish historians who thought that the Templars were established in Ireland by Strongbow (Richard de Clare, Lord of Strigoil, sometimes known as Richard Fitz-Gilbert), and inhabited strong stone castles from which they issued to indulge in bloody affrays with the native Irish. This has been redressed by twentieth-century historians who point out that the Templars have been blamed in Ireland for deeds that were not theirs.[1]

Similarly in Scotland, the Templars have become clothed in mystery and legends of cruelty appropriate to those of a conquering power. But they were invited into Scotland by King David I in 1128 and became his trusted advisers, almost persuading him to go on crusade. Nevertheless they were foreigners and eventually became symbols of an alien culture and humiliating submission to the English overlord, although not as MacInery suggests 'overwhelmingly English in race and sympathy'.[2] It is doubtful whether those brothers sent to Ireland or Scotland saw themselves as part of the English colonisation. They were members of a religious organisation and their role was to husband the resources they had been given so that these could be offered to the glory of God and the relief of the Holy Land.

Colonisation?

One of the charges levelled against the Templars in Ireland by nineteenth-century historians was that they were part of a colonising force that suppressed and dominated the native population. Twentieth-century historians have been more circumspect about this. B. Smith suggests that the concept of medieval Ireland as a colony is not a viable model as it did not destroy the ancient Irish lineage, although the new settlers helped to exploit underused resources.[3] There is no doubt that the Templars were part of this exploitation.

Although Strongbow led the initial conquest of Ireland for the Normans, it was Henry II, armed with a papal bull giving him permission to take Ireland into his dominions, who completed this task. The Treaty of Windsor, made with the King of Connaught in 1175, turned Henry into the High King of Ireland, and opened the way for a full-scale emigration into Ireland from England. The coming of the English changed Ireland's religious, social and economic structure. The Church was reorganised into parishes and tithes collected from these. The English shire system of local government was introduced and a stable coinage developed so that where before cattle had been the main currency of a pastoral people now there was a cash economy. Monasteries were founded with English officials, and great castles were erected as symbols of a political and military domination. R.R. Davies writes that the English reconstructed the Irish world to their standards.[4] This new world was one of opportunity for the settler. Into this land of opportunity came the Templars.

The Templars in Ireland

The first documentary evidence for the Templars in Ireland is dated 1177 when Matthew the Templar witnessed an Irish charter, but the first known grant of land was made in *c.* 1185 by Henry II who gave the Templars the vills of Clontarf and Crook, and ten carucates of land, later adding to this a marsh at Waterford, and a church dedicated to St Barry. This was followed by numerous other grants of land from members of the Anglo-Norman aristocracy, for example the Lacies and Montfichets, so that by 1308 the Irish lands were the third most valuable of all the Templar holdings and worth over £400 a year. Most of these lands were concentrated on the eastern seaboard of the country. These included lands and manors in Carlow, Louth, Kilkenny, Sligo and many other places. Where formerly there had been cattle grazing, the Templars started to grow wheat and soon had so much surplus that in 1225 they were given a licence to sell this wherever they wished in Ireland.

The tenants on their manors were mostly Irish, as shown in a plea roll from the time of Edward I. They were obliged to render service and to plough up lands that had formerly been pasture, leading to these manors being described as 'colonising manors' that imposed the conqueror's way of agriculture on the native population.

The Masters of the Temple in Ireland do not appear to have had a fixed residence, but as they are recorded as acting for the king in Dublin, this must have been their principal house. Elected from England most of them bear English or Anglo-Norman names.

Masters of the Templars in Ireland
Walter the Templar   *c.* 1180
Guarnerus

Hugh the Templar	*c.* 1200–10
Henry Foliot	*c.* 1210
Ralph de Southwark	1234
Roger le Waleis	1235–50
Herbert de Mancester	1257–73
Roger de Glastonbury	1278–88
Thomas de Toulouse	1288
Walter Bachelor	1295–1301
Peter de Malvern	1300
William de Waryne, became preceptor of Clontarf	1302–6
Henry Tanet	1307–8

Tanet was to give evidence against the Order at the trial.

The principal preceptory in Ireland was probably at Clontarf in County Dublin. Hore suggests that altogether there were nine preceptories:

Irish preceptories
Clonaul, Tipperary
Clontarf, County Dublin
Crook, Waterford
Kilbarry, Waterford
Kilclogan, Wexford
Kilergy, Carlow
Killure, Waterford
Kilsaran, Louth
Templehouse, Sligo

The last of these may have been a manor rather than a preceptory. Excavations revealed a hall set in a rectangular enclosure, and probably the layout would have been the same as seen at the Templars' English preceptories and manors. A hall, chamber, chapel and barns appear in the inventory for the manor of Kilclogan and confirm this. A considerable amount of silver was found in the chapel, including 17 silver spoons, a silver dish and two silver cups, whilst the priestly vestments were made of silk. Kilclogan was an exceptionally wealthy preceptory. Hore suggests that it was founded by the O'More family and they may have endowed it. As well as the usual furniture, its possessions included three small books, wax candles, wine, beef carcasses, mutton, bacon and lard in the kitchen, skins, canvas, and wool.[5]

Life in Ireland was difficult for the Order as they were surrounded by a hostile population, but on the other hand they were a considerable distance from London and this gave the Masters more latitude in what they did, and more opportunity for corruption. Two Irish Masters succumbed to temptation. Ralph of Southwark in the 1230s and, in the early fourteenth century, Walter Bachelor, who was excommunicated for stealing the Templars' property and taken to London for punishment by the general chapter. He was sentenced to eight weeks in the penitential cell in the New Temple where he died, and because he was excommunicated he could not be buried in consecrated ground.

It was Bachelor's death in what were seen as suspicious circumstances that interested the inquisitors in 1308. Those who had been present at the time were questioned about this many times. They claimed that Bachelor had died of natural causes, and had been allowed to confess his sins before he died, and was given a normal burial. Despite this, Bachelor's death added to the mystery surrounding the Templars' activities and in the nineteenth century Addison claimed to have identified the cell where he died in the New Temple. This was a small space within the church wall with two small apertures for ventilation. Addison's book on the Templars contains a graphic illustration of Bachelor, unconscious from a severe beating, being placed in the cell.[6] Addison had probably found the start of the stairway leading to the rood loft.

The Master in Ireland was an officer of the English crown and one of the auditors of the Irish exchequer. He sometimes acted as a mediator between the Anglo-Norman aristocracy and the Irish, and between Anglo-Irish rebels and the Plantagents. In 1234 the Templars tried to make peace between the rebellious Earl Richard of Cornwall and loyal members of the aristocracy. This time they were singularly unsuccessful because when the two sides met at the Curragh of Kildare the Templars lost control of the situation, and the conference ended up as an armed mêlée during which Earl Richard was mortally wounded.[7]

Other religious houses in Ireland were jealous of the Templars' privileges of freedom from tithes and taxes and the right to offer sanctuary to felons, and complained to Henry III about this. As one of the Templars' chief supporters he took no notice of this complaint. The Church also objected to the Templars' holding the advowsons of numerous Irish churches, and this added to their unpopularity. The trial of the Templars in Ireland, which was held in St Patrick's Cathedral in 1310, gave them opportunity to vent their anger.

Templars arrested in Ireland, 1308

Henry Tanet, Master but described as
   the prior
Henry de Aslackby
Richard de Bistlesham
Ralph de Bradley of Crook   Does not appear in the trial
Hugh de Broughton
William de Chonesby
John de Faversham
Henry de la Forde
Henry de la Forde junior
William Kilross, chaplain
Adam Langford
Peter de Malvern, warden of   Does not appear in the trial
   Kilclogan
Henry Montravers

Thomas le Palmer of Kilbarry	Does not appear in the trial
Robert de Pourbriggs	
Robert, preceptor of Rothronan	Does not appear in the trial
John Romayne	
Richard de Upleden	
William de Waryne, preceptor of Clonaul	Does not appear in the trial

Those who were arrested but not tried presumably died in prison. The predominance of English names is striking, and as only two Templars were arrested in Scotland it is possible that some of these were fugitives either from Scotland or England.

Some arms were found in the Irish houses – swords at Clontarf, and lances, a helmet and a balister at Kilclogan – and the manor house at Ballymean was described as a castle, it was so strongly defended.

The commissioners taking the inventories in 1308 used the Irish weight of a crannoc for corn. This was probably the equivalent of just under a quarter in English terms. The values of some of the Irish estates are shown in Table 7.1.

Although the Templars were producing a surplus of corn in Ireland, these and other inventories show that the pastoral way of life had not disappeared. An abnormal number of horses that were riding horses rather than draught horses suggests that the breeding of horses may have been one of the specialities of the Irish manors. Clonaul is an example of this where a number of high-value horses

Table 7.1 Value of a sample of Templar estates in Ireland, 1308[8]

Manor	Goods	Grain	Livestock
Clontarf	£4 0s 0d	£4 2s 0d	£66 6s 10d
Cooley	£3 19s 6d	£3 16s 4d	£10 16s 10d
Crook	£1 0s 0d	£3 12s 0d	£14 4s 0d
Kilsaran	£8 5s 5d	£10 0s 9d	£11 5s 0d

were found. The buildings show the usual complex of a hall, chamber and chapel surrounded by barns. Kilsaran is an interesting inventory as it includes some goods that suggest the Templars may have been encouraging the Irish cloth industry as there were six ells of white Irish cloth in store as well as robes of coloured wool. All of the Irish inventories show a richer variety of domestic goods than the English ones. This may have been because the commissioners arrived before the looters and the Irish houses give a more representative sample of what the average preceptory contained. At Kilsaran the goods and chattels were given into the custody of Adam, the vicar of Kilmedymok, to keep until these could be handed over to the king's keeper, Thomas of Kent. John de Egge took away the vessels, vestments and books from the chapel, and eventually all the remaining goods were packed up and sent to Dublin.

There is no doubt that the Templars' Irish possessions were profitable. On average each manor was worth £25 a year, on a par with the Templars' Northumbrian properties, and there were some similarities between the Irish estates and those in Northumberland with manors containing a mixture of upland and valleys, and lying in a situation in which crops could be destroyed and cattle rustled without warning.

The final comment on the Templars in Ireland is in the *Book of Howth*:

> *While they lived in wilful poverty*
> *These crossed knights in mantle white*
> *Their names spread in many far country*
> *For in their perfection was set delight*
> *Folk of devotion caught an appetite*
> *Therefore to increase gave them great cheer*
> *By which they increase . . .*
> *By process within a few year*
> *The number great of their religion*

And the face of the Templars
Gan spread wide in many a region
With towers, and castle they gave to them desire
Apparelled in virtue which brought in many wise . . .[9]

SCOTLAND

We know less about the Templars in Scotland than elsewhere in the British Isles. Their land does not appear in the 1185 inquest and there are no 1308 inventories for Scotland. Perhaps because of this a panoply of myth has developed around them that has obscured reality and cloaked them in mystery. Establishing where their land lay is complicated by the use of the description 'Temple land' in the sixteenth century for land that had never belonged to them, but to other religious foundations. Despite this we know that they were settled in Scotland as soon as they were in England. Hugh de Payens attracted the attention of David I of Scotland, who invited him north and gave him the land in Midlothian originally known as Balantrodoch, but now known as Temple, where one of the two Scottish preceptories was situated.

Ailred of Rievaulx writes that David surrounded himself with Templar advisers, and under their influence decided to go on crusade, but was prevented by the dismay of his subjects. David may have intended Scotland to become a separate province. Most of the grants of land in Scotland came from Norman families, and no Scottish family names appear as members of the Order in Scotland, although there were several examples of Templars described as de Scot, Scotho or Scotto in English preceptories who might have originated in Scotland.

The general chapter in England oversaw affairs in Scotland, even discussing mundane grants of land. Thus in 1234, with the agreement of the general chapter of London, the English Master granted to John, son of Richard the priest, a toft and two acres in Falkirk, and common pasture for 12 cattle, 60 sheep and two horses. Another grant made with the consent of the chapter at Temple Dinsley gave four perches of land in Perth to Christine of Perth.[10]

Main Templar possessions in Scotland
Place
Balantrodoch/Temple
Maryculter
East Fenton
Peffer
Swanston
Glasgow tenement
Temple/Kirk Liston
Callander Saltworks
Gullane

Balantrodoch or Temple

This was the site of the Templars most important preceptory in Scotland, sometimes referred to as Blancraddock. It was a fully functioning preceptory by 1175 when Brother Raan was granted a toft in Glasgow with the assent of the brothers of Balantrodoch.[12] Temple, as it became known, lies on a ridge above the South Esk river, 11 miles south of Edinburgh. The preceptory lay beside the river, about 150 yards north-west of the present village. Here they built a mill and a simple single-celled chapel (see Plate 7.1). Arable was grown in the valley bottom on an infield–outfield system and sheep grazed on the hills, but a great deal of the parish consisted of moss and wet clay, and by the sixteenth century this was a coal-mining village.[13] In the thirteenth century the coal and iron in the area were being exploited by the monks of nearby Newbattle Abbey, but the Templars do not seem to have taken advantage of these resources.

Plate 7.1 Ruins of the Templars' church at Temple, Lothian
Crown copyright: RCAHMS

Preceptors of Balantrodoch

Robert	1160
Ranulph Corbet	1174–99
Hugh de Conyers	c. 1233
Roger de Akiney	1278–90
Brian de Jay	1286–92
John de Sautre	1296
John de Husflete	1304–6
Walter de Clifton	1306–9

Brian de Jay and Christiane of Esperston

Almost single-handedly, Brian de Jay destroyed the reputation of the Templars in Scotland and sent them into history as cruel and ruthless men. De Jay probably came from a knightly family with land in the village of Jay in Shropshire. He was appointed as Master of Scotland in 1291, and his career is evidence that Templar officials passed between the two countries.

De Jay was a man born out of his time. Had he been born a hundred years earlier his energies could have been spent fighting the Saracens in defence of the Holy Land. As it was he was a crusader without a crusade, entering the Order in its twilight and becoming Master of Scotland at precisely the same time as the Templars withdrew from Acre to Cyprus. De Jay was to travel to Cyprus to consult with the Grand Master[14] and may have suffered some disillusion about the state of the Order and the likelihood of ever regaining Jerusalem. Without a crusade he espoused the cause of Edward I in Scotland, becoming his passionate supporter. This was to lead him to break the Templar Rule and probably becoming the model for the evil Templar, Sir Brian de Bois Guilbert, in Sir Walter Scott's *Ivanhoe*.

In July 1291 de Jay swore fealty to Edward I in Edinburgh Castle. It is not clear whether he did this on his own behalf or as a representative of the Order. Either way it was against the precepts of the Rule as it meant he acknowledged Edward I as his overlord when in theory only the Pope could stand in this position. It should be added that de Jay was not the only person swearing fealty to Edward that day. He was accompanied by, among others, the Abbot of Newbattle and the Master of the Hospitallers in Scotland, who was compromising himself in the same way. De Jay compounded his fault by bearing arms against Scotland in the 1298 campaign and was killed at the Battle of Falkirk, according to the English chroniclers fighting valiantly for the cause. It is for the affair of Christiane of Esperston that he is chiefly remembered in Scotland. The story is narrated in a document dated 1354.[15] This is a petition from Robert Simple,[16] son of Alexander, seeking the restitution of a tenement at Esperston that the Hospitallers had claimed when they took over the Templars' land. Esperston was a farm set some 800 feet above sea level above Temple in Midlothian. It had once been the property of Robert the Scot who left it to his daughter Christiane who married William, son of Gaufrid of Haukeston. Christiane's husband was more given to ease than work and conveyed the tenement during his lifetime to the Templars in return for board and lodging. Whilst he retired to a life of idleness at Balantrodoch, Christiane and her three sons remained in the tenement with barely enough to live on.

William had become a corrodian of the Templars, and as Christiane's husband he could devise her property as he wished. He can be seen as being as big a villain as de Jay, but it is possible that he went into the preceptory because he was terminally ill, as shortly afterwards he died. The property should then have reverted to Christiane, but the Templars wanted to keep it and decided to evict Christiane. The illegality of this act may have been the reason for them arriving in force to do this. Christiane refused to go. De Jay ordered his men to drag her out of the house. She clung to the doorpost and they could not get her to release her grip. At which point one of the Master's followers drew his sword and cut off the fingers clinging to the door, and she was expelled sobbing and shrieking.

There are symbolic elements in this part of the story. The innocent Scottish widow expelled from what was rightfully hers by the ruthless foreigner was one which was paralleled in the political situation in Scotland, with the English overlords stamping their authority over the Scots.

Christiane sought redress for her wrongs. The document says she went to Newbattle where the king, moved by her story and her injuries, ordered that the farm be restored to her. John Edwards suggests that the king in question was Edward I who was at Newbattle on 5 June 1296. G. Barrow thinks it was more likely to have been Alexander III or John Balliol, and he claims that Christiane and William were married in Alexander's reign.[17]

Esperston was restored to Christiane and she lived there peacefully until the Anglo-Scottish Wars when she was once more expelled. This is placing the Templars on the side of the English, and again could be an analogy for the two states. Barrow sees this as part of a stubborn desire on the part of the Scots to remain on the ancestral estate, and he names John de Sautre as the offending Master this time. Two years later Brian de Jay was back, this time at the head of a troop of Welsh mercenary soldiers whom he was conducting to meet up with Edward I at Kirk Liston. On the way they stopped to rest at Balantrodoch.

Richard Cook, Christiane's eldest son, with more bravado than good sense, came to him to beg for the return of his mother's property. De Jay dissembled and somehow managed to persuade Cook to act as a guide for the Welsh troops on the morrow, whilst striking a bargain with the Welsh captain that he would kill Cook on the way. The murder took place at Clerkington Wood on the banks of the South Esk river, now known as Rosebery. Cook's body was despoiled and left. De Jay was now guilty of conspiracy to murder, and murder was one charge that a Templar could be tried for in the king's court. But de Jay died a few days later at Falkirk and the Templars remained in possession of Esperston until their suppression in 1312. At this point William, Christiane's younger son, went to Robert Bruce and asked him to restore the lands, which he did. But William fell on hard times and sold the farm to Alexander Simple, which is why Robert Simple brought the petition claiming the lands were his. Was this an entirely fabricated story dreamt up by Robert Simple to add background to his claim, or was it a literary device to show the perfidy of the English and the evil of the Templars? The document itself appears to have been written in the fourteenth century. It is on parchment in Latin, and would have been authenticated by the National Archives before it was catalogued. At least one of the jurymen, William Sleigh, who gives evidence about the claim, appears in other documents from the 1350s.[18] But no mention of these crimes was made by witnesses at the trial of the Scottish Templars. Although rumours about de Jay's uncharitable behaviour do appear, these events were far worse. Was this because the inquisitors asked the wrong questions, or spoke to the wrong people? By the time the story surfaces it is at least two generations old, and may have become exaggerated in its telling.

Maryculter

Maryculter on the lower Dee was granted to the Templars by William the Lion, but the preceptory was not built until Walter Bisset added more land, so that in all it amounted to some 8,000 acres. It was separated from Peterculter and Kelso Abbey by the River Dee and although few details exist about its agriculture, it can be deduced that this would have been similar to that on the Kelso estates. These had a hamlet where cottars held a few acres and beyond that the 'husbandland' with holdings of about 26 acres held for a cash rent and services that included harvesting, sheep-shearing, carrying peat and cutting wood.[19]

As there was no bridge over the Dee at this point in 1287, the Templars built a chapel for their tenants on their side of the river. This contravened Walter Bisset's original grant that gave protection to Kelso Abbey's rights and the monks saw this chapel as a direct threat to part of their income. Lengthy litigation followed. The Templars claimed they had built the chapel for the good of the souls of their tenants because the river was wide and swift at this point and could not be crossed safely. Eventually Maryculter was made into a separate parish for which the Templars were to pay Kelso Abbey eight and a half marks a year. This payment was to be made at Balantrodoch.[20] The chapel is an ivyclad ruin, but the graveyard remains by the Dee.

The Legend of Maryculter

Like Balantrodoch, a legend grew up about the Templars at Maryculter. This was written down by J.A. Henderson in 1892. It concerns a Templar called Godfrey Wedderburn, a native of Maryculter, who joined the Order and went east, where, before a battle commenced, he challenged a Saracen leader to single combat and was severely wounded. After the battle he recovered consciousness and made his way to a well to get water where he fell asleep. He awoke to see a beautiful Saracen maid watching him. She was the daughter of the Saracen leader.

She hid him in a cave and nursed him better, giving him a golden ring as a charm to help the process. Of course they fell in love, but Wedderburn, being a Templar, could not fulfil this love so left, rejoined the Templars and eventually returned to Maryculter. Heartbroken, the Saracen maid followed him and somehow entered the preceptory, was discovered by the Master and roughly ejected. Wedderburn, seeing this, flew into a rage and knocked the

Master to the ground, and for this act was sentenced to death. He was led out to a spot used by the Order to punish disobedient members and was stabbed to death with his own dagger. As he fell to the ground the hills and dales resounded to a terrible scream. The Saracen maid appeared and fell on Wedderburn's chest. She drew out the golden ring she had given him and told the Master to put it on if he dared. The Master drew it on and immediately a bolt of blue fire struck him. The Saracen maid seized Wedderburn's dagger and killed herself. Nevermore would the Templars visit that spot again. A charm was cast on the fields and a blue light was sometimes seen hovering there. Wedderburn's body was buried in the Templars' chapel and the bloodless ghost of the Saracen maid can be seen hovering over it. On dark nights a fully armed knight gallops into the glen and over Kingussie Hill uttering thunderous war cries, and the wraith of a raven-haired maid can be seen sitting beside the beds of the dying in Culter.[21]

In essence, this is Sir Walter Scott's *The Talisman* translated into the Scottish glens. Was Henderson merely retelling a version of this tale, or did Sir Walter Scott hear this legend and place his story in the Holy Land? The tale has elements of the classic *Romeo and Juliet* love story in it, and it also contains many misconceptions about the Templars and their military role in the British Isles. It could be an example of a folk tale rationalising unexplained natural events. The screams and war cries could be wind funnelled up the glen, and the hovering blue fire marsh gas above the peat bogs. Henderson adds to his description of Maryculter by stating that effigies of knights in full armour can be seen in the graveyard, of which all trace has disappeared.

The Templars in the burghs

As well as land in the countryside both the Templars and the Hospitallers had at least one tenement in each of the Scottish burghs, granted to them by Alexander II. All of these tenements allegedly bore a cross, showing that it belonged to one of the military orders, and its tenants had privileges of freedom from taxes and tolls. The location of the tenements can be traced through the eighteenth-century *Charter Book of the Earl of Haddington*. The earl had 'special powers of warrant and commission of all vassals and temple lands holden in the kingdom of Scotland as well as in the burghs as in the country'.[22]

In Edinburgh the Templars' property lay at the head of Cowgate, bounded on the east by Stinking Close and the High Street and Grassmarket on the west. This property included four cellars and the right to draw water from the well in the close. They also had a dwelling house on the Fore Stairs with a booth (shop) underneath a house (open hall), a hall chamber and a high loft. Other properties included a tenement on the grass mound at the north of the castle, with the castle wall forming one boundary of it, and a tenement in Greyfriars Park.

The St Andrews tenement lay at the Mercat Cross and in the eighteenth century was known as New College. In Aberdeen the tenement was on the east side of Castle Gate, in Haddington on Mealls Street, and in the High Town of Lanark. The privileges the tenants of these properties claimed had been granted to the Templars by Alexander II. These included freedom from tolls and customs when buying and selling in markets, freedom from plaints in court, from attending assizes, from working on building castles, bridges or bulwarks, freedom of passage, and freedom from the mercat toll. In addition, tenants had the right to root out woods where they pleased without licence, protection from persecution and the theft of their goods, corn and cattle, and freedom from prosecution in the king's court except for the crimes of murder, arson or rape. The economic benefits of these to the Templars and their tenants were incalculable and distinguishing the houses attached to these privileges brought the Templars out of the countryside into the urban spotlight. The tenants of these tenements were still invoking these privileges in the eighteenth century, showing how the Templars' influence in Scotland remained even after the knights themselves had gone.

Roslin Chapel and the Templars

One place in Scotland where the Templars' presence lingers is in Roslin Chapel, which ironically was not built until over a hundred years after the Order's suppression.[23] The chapel was founded in 1446 by Sir William St Clair as a collegiate chapel where colleges of priests could sing perpetual masses for the souls of his family. From the outside the chapel looks as if it is a fairly plain fifteenth-century building, possibly incomplete, but possessing the characteristic features of fifteenth-century architecture – flying buttresses, pinnacles and gables (Plate 7.2). Inside, the chapel looks as if it was designed by the architect of King's College Chapel, Cambridge, on speed. Every surface is encrusted with carvings and decoration (Plate 7.3). Roslin is where the chapel is situated, but the chapel is generally known as Rosslyn.

This was a vastly expensive chapel to build. Some of the workmen probably came from Paris as continental influences can be seen in some of the carvings. But others were local. For example, the east chapel is modelled on the ambulatory of Glasgow Cathedral.[24] Perhaps bringing together local and foreign craftsmen spurred them on to ever more fantastical work, and Roslin Chapel is a tribute to the spirit of competition. Competition and craft jealousy certainly surrounds the richly carved apprentice pillar that forms the south pier of the eastern chapels. This pillar is unique in church architecture but is supposed to have been modelled on a drawing of a similar pillar sent from Rome. So difficult did this look that the master mason decided to go to look at the original. Whilst he was away his apprentice made the pillar. When the master mason

Plate 7.2 Exterior of Roslin Chapel, Lothian
Crown copyright: RCAHMS

Plate 7.3 Interior of Roslin Chapel, Lothian, from an engraving by T. Allom, of Views of Scotland Crown copyright: RCAHMS

returned and saw this he slew the apprentice out of jealousy. The head of a young man in the south-west corner of the choir is supposed to be the apprentice, a weeping woman his mother, and a surly looking older man the master mason. Crowden notes that there are similar stories attached to other pieces of art, and suggests that the apprentice pillar should be known as the Prentice Pillar as it was the work of the members of a family called Prentys who were prestigious alabastermen from Chellaston in Derbyshire and who were known to be working in Scotland during the fifteenth century.[25]

The riot of images in the chapel have produced many theories as to what these mean and whether the chapel hides a secret. It has been suggested that this is the grail chapel and the Holy Grail, guarded by knights in full armour, lies beneath the floor of the underground sacristy. Theories on Roslin Chapel will be discussed in the last chapter of this book, but at present we have to ask why the chapel is associated with the Templars when the Order was suppressed 100 years before it was built. The key to this is the gravestone of William St Clair, who died fighting the Moors in Spain whilst taking Robert the Bruce's heart to be buried in the Holy Land. This has a floriated cross on it that is thought to be the emblem of the Templars. Thus an ancestor of the St Clairs is thought to have been a Templar. Further back in time there is a tradition that Hugh de Payens, the founder of the Order, was married to a Katherine St Clair. Other Templar images can be seen in the chapel, and the traditional role of the St Clair/Sinclairs as hereditary Grand Masters of the Scottish Freemasons completes the circle.

There is no documentary evidence linking the St Clairs to the medieval Templars, and at the trial of the Templars in Scotland Henry and William St Clair gave evidence against them. Only two Templars were arrested in Scotland and both of them were English – Walter Clifton, preceptor of Balantrodoch, and William Middleton from Maryculter. This has given rise to the suspicion that there were other Templars in Scotland who had gone into hiding, and had been joined in the fastness of glens and mountains by Templars from elsewhere, where they reformed the Order and eventually came back into the public domain as Freemasons. This renegade band of Templars is credited with helping Robert the Bruce to win the Battle of Bannockburn.

The Templars and Bannockburn

The Battle of Bannockburn is seen as the culminating event of the Scottish War of Independence, a struggle that is seen in terms of the weaker native population against a strong and arrogant English oppressor. It should be pointed out that the independence being fought for at Bannockburn was the replacement of one set of Anglo-Norman victors by another. The three major claimants to the Scottish throne who came before Edward I in 1291 all had Norman ancestry; Bruce, Balliol and Hastings had land and relations on both sides of the border and in Normandy, whilst the refugees who fled to England after the battle and were given Templar land to live on by Edward II have Scottish names, for example John of Argyle, Margery the widow of Duncan Frendochart, David and Adam Gordon, Duncan MacDougal.[26] It would have been fitting, therefore, if the victory had been achieved through the intervention of a body of French-speaking foreigners.

Bruce's army at Bannockburn was composed mainly of 6,000 foot soldiers. It was far smaller than the English army that had battalions of mounted knights, and Bruce had no experience of pitched battle. The turning point of the battle came when a supplementary force appeared on the hills behind Bruce, at which the English knights took fright and fled. Translations of chronicle accounts of the battle suggest that these reinforcements were 'camp followers' from Argyle. Other interpretations add that these were reinforcements with cropped heads and long beards, bearing the

Beausant banner of the Templars. Immediately recognisable, they struck fear into the heart of the English knights. These were supposedly renegade Templars from Ireland and La Rochelle who had taken refuge in Kintyre, Argyllshire. They had trained Bruce's army and planned his strategy, and they were responsible for the victory.[27]

There is no evidence for these suppositions, and they diminish Bruce's achievements by suggesting that these were only possible with outside help. The Knights Templar in the British Isles had little or no experience of open battle, and why should they have been supporting Bruce against Edward II when on the whole Edward had been particularly lenient towards them? This story is evidence of the power of the Templars on the public imagination, and of the isolated and mysterious nature of medieval Scotland and interpretations of it.

CHAPTER EIGHT

THE TEMPLARS AND THE PLANTAGENETS

In the preceding chapters we have seen the Templars in their role as monks, farmers and landlords. The Templars in the west also took on the role of advisers to the king, royal officials, ambassadors and negotiators. One of Hugh de Payens aims in coming west in 1128 may have been not only to gain recognition for the Order, but to place its members where they would have the secular overlord's ear and could promote the benefits to his soul of going on crusade, as they did in the case of David I of Scotland. Their role at court was to alter during the twelfth century from one in which they gave counsel on the crusades and affairs in the Holy Land to one where they were giving advice to the king on the affairs of his realm and overseas, and taking charge of his finances. In these dealings the Templars could be trusted as members of a religious order, and as an international order their advice should have been impartial, and aimed at the best for all concerned. But they were in an ambiguous position. They owed allegiance only to the Pope and in a squabble between the monarch and the Church were duty-bound to promote the Church's interest. As an institution without boundaries they had to take care to show they were aloof from international struggles, as frequently occurred between England and France, and in the fourteenth century between England and Scotland. They also had to be careful in internal politics not to be bribed by offers of property to favour one side over another, and they had especially to eschew any involvement that might result in the spilling of Christian blood.

Templars held high positions in the courts of France, Portugal and Aragon. Alan Forey suggests that the natural place of the provincial Master was at the side of the king. He shows that in Aragon the Master had special responsibilities such as acting as tutor to the royal sons, as well as acting as mediator between the king and his nobility and representing the king in Rome. At the same time he had to keep out of local politics.[1] The overall aim of the Templars' political role was to maintain the Order's rights and privileges.

THE TEMPLARS AND THE NORMAN KINGS

When Hugh de Payens came west in 1128 to seek out aid from Europe he tracked down Henry I of England in Normandy. Henry spent the whole of that year in Normandy, engaged in war with France, but he paused long enough in this activity to give Hugh the letters of permission he needed to travel to England and get support for the Order. Henry of Huntingdon describes Henry I as possessed of sagacity and foresight, but added that others said he was gross, and avaricious, imposing high taxes on his realm, as well as being cruel and wanton.[2] Henry of Huntingdon illustrates one of the problems of using medieval chronicles as a source. Those writing after the subject's death, as Henry of Huntingdon was, could reflect on the subject and interpret events in their wider context. Those writing at the time were likely to be extremely partisan.

There is no record of Henry granting any land to the Templars himself, but by the time he died in 1135 the Templars were established in England, and had probably built part of the Old Temple in London. Henry's successor Stephen was chosen as king by the barons and the citizens of London, who ignored the prior claim of Henry's daughter, the Empress Matilda. Before his death Henry had made the barons swear fealty to her. They reneged on this oath and paid homage to Stephen. The author of the anonymous *Gesta Stephani Regis Angolorum* shows Stephen as a generous, humble and affable man. A military commander who excelled in war, strong and discrete, and ready to listen to commoners who came to him with pleas. Writing after the events and in the reign of Henry II, Walter Map describes Stephen as 'a man distinguished in arms, but in other respects almost a fool, save that he was rather inclined to the side of evil'.[3]

It was the generosity of Stephen and his queen, Matilda, that made the Templars into major landholders in England. Cressing, Witham and Cowley were all royal gifts, whilst the Empress gave them rights of pasture in Shotover Forest. Apart from retrieving the body of Geoffrey de Mandeville, the Templars were not involved in the struggle for the crown. They were busy establishing their preceptories, and were also preoccupied with events in the east. Stephen's reign coincided with one of the most successful periods for the Christian armies in the Holy Land, culminating in the Second Crusade and the Fall of Ascalon to the Franks. The Templars' energies were focused on this and providing resources for their brethren rather than on internal politics.

Although Stephen's reign is known as the 'anarchy' and described by Henry of Huntingdon as a period when 'slaughter, fire and rapine spread throughout the land',[4] an analysis of events shows these to be more circumscribed than Huntingdon and other ecclesiastical chroniclers suggest. Some bishops and abbeys were caught up in events, but this was a war of castle sieges with the armies moving from castle to castle. The effect on the population around the castles would have been dramatic, but outside the war zone they would not have been affected. The struggle did not get any further north than Lincoln, and it was concentrated in the west and south-west around the possessions of the Empress's half-brother, Robert of Gloucester. It is doubtful whether the initial uprising of

Baldwin de Redvers and William of Bathampton was aimed at placing the Empress on the throne as their main concern was the restitution of lands they had lost.

One measure of how both sides tried to woo the Templars comes from the number of grants of lands and rents. The *Gesta Stephani* has a list of supporters for both parties. The count is based only on those who remained on the same side throughout, and does not include the royal family. The 1185 Inquest shows that the Templars received 37 grants during this period, of which 21 came from supporters of Stephen and 11 from Matilda. In the reign of Matilda's son the number of grants to the Templars doubled. This was due to the reinstatement of a relatively stable kingdom, successes in the Holy Land and a growing awareness that a grant to the Templars could earn absolution for sins.

THE TEMPLARS AND THE PLANTAGENETS

An ancient legend tells that the ancestress of the Plantagenets was a witch named Melusine who one day flew out of the window of her earthly castle never to return. Bernard of Clairvaux, no doubt familiar with the legend, when irritated beyond endurance by a member of Melusine's descendants, proclaimed, 'From the Devil they came, to the Devil they will go.' This colourful and short-tempered bunch are known to us as the Plantagenets but to themselves as Angevins from the House of Anjou (Plate 8.1). Plantagenet was a nickname used for Geoffrey of Anjou, Henry II's father who wore a sprig of broom, or *planta genesta*, in his helmet.

Henry II was the child of a proud and disappointed woman and a handsome but self-centred man. He began his reign in England at the age of 21, and Henry of Huntingdon hailed him as England's saviour.[5] By this time he had already made a scandalous marriage to Eleanor of Aquitaine, the divorced wife of the King of France and 10 years his senior. Walter Map described Henry as a lawmaker,

Plate 8.1 The Plantagenet kings. King John wears his crown askew
BL Ms Claudius D Xı fol. 9
The British Library

affable and modest, with abundant energy.[6] Others were less complimentary, noting his bad temper and his blasphemy.

Henry was quick to favour the Templars, granting them annual alms of one mark from every sheriff's farm. These annual payments can be traced through the Pipe Rolls until the Order's suppression. Henry II's reign marks the beginning of the Templars' public life as councillors and advisers to the king at home and abroad. Roger the Templar became Henry's councillor.[7] Henry's vast possessions included Normandy and Anjou held on his part, and Aquitaine, his wife's duchy. This made him an important player on the international stage and he was soon negotiating with other European princes to cement treaties and alliances through the marriages of his children. His daughters Matilda, Joanna and Eleanor married the Duke of Saxony, King of Castile and the King of Sicily respectively, and his third son, Geoffrey, married the Duchess of Brittainy, thus securing a friendly neighbour on Normandy's flank. The most important matches were to be those made by Henry's eldest sons, Henry and Richard. At this time England and France were almost permanently at war. If France could be secured through a double marriage of Louis of France's daughters to Henry's sons, this should have resulted in peace and, because Louis had no male heir, the likelihood of one of the elder sons ascending to the French throne as well as to the English crown. Peace with France would also give Henry the chance to fulfil another of his ambitions and go on crusade.

During Henry's reign a religious fervour was whipped up by the preaching of the Second Crusade and towards the end of the reign the news of the Battle of Hattin and the defeat of the Christian army filtered through to the west. As a man of action whose immortal soul was in danger, taking the cross would have seemed like an excellent way to redemption. In the event Henry was frustrated in this, but he was meticulous in enforcing the Saladin tithe in England, and in his will he left 5,000 marks each to the Templars and the Hospitallers in Jerusalem.

The treaty with France was to be cemented with the marriage of Henry, the elder son, to Marguerite, the King of France's elder daughter, and Richard, the second son, to Louis's younger daughter Alys. Marguerite's dowry was to include the castles of Gisors and Neafle in the Vexin. This was an important prize for Henry and these castles controlled the north-east border between his posses- sions and France. Until the marriage was solemnised the Templars were to hold the castles in trust. This shows that both kings had confidence in the Templars and it indicates the development of their role in international politics. Malcolm Barber suggests that they were successful in this role because of their objectivity.[8] Louis of France would have disagreed with this assessment. When the news came to Henry that Louis was to be remarried and there- fore might produce a male heir, he speedily arranged the marriage of Prince Henry to Marguerite of France.[9] He then asked the Templars to release the Gisors and Neafle castles which they did with alacrity.

Roger of Howden writes that the castles were handed over to Henry by the authority of three Templars, Robert de Pirou, Tostes de Saint Omer and Richard Hastings, the Master of the Templars in England, and they agreed to Henry's request because it seemed right. The King of France, he continues, was very angry and ex- pelled the three from the kingdom of France, but the King of England was greatly obliged.[10]

Why did the Templars break their trust in this way and show partiality to Henry, whose act was clearly against the spirit of the agreement with France? Did they fear reprisals from Henry, who was known to be ruthless when roused? Henry controlled an enorm- ous amount of land in south-west France, including Bordeaux, where the Templars had an important preceptory, and La Rochelle, where the Templars' Atlantic fleet was stationed and from where they shipped Gascon wine. Did this have anything to do with the decision? It seems to have been a unilateral decision by the three

Templars mentioned and there is no evidence that this was discussed at a chapter. Perhaps they did what they thought best at the time.

Henry was a man who liked to get his own way. This was to bring him into armed conflict with his own sons, and famously with Thomas Becket, his Archbishop of Canterbury, who, as a result of this, was to be murdered in his own cathedral. The Pope sentenced the murderers to go on a pilgrimage as absolution, with some suggestion that he might have intended them to join the Templars. In the event, after a year holed up in Knaresborough Castle, two of the assassins, Hugh de Morville and William de Tracy, departed on pilgrimage. De Morville gave the Templars the whole vill of Sowerby as part of his absolution, and a third member of the gang, Reginald Fitz-Urse, granted them the whole vill of Wileton in Somerset.

The Templars were involved in the collection of the Saladin tithe for Henry and by 1185 had safe-keeping of part of the royal treasury. This is evidence of Henry's trust in the Templars, but not all Templars were worthy of this. In 1188 Gilbert of Hoxton, a Templar, was charged with stealing money designated for the crusade. He was spared by the king, and handed over to the Master of the Temple in London to be punished. We do not know what happened to him.

Henry died in 1189. He was still at war with his surviving sons, and when Richard, now the heir to the throne of England, came into the room where his father's corpse lay, blood is supposed to have gushed from it as evidence of Richard's responsibility for his father's death. Richard was crowned on 3 September 1189. His mind was already focused on the east and preparations for his crusade. Desperate for cash, he sold crown offices and lands and offered to pawn the crown jewels. The Templars privileges and possessions were confirmed on 6 October 1189, and he granted them assarts at Garway, Merton and Cowley in Oxfordshire and elsewhere. Richard left England for Normandy in December 1189. The kingdom was almost bankrupt.

The Third Crusade was the result of an aggressive campaign in the Holy Land by Saladin and the loss of Jerusalem. The Templars played a diplomatic role as the crusaders travelled east, mediating between Richard and Philip Augustus, King of France, and eventually being given charge of Messina. The Templars were with Richard when he took Cyprus in 1191, and eventually purchased it from him for 25,000 marks, re-selling it to Guy of Lusingnan the next year for the same amount. It was claimed that during their ownership they levied extortionate taxes in order to make a profit, but there is no evidence for this. But it is during Richard's reign that rumours start in England about the Templars' pride and avarice. According to Gerald of Wales and Roger Howden, Richard is reputed to have said that he would marry his daughter pride to the Templars because they were as proud as Lucifer.

Richard's expedition to the Holy Land may have had a dynastic reason as well as fulfilling a religious vow. When Heraclius Patriarch of Jerusalem was in London to dedicate the New Temple in 1185 he offered the kingdom of Jerusalem to Henry II for his second son, Richard. Henry refused, but this offer may have stuck in Richard's mind. J.O. Prestwich and John Gillingham argue that much of Richard's strategy in Europe and the Holy Land was concerned with the maintenance of the Angevin inheritance of which Jerusalem was part.[11] When Richard left the Holy Land for Europe in 1192 he went in the company of four Templars, and may have been wearing a Templar's mantle as a disguise. But he was recognised as he crossed the territory of the Duke of Austria, with whom he had quarrelled during the crusade, was taken prisoner and held for a ransom of 150,000 marks. The ransom money was to be collected by a levy of 20s on all property and income of the laity and clergy in Richard's dominions, and all privileges were suspended. This included those held by the Templars. They also had to pay a tax on the land they held as knights fees, and a 25 per cent tax levied on all ecclesiastical foundations would have netted about £1,000 from them.

It was during Richard's captivity and the attempts to raise the ransom that legends grew up about Robin Hood and wicked Prince John, culminating in the anonymous return of Richard as the champion of the oppressed. This period entered into fiction in Sir Walter Scott's *Ivanhoe*, in which the Templars play a major part as scheming villains. There is no evidence regarding the Templars' role in the collection of Richard's ransom. We can only surmise that they would have remained loyal to Richard as an anointed king and a fellow crusader who had fought beside their brothers. Nevertheless, when Richard died in 1199 and was succeeded by his brother, the time-serving John, the Templars were quick to ingratiate themselves with him, giving him a palfrey and paying him £1,000 for the confirmation of their rights and privileges.

Medieval chroniclers are almost universal in condemning John. Secular chronicles condemn him for the loss of Normandy and his espousal of foreign advisers; ecclesiastical chroniclers because his quarrel with the Church placed the kingdom under an interdict. Matthew Paris thought that John's reign was a failure because he was evil, and an analogy can be drawn with Paris's conclusion that Jerusalem was lost because of the Templars' pride. John's quarrel with the Church started over the election of the Archbishop of Canterbury. John wanted John de Gray, the Bishop of Norwich, to succeed Hubert Walter, who had died in 1199, but the bishops elected Reginald, the prior of Canterbury. John forced another election at which de Gray was chosen. The Pope refused to accept either candidate and instead nominated Stephen Langton, an English theologian and teacher at the University of Paris. A furious John expelled the monks from Canterbury and refused to let Langton enter the country. The Pope consecrated him at Viterbo, and threatened that unless John accepted him an interdict would be placed on the country. This would mean that the clergy would no longer perform their duties, except the baptism of infants and the confession of the dying. The interdict was proclaimed on

24 March 1206, and John gleefully seized all clerical property. With the Pope's protection withdrawn, Geoffrey Fitz-Peter the justiciar made himself responsible for the Knights Templar.

There was a financial advantage to the Templars in this situation as they were permitted to open parish churches once a year in a country under an interdict and perform the divine office, and could bury the dead in their consecrated ground. But the spiritual disadvantages to the country outweighed this. In 1209 John was excommunicated and by 1211 only one bishop remained in England. When the Pope sent his legate Pandulph to negotiate with John, he went to the Templars' house at Dover, on the Western Heights. John and his retinue joined him there, and two Templars acted as mediators between the legate and the king. The account given by Roger Wendover suggests that the parties were in different rooms, and the Templars plied between them reporting what the other had said. 'We are repeating to you, O mighty king, on the part of Pandulph the servant of the Lord Pope that is for your advantage and the kingdom's profit to have a conference together; and propose how peace may be made, that will reconcile you to almighty God and the church . . .' Wendover adds that this is the truth and what the Templars remember saying. After much negotiation a charter was drawn up in which John, with the mandate of his barons and for the sake of all their souls and the kingdom, agreed to hand the kingdom over to the Pope and pay homage for this. On 15 May 1213 this was done at the Templars' house at Dover, and the kingdoms of England and Ireland were handed over to the Pope.[12] John paid homage to the Pope as his overlord and received absolution, paying nine golden marks for this, some versions suggesting that these were borrowed from the Templars.

The Templars must have been involved in a considerable amount of behind-the-scenes diplomatic activity before the meeting between John and Pandulph. Frequent trips to Rome would have been necessary, and the Templars advising John had to make sure they did not alienate him. One of the anonymous Templars who brought about the reconciliation may have been Aymeric St Mawr, Master of the Templars in England, who was at John's side during another crisis when he was forced to set his seal on the Magna Carta. St Mawr had remained loyal to John throughout the Barons' War and he advised John to submit and agree to the charter. The night before setting out for Runnymede was spent at the New Temple, and St Mawr is listed as one of the observers at Runnymede.

The other Templar at Dover may have been Brother Roger, who became John's almoner in 1215 and agent for the regulation of seaborne commerce between England and Gascony. During John's reign the Templars appear to have been one of the chief importers of Gascon wine, even supplying it to the royal household.

John's reign came to an ignominious end with him on the run from a French prince who had been invited to invade the country by his discontented barons. Many historians dwell on the failures of his reign, but he left an improved bureaucracy with a workable exchequer and chancery, and he laid the foundations of the royal navy. The Templars supported him throughout his reign, and it was their support and the wisdom of William Marshal, one of their associate members, that helped to secure the kingdom for the infant Henry III.

HENRY III AND THE TEMPLARS

The Templars' loyalty to his father and the influence of William Marshal resulted in a beneficial relationship between Henry III and the Templars. They became his advisers, officials and treasurers, and his reign has been seen as the apex of the Templars' influence in England. In July 1231 Henry made it known that he wished to be buried in the New Temple and gave the Temple a grant of £8 to support three chaplains to celebrate mass daily for his soul, the souls of all Christian people and the faithful departed. Part of the manor of Roel/Rothley was given to them as down payment for a burial place. Four years later in July 1235 Henry again gave notification that he wished to be buried in the New Temple.[13] Henry changed his mind about his burial place, and was eventually buried in Westminster Abbey that he had remodelled.

The importance of the New Temple as an administrative centre appears early in Henry's reign when, in 1220, the vice-chancellor is told that if he leaves London he is to deposit any money he has received there, and to give the Great Seal of England into the Master's care.[14] Brother Geoffrey from the New Temple was already acting as an envoy for the king when he was appointed as king's almoner in 1229, succeeding another Templar, Brother Roger. His tasks as almoner and keeper of the wardrobe included receiving and disbursing monies for the king, and purchasing materials for the king to give to the poor. In 1233, as keeper of the wardrobe, he purchased 450 ells of russet cloth in Oxford which was to be carried to Gloucester and made into gowns for the poor, to be distributed at the Easter court. As keeper of the king's wardrobe he was responsible for the transport of Henry's robes wherever he wanted to wear them on a state occasion. He was also responsible for equipping military expeditions and buying in equipment, such as a mangonel and stones for use at the Siege of Bedford. He handled large sums of money that had to be accounted for every year. The patent appointing Geoffrey made it clear that he personally was responsible for the money and not the Templars as a corporate body.

Wardrobe accounts of Geoffrey the Templar

1236–37	Received	£9,142
	Expenditure	£5,176
1237–38	Received	£2,810
	Expenditure	£7,186
1238–40	Received	£21,010
	Expenditure	£4,062[15]

Expenses went on robes, hospitality in the royal household, campaign expenses and shipping. Matthew Paris, who rarely had a good word to say for the Templars, wrote that Geoffrey was unpopular with court and commoners, and that the king reproached him for too great a subservience to Rome, and dismissed him. T.F. Tout accepts Paris's version, and adds that Geoffrey was a bitter persecuter of the Jews, extracting one-third of their substance from them.[16] He is referring to the Templars' collection of the Jewish tallage for the king. In reality, Geoffrey was dismissed because he refused to sign a writ giving the queen's uncle, the Count of Flanders, a toll of 4d on every sack of English wool exported to Flanders. This imposition would have stifled exports, and although it could be argued that, as the Templars were exporters of wool themselves, Geoffrey refused out of self-interest, it lost him his position. F.M. Powicke thinks that Geoffrey showed too much independence of spirit whilst in the post and his refusal to do the king's wishes in this event led to his dismissal. But the king might also have been looking for a reason to get rid of Geoffrey because he wanted the post for one of the queen's relatives.[17] Henry does not seem to have had a personal motive as he continued to give Geoffrey gifts of wine, and part of the wardrobe was still at the New Temple in 1246.[18]

THE FALL OF HUBERT DE BURGH

As the boy king moved into manhood he became increasingly unpopular because he surrounded himself with new men and foreigners. Hubert de Burgh was one of the new men, and his affairs were to become entangled with those of the Templars. An impoverished Norfolk squire, de Burgh decided to make his fortune at court. By 1198 he was John's chamberlain, and was soon amassing manors and offices that were to make him one of the wealthiest men in the kingdom. Like the Master of the Templars, he stood by

John during the Barons' War, and for his loyalty was rewarded with the office of justiciar, the highest judicial office in the land. He kept this office during Henry III's minority and continued to add to his wealth which irritated the old nobility, who resented his dictatorial bearing, and the Church, which was jealous of his wealth. His particular enemy was Peter des Roches, Bishop of Winchester. In 1232 he accused de Burgh of acquiring offices, lands and treasure by artifice, giving the king bad counsel, stealing Margaret, the daughter of William the Lion of Scotland, and marrying her himself, plotting with the Pope to rob Henry of his inheritance, not rendering satisfactory accounts, wasting money at the Siege of Bedford and loosing control of La Rochelle through his negligence. De Burgh fled into sanctuary but was brought out and placed in the Tower of London.

The evidence throughout Henry's reign shows that he was easily persuaded by others, and at this time he was also desperately short of funds. Rumours were put abroad that de Burgh had deposited a fabulous treasure with the Templars, and that this included articles stolen from the king. Robert, the Master of the Temple, was sent for, and admitted that de Burgh had deposited treasure in the New Temple, but he did not know how much and, as it was under his care, he could not release it without permission from the depositor. Henry suggested that as much of it was stolen from him it belonged to him anyway. The Templar was adamant, and pointed out that only de Burgh had the keys to the treasure chest. Des Roches's nephew, Peter de Rievaux, was sent to speak to de Burgh in the Tower. The official version is that he told de Burgh that the king had need of his treasure and de Burgh meekly handed over the keys. It is more likely that he went with permission to put forward a deal to de Burgh as shortly after he handed over the keys he was released from the Tower and put on open arrest in Devizes Castle.[19]

The chronicles such as those of Matthew Paris and Roger Wendover exaggerated the amount of the treasure. They suggested that there was at least 8,000lbs of silver and 140 cups of gold and silver. The inventory shows this not to be the case.

The inventory of Hubert de Burgh's treasure in the New Temple

2 gold rings, one with a *balas* ruby, the other with an emerald

A gold brooch with sapphires and garnets

12 silk girdles

3 circlets of gold, one of which was the old king's old treasure with sapphires, and the other two of Paris work and smaller

A great cup with figures in relief

28 cups of silver gilt working in relief, £125 6s 5d

57 cups of silver gilt, engraved, £183 1s 11d

64 cups of silver gilt, plain, £199 3s 9d

9 cups of white silver, £23 14s 6d

9 silver justs, 8 gilt and 1 white, £55 9s 3d

22 pairs of basons, £81 1s 9d

7 porringers, 3 salt cellars of silver, £18 19s

1 crystal phial with silver gilt fitting

2 silver candlelabras, £5 9s 6d

In pennies, £150

Also the treasure of Margaret his wife

A silver cross, double gilt with a ruby and an emerald, relics and figures of St Mary and St John

A silver porringer with a font, £1 7s 3d

A gryphons egg cup, £1

2 white cups, £4 10s

2 other cups of unknown weight

2 silver gilt cups, plain, £4 6s

The value was based on the weight of the article.

Despite having a bag of £150 in pennies (probably golden pennies), de Burgh needed ready money and had mortgaged the manor of Banstead in Surrey to the Templars.

Like de Burgh, Henry III also built up a store of treasure. His was in gold. D.A. Carpenter shows that gold was crucial to Henry's financial activities. He started collecting it in 1243, but this was spent on the Gascony campaign of 1253–54. At least part of this golden treasure was kept in the New Temple because in July 1245 the king sent a mandate to Peter de Chaucepore that all the gold lying at the New Temple in bezants, bars and spangles, was to be weighed by the mark.[20] A second collection was started at the end of 1254 and sold in France and London in 1260–61. Much of this later collection came from the confiscation of Jewish property and fines levied on monastic houses which were forced to hand in their charter of privileges to Henry and have them re-issued for a price. The Templars were affected by this, paying £151 to Henry for the confirmation of their charter.

One reason that is advanced for Henry's fixation with gold is that he was collecting it to take on crusade with him. However, as Carpenter points out, there was no need for crusaders to carry bullion with them as this could be paid into a local house of the Templars and drawn out by a letter of credit in the Holy Land.[21]

Henry's golden treasure was in bezants, money, cups, gold leaf and gold dust. It was worth 28,390 silver marks, about £18,926, considerably more than de Burgh's treasure which, at an estimated value of £1,000, was worth only a fraction of the king's. The only item de Burgh could have been obtained by artifice was the old king's circlet.

HENRY III, THE CRUSADES AND SIMON DE MONTFORT

In 1250 Henry III took the Cross, an action that was to have far-reaching consequences. It is possible that this was a public relations exercise and he had no intention of going east but intended to redeem his vow by payments to the Pope. In 1254 the Pope converted Henry's vow to go on crusade to one by which he would conquer the kingdoms of Naples and Sicily for the Pope. When this was complete, Henry's second son, the Lord Edmund, would be declared King of Sicily. A Sicilian tithe was collected and the Pope put an army in the field, but it was defeated. The bill for this expedition was sent to Henry. It was three times his annual revenue. In 1258 the papal legate arrived in England to collect the first instalment of the debt, and Henry was told he must pay the rest within a year and bind himself to go to Naples and conquer it, or be excommunicated. In a panic Henry appealed to his barons for help.

At this point Simon de Montfort, Earl of Leicester and Henry's brother-in-law, emerged as leader of a reforming party of barons. Historians and chroniclers are divided as to whether de Montfort was a liberal and the father of the English Parliament, or a self-seeking villain who massacred the Jews and met his just deserts at the Battle of Evesham. Henry always seems to have been suspicious of him, and a commission that included a Templar was sent to investigate the way in which he governed Gascony when he was its seneschal. The Templars supported Henry as the anointed king, but whilst the barons were deliberating on what to do, they met daily, sometimes at the New Temple.[22]

The result of these deliberations were the Provisions of Oxford that proposed that the king should rule through a council of 24 barons. The barons demanded that Henry should dismiss the alien clerks and officials that surrounded him, and send his Lusignan half-brothers back from whence they came. If Henry agreed to this, the barons would help to raise the Pope's fine. The Lusignan brothers were given a safe-conduct to cross from Dover to France, taking 300 marks each with them. The rest of their wealth was to be paid into the treasury of the New Temple. Henry was to follow them in 1259 and stayed in France from November 1259 to April 1260. When he returned he resumed authority of the country, issuing a proclamation against the aliens Simon de Montfort had introduced to the country. By summer 1263 the Welsh were in arms, the barons in revolt and the country was plunged into civil war. Henry fled to the safety of the Tower of London where Edward, his eldest son, found him when he returned from fortifying Dover Castle, almost alone and without money. Edward, ever resourceful, knew where to find funds. With a body of his knights he marched on the New Temple, broke into the treasury and seized £1,000. Later Henry was to express regret at this action. The incident shows the vulnerability of the Temple to a concentrated armed attack, but we should consider whether breaking into the precincts was a symbolic act to cover for the Templars giving Edward the money. Whether or not this was the case, this was the signal for a breakdown of public order in London.

The Templars were not involved in the war with de Montfort, but when Parliament was convened the Master of the Temple, with the heads of other religious houses, was invited to attend, and continued to do so throughout the thirteenth century. The 1299 Parliament was held at the New Temple, and important visitors from abroad were lodged there at the king's expense.

On their accessions, Edward I and Edward II confirmed the Templars' privileges. Edward I used the Templars as envoys to Scotland, and continued to send them gifts of wine and venison. There is no evidence that either of the Edwards viewed the Order with anything other than respect. Throughout the colourful and often violent rule of the Plantagenets the Templars managed to maintain a political equilibrium. They supported the anointed king, but not against the Pope, who was their nominal overlord. They served the crown as officers and ambassadors, handling large sums of money for the king, and negotiating through delicate situations. This is the public face of the Order and it is far removed from the isolated rural preceptories where many of the brothers ended their days.

CHAPTER NINE

THE TEMPLARS AS BANKERS

The settlement of the Templars in the British Isles coincided with the growth of an international money economy. The crown and members of the nobility who had lands on both sides of the Channel needed a mechanism to transfer revenues backwards and forwards between their estates; trade and commerce needed to exchange foreign currency into sterling, and vice versa; kings and merchants needed credit to finance their operations. The Templars already had experience in money management and in transporting cash over long distances, and because crusaders needed to be able to draw on funds once they reached the Holy Land without being weighed down with bullion, the Templars had developed a system which transferred money between their preceptories on paper rather than as specie. As they were an international organisation with a network of communication they were able to do this easily.

As well as issuing international credit notes they also acted as couriers, carrying large sums of money overseas. They arranged and paid ransoms and jointures, collected and stored taxes and royal revenues, and offered a safe-deposit service. To do this they developed an international reputation for efficient book-keeping and financial expertise that would only be superseded by the Italian bankers in the fourteenth century. It was the large sums of money they handled that led to the notion that they were extremely wealthy, and to them being accused of avarice.

When money became a fact of everyday life in the twelfth century it created moral tensions within religious communities. Fundraising became a recognised part of their activities. This led to a number of theological debates on how a religious order should dispose of its surplus cash. Should this be to purchase relics that would add to the sanctity of the house, attract pilgrims and add to revenues? Should it be used to build larger and more glorious churches, should it be used to feed the poor, or loaned to those in need? These debates passed the Templars by because their surplus was already spoken for, it was sent to the Holy Land to keep their army in the field. What was different between the Templars and more orthodox monastic orders was that the Templars were handling large sums of other people's money.

Dealing with the financial affairs of others brought them into the political arena and placed them in a peculiar relationship based on power and trust, a relationship that was often unstable and reversible. This can be seen in the Lord Edward's dealings with the Templars in 1263. They held the £1,000 he stole from the Temple on trust, and whilst they held the keys to the chest they were in control. Edward broke that trust, and reversed the balance of power by taking the money by force.[1] Banking, trust and credit relations in the Middle Ages meant those providing these services were vulnerable to political allegations of corruption, and to violent attack.

THE TEMPLARS, THE EXCHEQUER AND BOOK-KEEPING

In 1177 a tract was written that consisted of a dialogue between two exchequer officials. It discussed the exchequer's origin, its duties and how it recorded and audited the revenues it received. The exchequer itself, as described in the dialogue, was a quadrangular board 10 feet long by 5 feet wide with a raised edge. On the board was a black cloth marked with white lines one foot apart. Coins were placed within the spaces formed by the lines. Although the dialogue does not specify this, it is sometimes assumed that horizontal lines were added to form squares and a chequer-board effect. It is more likely that only vertical lines or rods were laid down and the board was used as an abacus.[2] The Templars received a chequer board for counting in May 1238 along with other office furniture, including wax for seals, sacks for putting money in and benches for clerks to sit on.[3]

The New Temple was not the exchequer but the 'treasury' where the exchequer lodged its revenues. It was also the place where taxes were received, brought by the county sheriffs, or by a Templar and escort who received the provincial tax revenue and was responsible for bringing this to London. In May 1238 a mandate was sent by the king to the bailiffs of Bristol telling them to supply good barrels and good carts to John de Plessis, Brother Robert the Templar and a Hospitaller so that they could transport the king's revenues from the tax of the thirtieth to the New Temple in London.[4]

When the county sheriff arrived at the Temple with the shire revenue this was received by the treasurer. He may also have been the treasurer of the Temple, or a separate official. The money was counted and recorded by tellers who remembered the amounts by notches on tally sticks. The final amount was recorded in a roll, and in the presence of an usher and a watchman the money was placed boxes that were put into a chest with a double lock that needed two key holders to open it.[5] If the money inside was part of the royal revenue a royal writ was needed before it could be paid out. It is these writs that help us to reconstruct the Templars' financial activities in the British Isles.

A written record was kept by the Templars of the financial transactions they were involved in, but unfortunately those for the New Temple have not survived. Some idea of what these may have told

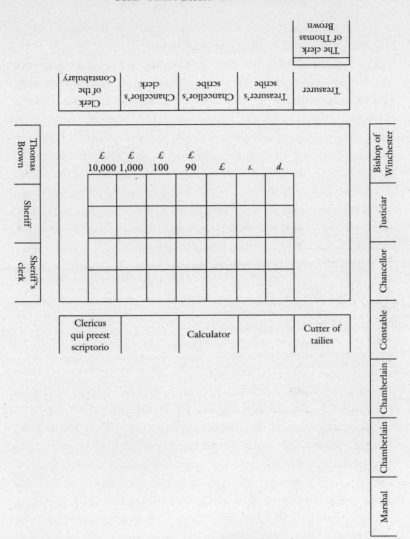

Plate 9.1 Diagram of the layout of the Exchequer
Re-drawn from Richard son of Nigel, *Dialogus de Scaccario*, ed.,
Hughes, A.C. Crum and C. Johnson, Oxford: Clarendon Press, 1902

us comes from the day book of the Paris Temple that has survived and which has been analysed by J. Piquet.[6]

The basic principle of accounting is that all transactions should be recorded twice. Once on the debit and once on the credit side, that is double-entry book-keeping. This integrates a real and a nominal sum, and helps the books to balance. This system was in use by the 1150s, and was first arranged in paragraph form entries following each other rather than on opposite pages. A variant was used by the Paris Templars with each client's account having a number and particulars of remittances and withdrawals listed in sequence. Accounts were sent to the client three times a year, at Ascension Day, All Saints, and Candlemass. A typical account is that of the Queen-mother of France for Candlemass 1242.

1242 Candlemass account of the Queen-mother of France with the Paris Templars

Paid in, 5,449 livres Tournois
Paid out, 718 livres Tournois
Received from reeves, 560 livres Tournois
Received from baillies, 951 livres Tournois[7]

Had they survived, a similar scheme would have been visible in account books for the Templars in the British Isles.

Piquet suggests that the Templars became financiers accidentally because their precincts were secure and as a military order they could defend these.[8] This was not the case in London where the New Temple was broken into several times and money removed: by Richard, Earl of Cornwall, in 1254, by Edward I in 1263 and 1294, and by Edward II in 1307. But these were royal princes and the violence may have been symbolic. A story recounted by John of Joinville about raising Louis IX's ransom bears this out. The Templars would not release funds for this without the written permission of the depositors, but they stood by whilst Joinville with raised sword opened the chests and barrels where the money was stored.[9]

The Templars' international network and their expertise in transporting money safely over long distances made them an obvious choice for kings and princes as well as crusaders to use as financiers. Initially this gave them a high profile at the courts of Europe and an advantage over the Italian bankers who became their rivals. But the Templars were probably not undertaking what were often hazardous transactions without reward. How did they make a profit from their banking activities? Did the depositor pay a percentage to the Templars, or grant them lands or rents in exchange for their services? Did they give interest on deposited money, or take it from loans? Answering these questions is difficult. First, because the evidence produced by the Templars themselves does not exist, and secondly because that which does survive was produced for the public domain and tells us little about the actual transactions themselves. All we know is that it happened, we do not know on what terms. From the *Paris Day Book* recording transactions it appears that if an account was closed the Templars had half of what remained in it, but as many British accounts were in debit this was no reward. Using official sources such as the Close, Liberate and Patent Rolls, seven types of financial activity in Britain can be distinguished.

The Templars' financial services in the British Isles

1. Current accounts with regular payments of money in and expenses paid out of this money on the written authority of the account holder.
2. Safe-deposit facilities for money, jewels and other treasure.
3. Loans and credit.
4. The transmission of money over international boundaries, either as cash or as letters of credit.
5. Trustees for the payment of annuities.
6. Tax collectors and receivers.
7. The New Temple acting as a recognised place where debts between private citizens could be repaid.

HENRY III'S CURRENT ACCOUNT

Henry's current account is being used as a case study because it provides the best evidence of the way in which the New Temple operated. Henry's father, King John, had started the family tradition of banking with the New Temple. He had money on deposit there in 1202, put the crown jewels into its safe-deposit, and in

Great Seal of Henry III.

Plate 9.2 The Great Seal of Henry III
From *Annals of England*, 1876

1212 deposited 100 marks there to be paid out to his nephew, Otto IV of Germany. A further 7,000 marks were deposited in 1214; 6,000 of these were intended for the papal legate. It is doubtful whether much of John's deposits remained when Henry came to the throne in 1216. However, Henry would have received annual revenues from the county farms and other taxes, and revenues from the royal estates. As has been shown, he was to amass a golden treasure, but that was more in the line of personal savings. His current account with the Templars was more official.

1220–29
Deposits   £1,433 7s 9d   Withdrawals   £275 19s 5d

Withdrawals were for work on Windsor Castle and in Wales and a deposit of £1,000 was intended for Richard, Earl of Cornwall, although there is no record of it being withdrawn.

1230–39
Deposits   £26 6s 4d   Withdrawals   £6,956 6s 4d

Henry's financial situation was not as desperate as this implies. Added to his revenues were the taxes and fines recorded in the Pipe Rolls and the Jewish tallage that at this time amounted to between £9,000 and £20,000.

1240–49
Deposits   £14,695 7s 0d   Withdrawals   £2,418 3s 9d

Withdrawals were to buy horses and other military expenses. £9,000 of the deposits came from the Jewish tallage.

1250–59
Deposits   £333   Withdrawals   £9,501 2s 0d

The sole deposit in the account at the New Temple came again from the Jewish tallage.

1220–59

Deposits (to the nearest £) £16,487   Withdrawals £19,150

The account at the Temple was in debit of £2,663

The *Receipts and Issues Roll of 1241–42* shows receipts of £34,427 and withdrawals of £38,105, leaving a debit of £3,678, 11 per cent[10] of deposits compared to 16 per cent of the deposits at the New Temple, but close enough to suggest that Henry was overspending by about 13 per cent of his annual income. The receipts shown in the *Great Roll of the Pipe* show this to have been about £30,000 a year, of which the Jewish tallage sometimes accounted for one-third.[11] This can be compared with the revenues received in the Paris Temple for the King of France, Philip IV that amounted to annual deposits of about £800,000. Despite this, his account with the Templars was in debit on at least eight occasions.[12]

A considerable amount of the crown's revenues went on the war effort. Between 1294 and 1298 Edward I spent £750,000 pursuing the wars against Scotland and France.[13] Other members of Henry's family had accounts at the New Temple, including William de Valence, as did clerics, including the Bishops of Rochester and Lichfield. Accounts apart from those of the king only enter the records when the account holder was in trouble and the account was sequestered. This means that there were probably many more account holders for whom no record survives.

Banking services usually incur some fee. Many of the Templars' customers would have been able to offer privileges and gifts in return for the Templars' services. Henry III was very generous to the Order, giving them manors, assarts, grants of cash, and gifts of wine and venison. There is no evidence that any interest was paid on current accounts. Another way in which the Templars could have gained profit from the accounts was by making the money deposited work for them on paper through lending it on letters of credit.

THE TEMPLARS AS CREDITORS

In the east one reason the Templars loaned money was to ransom Christian knights from the Saracens, and this function may have been one reason for accruing a surplus. This particular service was extended into the west, for example King John arranged for the Templars to pay the ransom of three of his knights captured in France.[14] Money was also loaned to crusaders desperate for cash, and they often pledged goods and land to the Templars since an essential part of the credit transaction is security on the loan. The Pope facilitated these transactions by allowing those going on crusade or intending to donate funds for the crusade to pledge property or pawn sacred vessels.[15] Custom extended into secular fields. Henry III borrowed 800 marks in 1221, using the manor of Godmanchester as security. In 1224, 330 marks of this was still outstanding.[16]

Securities such as this freed the lender from the sin of usury, and bonds between creditor and debtor usually contained a clause stating that if the loan was not repaid on time a penalty amount would be added to the sum. Although the bonds no longer exist, it would appear from indirect evidence that this was the system used by the Templars. When King John died in 1216, leaving an outstanding loan of 1,000 marks with the Templars of Poitou, this was repaid by his son with the sum of 1,175 marks.[17] Throughout his reign John borrowed money from the Templars in England and in France, and was eventually forced to grant the preceptories in Poitiers and Bordeaux part of his French revenues to repay these. Henry III was also a frequent borrower in the 1230s–40s, borrowing amounts of up to £1,000 that were repaid from his annual revenues. Edward I tended to borrow from the Italian merchants rather than the Templars, but credit arrangements were often very complicated and debts could be sold on to other creditors, creating a network of debtors. In 1274 Edward ordered Brother Warin, treasurer of the New Temple, to deliver £20,000 received from the Jewish tallage to Luke de Lucca, the king's merchant.[18] De Lucca was an Italian banker, and this is a good example of how the king's annual revenue was eaten up by his debts. Often royal debts were repaid to a third party by the Templars. In September 1254 a mandate from Henry III to the barons of the exchequer announced that the war in Gascony was over and the king would return to England after a pilgrimage to Pontigny, but before that he needed to repay a debt of 4,000 marks. He requested that this amount be given to the Masters of the Templars and the Hospitallers and they were to ensure that 2,000–3,000 marks of the amount were to be sent to Paris as a repayment instalment. In June 1255 Alan of Kent, a Templar, took 1,140 marks to Toulouse to repay a debt of 1,080 marks that the king owed to three merchants. Fifty-five marks were to be given to the keeper of the king's wardrobe, and Alan was given five marks for his expenses.[19]

It was not only in the British Isles that the Templars were royal creditors; they loaned money to other European princes, including the Kings of France and of Aragon.[20] Borrowing money was an accepted part of the medieval king's economic policy and an accepted part of the Templars' function in medieval society.

On another level, extending credit helped to facilitate trade, as much medieval commerce operated on a sale and credit basis involving deferred payment for goods purchased. The Templars were involved in this through the sale of their wool. In 1298, for example, they sold 16 sacks of wool from Bruer, Eagle and Willoughton worth £134 15s 7d to the king's agent in February with the promise that the amount would be paid a fortnight after Easter. Other debts for wool purchased from the Templars by merchants on a sale and credit arrangement were still outstanding in 1310.[21]

The New Temple was a recognised place for the repayment of debts between private individuals. In 1260 Richard de Ses owed £40 to Walter of Radham, which was to be repaid at the New

Temple, and in 1267 William Marmion of Wintersey agreed to repay his debt of 200 marks to Robert Aguylf in instalments at the New Temple.[22] Often it meant that the parties involved had to travel considerable distances to get to London and pay the debt, but the New Temple was deemed to be a secure place, there were lawyers close by should there be any disagreement, and one of the Temple brethren would make an impartial and honest witness to the transaction.

FOREIGN EXCHANGE, THE TRANSPORT OF MONEY AND TRUSTEESHIPS

In 1238 Henry III issued a mandate to William Hardelton that he was to take all the old pennies and half-pennies that the Templars had and exchange these for the new ones that had been minted for the use of the king abroad.[23]

Carrying specie from one country to another was dangerous. The money was heavy and as the carts carrying it could only move slowly, it was a source of temptation to nimble-footed thieves. It needed an armed guard to protect it that added to the expense of transportation, and there was always the likelihood that it would be lost at sea. Those going on crusade were especially reluctant to load their saddle bags with cash, and to aid them the Templars developed a system whereby the crusader could deposit money in one preceptory, and receive letters of credit to enable him to withdraw it from others as he travelled. This was an early form of credit transfer in which the money itself did not have to be exchanged for local currency or cross international borders.

This service was soon extended to others not going on crusade. Debt incurred in one country could be paid in at a preceptory in another country. In 1228 the sum of 11 marks and 20d was paid at the London Temple to be drawn out in Paris, and in 1244, 500 marks was paid by Henry III to the New Temple to be withdrawn by the brethren in Gascony who had loaned the king this amount.[24] However, despite these examples, the evidence that has survived shows that the King of England preferred to transfer the actual cash. This is illustrated by the travels of Brother Alan of Kent (Plate 9.3).

The travels of Brother Alan

In February 1254 Brother Alan was given £1,500 to carry to Paris for the use of the Count of Toulouse. He was told to keep the money 'safely, saving peril at sea, fire and a greater force of thieves coming upon him'. The money was paid at Paris in mid-Lent in the presence of Peter of Montfort. It represented compensation for damage done to the count's lands during the Gascon Wars.

In May Alan returned to France with a further £1,460 for the count. This time he was met in Paris by the king's messenger, William Bardolph, who was to take the money on to Gascony. We know Alan had returned to England by June as he was paid 24 marks for his expenses in that month. In August he was on his travels again, taking 4,671 marks to the king in Gascony, returning to collect a further 4,000 marks to take across to the king. This time he was allowed 60 marks expenses. His year ended with another Channel crossing to deliver 4,000 marks to Alberic de Fecamp, the keeper of the king's wardrobe. In March 1255 the constable of Dover was told to find a safe and speedy passage for Alan, two other brethren, their horses and harness, and in June 1255 it was Alan who delivered the king's repayment of 1,080 marks he had borrowed in Toulouse.[25] Between 1154 and 1155 Alan carried £11,406 abroad for Henry. This amounted to 38 per cent of Henry's annual revenues.

Why did Henry send cash rather than letters of credit? There were some purposes for which he needed to have cash, such as paying his troops and buying provisions, and if the money was

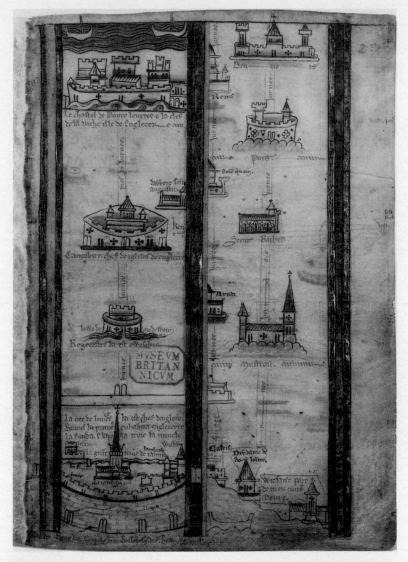

Plate 9.3 The route from London to France as taken by Brother Alan
BL Royal Ms 14c VII fol. 2
The British Library

transported in marks it would have been acceptable in Gascony as well as in England as the mark was the equivalent of the twenty-first-century euro.

THE TEMPLARS AS TRUSTEES

The Templars also acted as trustees for the payment of annuities, widows' jointures and pensions. They paid Queen Berengaria's jointure, and in 1257 paid the final instalment of the 30,000 mark dowry when Henry III's sister Isabella married the Holy Roman Emperor, Frederick I. Two years later they were the trustees for the dowry of Henry's daughter Eleanor on her marriage to Simon de Montfort. The dowry of Isabella, sister of Alexander III of Scotland, was paid through the Temple in 1228, and that of Alice de Valence on her marriage to Gilbert de Clare. They were also responsible for the repayment of the debt of £70,000 that Edward I owed to Louis IX of France, paying this in instalments of 10,000 marks a year from 1269–c. 1280. In addition, the Templars paid the annual pension awarded to the Count of Flanders, and to a number of other pensioners of the English crown.

The Templars often acted as intermediaries and trustees in wardship cases. Royal wards, heirs and heiresses to large estates, were valuable acquisitions and much sought after by the medieval barons. Not only did the keeper of the ward gather in the estate revenues whilst the ward was under age, but he could sell the marriage of the ward to the highest bidder. When the ward took matters into his or her own hands and married without permission, compensation had to paid to the ward's guardian. The Templars became the intermediaries who collected the fine from the guilty parties and paid it to the guardian. An example of this happened in 1253 when Alan Fitz-Roald married Maud, the daughter of Peter Goldington and ward of Arnold Ferdly, without permission. Alan and Maud agreed by covenant to pay Arnold 260 marks by instalments deposited with the Templars.[26] In these transactions the Templars were chosen because they had a reputation for impartiality and honesty.

During the thirteenth century over a million marks passed through the New Temple treasury, and the involvement of the Templars with financial activities came to overshadow their military and religious roles. It placed them on the political stage to such a degree that sometimes it was difficult to distinguish where the royal treasury stopped and the Templars' treasury began, and at least two treasurers of the New Temple were also royal treasurers. This preoccupation with money and its administration was at odds with their vows as a religious organisation, and although the Hospitallers were also involved in financial affairs, it was the Templars who achieved the higher profile; visible as tax collectors, creditors and the king's financial security guards, they became the objects of suspicion. But despite the large amount of money and jewels passing through and deposited in the New Temple little of it belonged to the Templars themselves. Judging by the small amount of wealth found in 1308, it would appear that their revenues were disbursed to the east as soon as they were received.

Misunderstanding about the funds passing through the Templars' preceptories was to contribute to their downfall, and give rise to the tradition of their immense wealth and missing treasure.

CHAPTER TEN

THE TRIAL AND FALL OF THE
TEMPLARS

In 1291 Acre fell to the Saracens and the Christian armies withdrew from the Holy Land. The Templars went to Cyprus, an island they had once briefly owned. In the post-mortem following the loss of Palestine the military orders were accused of causing this through their pride, avarice and corruption. Old accusations were revived about the Templars fraternising with the enemy, their cowardice, and love of plunder, whilst the rivalry between the military orders was seen as a hindrance to regaining the Holy Land.

The Templars were in a vulnerable position. Their main purpose, the defence of the Holy Land, had been torn away from them, they were failing to recruit new members, and the existing Order was increasingly elderly. They depended on the protection of the Pope and their special privileges to get them through this awkward patch. The election of Jacques de Molay in 1293 heralded a brief revival of the Order's fighting spirit. He tried to boost recruitment by attempting to regain a foothold in Palestine, establishing a base on the Island of Tortosa. When this was exterminated by the Egyptians in 1302 the Order's final chapter had begun.

The only way in which there was any possibility of the Christians regaining the Holy Land was through a fully fledged crusade that would unite all Christian nations in a supreme effort. The amalgamation of the rival military orders of the Templars and the Hospitallers was seen as being an imperative part of this. It would bring a return to the original values of the Orders, and harmony instead of discord.

In 1306 Jacques de Molay and Fulk of Villaret, Grand Master of the Hospitallers were invited to meet Clement in Poitiers to discuss the possibility of a new crusade and the merging of the two Orders. De Molay arrived with an estimate that an army at least 20,000 strong would be needed to re-take Palestine, and an unshakeable conviction that the military orders should not be merged. It has been argued that this is evidence of de Molay's essential conservatism and lack of flexibility that would contribute to the Order's downfall.[1] Despite this de Molay attempted to appease the Pope by presenting a list of pros and cons for the merging of the Orders. Against the merger he stressed the practical difficulties involved, such as which preceptories should be closed and who would receive and manage the revenues. He argued that the rivalry between the Templars and the Hospitallers was healthy, spurring them on to greater efforts in the field. For the merger, he grudgingly admitted that it would make both Orders less vulnerable to outside persecution, and would save on expenses. He gave no indication that he would agree to a merger, but he did offer to convene a council to advise the Pope on how to set a new crusade in motion.

The Pope might have dismissed de Molay's analysis and concentrated on the mobilisation of a Christian army had not the papacy and crusading policy moved from religious idealism into the political arena. Secular leaders, especially the King of France, were questioning the Pope's authority, and Philip IV of France had already destroyed the credibility of one pope, Boniface VIII, by accusing him of heresy, idolatry, sodomy, murder and simony. Boniface died before Philip could bring him to trial, but not before the French councillor, Guillaume de Nogaret, had insulted and arrested him.

The election of Clement V after Boniface's death brought matters to a head. Clement was weak and ailing and dominated by Philip, who held over him the threat of a posthumous trial of Boniface that would reveal the corruption in the papacy. The King of France and the papacy were on a collision course with the Templars caught in the middle. They owed allegiance to the Pope and were under his protection, but a large number of the Order were resident in France, where they could be seen as a threat against civil authority should it come to an outright confrontation between the king and the Pope. By devious means, Philip was to marginalise the Templars and pull Clement into his web of persecution, and this would result in the suppression of the Order. T. Parker reflects that this was part of the 'age-old rivalry between church and state in France, where currently the ambitious and ruthless king, Philip IV (the Fair) was vying for control with the weak and vacillating pope, Clement V . . .'[2] Philip instigated the persecution of the Templars, but this would not have been possible had the climate of public opinion not been ready to accept the charges levelled against them. Although it has often been suggested that it was Philip's parlous economic state that led him to cast around for a solution to his economic difficulties and light upon the Templars and their possessions, the reasons behind the charges against the Order were more complex than mere economics. However, that may have been the necessity that spurred Philip into action. Even though he had an annual income of 800,000 livres tournois, three times that of the English crown, by the early 1300s the wars with England in Gascony, and in the Low Countries, had left the treasury empty. Philip resorted to debasing the currency, increasing taxation and confiscating the money and goods of aliens such as the Italian bankers and the Jews. Still this was not enough. He was desperate for cash. The Templars handled large amounts of money, and they had vast annual revenues. They were reputed to own large stores of treasure. It was no surprise that they were next on the list of Philip's confiscations.

Financial reasons may have been one of the reasons Philip wanted to destroy the Order, but he was a man of deep religious piety, and to him the Templars were corrupt. He believed that he was acting for God, and that he was the charismatic leader that could lead a new crusade to victory. Like the Pope, he saw the amalgamation of the military orders as necessary to this, and he saw himself as the hereditary Grand Master of the new Order formed by this. The Templars' refusal to consider the amalgamation festered with him, and gave him another reason to seek their destruction.[3]

There is yet a deeper meaning behind Philip's actions. The early fourteenth century was a superstitious age with a real fear of sorcery and the evil it could create. Rationalist explanations discount the fear of magic and religious idealism as one of the prime reasons behind the fall of the Templars, and have seen the sections of the charges against the Order that refer to idolatry, raising devils, and the use of totems to gain power as the work of the inquisitors' imaginations. Imaginative as these may have been, those drawing up the charges believed in them, and believed that it was possible to change the course of life by using magic, witchcraft and demonology. They also believed that it was the Templars' dabbling with the occult that had helped to lose the Holy Land. The Templars had fallen short of the ideal, and they had made secular and ecclesiastical enemies, especially among the orders dedicated to poverty, such as the Franciscans. The secrecy that surrounded the Order allowed rumours to grow, and it was this secrecy that meant that no outsider knew for sure what went on in the preceptories that allowed a Gascon, Esquin de Floyran, to tell the stories that would become the basis of the charges against the Templars.[4]

De Floyran had first told his stories at the Aragonese court, but James II refused to believe him, and appears to have been so sure that these were not true that he promised de Floyran rents and money from the Order's possessions should he be able to verify them.[5] De Floyran, who was possibly a renegade Templar, travelled on to France where Philip IV was eager to believe him. De Floyran told him that the Templars put loyalty to the Order before moral principles, and were addicted to immorality. They spat on the cross, denied the sacraments and worshipped idols, murdering any member who refused to do this, and, through secret correspondence with the infidel, they had betrayed the Holy Land. With this and other evidence fed to him by his spies, Philip now had enough information to move against the Templars and accuse them of abominable crimes. Secret orders were sent out to the seneschals and baillies of France instructing them to arrest every Templar at dawn on Friday 13 October 1307.

THE TEMPLARS IN 1307

In France the Templars were taken by surprise. Jacques de Molay, who had taken up temporary residence there, seems to have had no suspicion of impending events. He had visited the Pope in September 1307 and had been on what appeared to be good terms with the king, acting as a pallbearer for the king's sister-in-law the day before the arrests.

In the British Isles the Templars' life continued much as before during the early years of the fourteenth century. They continued to acquire land, and were given a licence to crenellate Temple Bruer in 1306. On his accession Edward II had seized £50,000 worth of gold, silver and jewels placed in the New Temple by his father, and had given these to his favourite, Piers Gaveston, but the chroniclers saw this as evidence of the young king's extravagance rather than the Templars' negligence.

They were unpopular in some areas, especially with other religious orders. This would become obvious at their trial. There were also the usual local squabbles of rights to land, and it would appear that some preceptories were looted after the arrests. This may indicate local dislike and a desire for revenge, but as most of what was taken was food, it was more likely to have been the local population taking a chance when they saw it offered.

Edward II had only been on the throne four months when the French Templars were arrested. He was much more sceptical about the charges against the Order, and when he received notification of the allegations and arrests from Philip IV on 16 October he treated this with incredulity. In his reply he defended the Templars, telling Philip that he had discussed this with his barons and priests and they did not believe the charges. He went even further, writing to the Kings of Aragon, Castile, Portugal and Sicily in December 1307, urging them to ignore the charges against the Order and asking them to remember the Templars' devotion, honesty and long service to the Christian faith.

Philip IV was Edward's future father-in-law. He was not amused by Edward's reaction and was even less entranced by his future son-in-law when he wrote to Pope Clement expressing his disgust at the arrests. Philip had usurped papal power in making the arrests, being sure that Clement would not retaliate. If another monarch such as Edward now supported the Templars and argued against the credibility of the arrests, at best Philip's plans would crumble, and at worst he could be caught in a war with England on one front and the papal army on another. He had sent Clement a list of the charges and, like Edward, he had refused to believe them. Philip resorted to blackmail. He threatened to re-open the case against Boniface and bring the papacy as an institution into disrepute. Clement gave way and agreed to an inquiry into the Templars' affairs, but he denounced the arrests and refused to let the papal inquisitors examine the prisoners. Once more Philip raised the spectre of Boniface. Clement capitulated and issued a bull against the Templars.

THE CHARGES

104 articles were brought against the French Templars, 74 against the British Templars, based on the French charges. The accusations

were taken from what Philip's informers had told him, and confessions made by French Templars under torture shortly after their arrests. In other words, these were charges to which the accused had already confessed guilt, and the object of any inquiry into the charges would be to convict the already guilty rather than discover the truth.

Historians have defined six groups of articles referring to reception into the Order, idolatry, heresy, sodomy, charity and the acquisition of property, and secrecy of proceedings.

Articles on reception into the Order

Initiates were received in secret with only members of the Order present. At their reception they were told to deny Christ, and sometimes God, the Blessed Virgin and all the saints. They were made to spit on the cross, or an image of Jesus, to trample the cross under foot, or urinate on it. Brethren also urinated on the cross during Holy Week. The initiate was taught that Christ was not the true God but was a false prophet who had not suffered on the cross for the redemption of the human race, and therefore there was no hope of receiving salvation through Jesus.

Those being received were kissed on the mouth by the Master, and sometimes on the navel, buttocks or the base of the spine, or on the penis. They were given a small cord to wear at all times which had touched an idol, and were made to swear they would never leave the Order. Anyone who refused to do these things was killed or imprisoned.

Articles on idolatry

The Templars adored a cat that appeared in their assembly, and each province had its own idol. Some had idols with three faces, some one, others had skulls. These were adored in chapters and assemblies, as gods and saviours. The idols gave the Templars riches, made trees flower and the land germinate. They touched these idols with a cord worn next to the flesh or the shirt, day and night.

Articles on heresy

They did not believe in the sacraments or that the host was the body of Christ, and their priests did not consecrate it or speak the canon of the mass. If a Templar was present at a mass in an outside church, he must avert his eyes when the host was raised. The Master gave absolution from sin to the brothers, and Templars could only confess to another brother.

Articles on sodomy

At their reception the brothers were told that they could have carnal relations together as this was allowed, and they should comply as it was not a sin.

Articles on charity and the acquisition of property

The Order did not make charitable donations or give hospitality as other religious orders did. They did not accord it a sin to acquire property by illegal means or commit perjury to do this.

Articles on secrecy

Meetings were held at night after all the servants were sent away. These took place behind locked doors and with a guard posted on the church roof.

All of these things were done in Cyprus and all other kingdoms in the presence and the knowledge of the Grand Master who had confessed to this, and no effort had been made to stop these abominations.

It is the articles on the denial of Christ as redeemer and the worship of heads that has led to speculation that the Templars were trying to found a new religion based on Gnosticism. This has given rise to the theory that one of the heads was the Head of God, a theory that will be discussed in the following chapter. However, many of these articles were accusations made against all heretics and other marginal groups in the Middle Ages, and take a standard form. For example, the Cathars were accused of the same errors, including sodomy and the worship of a cat. The articles were designed to shock the public into condemning the accused and create a wave of horror and disgust that would make any sentence given appear to be just. Some of the charges echo those made by de Floyran, but he in turn may have been using a standard format. In the case of the Templars the charges were made more credible because this was an all-male order that conducted much of its business in secret.

Neither were the charges plucked out of thin air, but had a sound theological grounding. Heresy and idolatry were bracketed together with sorcery in Revelation XXIV.8: 'Sorcerers are included with murderers and idolators, and are to be cast into a lake of fire.' There had been papal bulls in 1258 and 1303 that dealt with sorcery and heresy in the same clauses. Sodomy and sorcery were also deemed to be in the same league as, and to be part of, heretical leanings. The ultimate punishment for sodomy was also burning. Again there was a sound biblical justification for this in the punishment of the city of Sodom described in Genesis, despite the fact that much hinges on the word 'to know', and the evil of Sodom may not have been homosexuality but lack of hospitality.

Homosexuality was not only a sexual deviance but also a social deviation that could threaten the structure of society, and it was no accident that twelfth-century theologians equated homosexuality with the infidel, and advised treating it as treason.[6] Accusing the Templars of this helped to criminalise them, and as it was also one of the accusations made against the Cathars it helped to place them in the public mind with other heretics. The articles referring to the Order's secret meetings at night are part of the paranoia about the power of the occult and the dark, and conspiracies against the state. By implication, something done under the cover of night must be wrong. But what we must not lose sight of is that the evidence for these articles had come from the confessions of the French Templars. All the Order could hope to do was to retract these and show they were extracted under pressure, and were not true.

THE FRENCH PROCESS

The Templars were under the protection of the Pope, and Philip IV had flouted his authority when he ordered the arrests. His orders stated that those arresting the Templars should make sure that confessions were obtained by any means. Any means included sleep deprivation, physical humiliation and torture. By these means papal inquisitors acquired the evidence that was put into the articles. The French Templars agreed that they denied Christ and defiled the cross, they agreed that they worshipped an idol, they agreed to the carnal kisses at reception into the Order and the acceptance of homosexuality as normal, they agreed that the Master could give absolution for sins, and the perversion of the sacrament. Even the Grand Master and high officials confessed to these sins.

In the twenty-first century we are familiar with the extreme heroism exhibited under torture by victims of the Nazis and other repressive regimes. From the ease with which these confessions were given, it may seem that the Templars were less than heroic under stress, and we may wonder why these men, who had taken religious vows and were ostensibly the heirs of the knights who fought and died at the Battle of Hattin, crumbled so easily. Evidence of the nature of the torture came to light later. One brother showed the papal commission a bag containing bones from his feet that had fallen out when they were roasted, and Jacques de Molay exhibited his stick-like skinned limbs and testicles. Many Templars died under torture. They might have withstood these trials had they not been in fear of dying without absolution and being sentenced to everlasting torture in Hell.

In February 1308 Clement at last asserted his authority and suspended proceedings against the Templars. He demanded that Philip release the Templars to him for a papal inquisition, and in June 1308, 72 Templars were despatched to him in Poitiers. Malcolm Barber suggests that they were carefully chosen from those who were not going to retract their confessions.[7]

Actions taken by Philip unilaterally did not affect the actions of other western princes, but actions and bulls sent out by the Pope did. If the Pope agreed that the Templars were guilty, other rulers must concur with his decision and examine Templars in their own lands, or risk excommunication. The Templars needed the Pope's support, and he should have given them protection. There is evidence that at least he tried to slow down the proceedings by picking up points of privilege and procedure. But by May 1309 the torture had recommenced, this time by the papal inquisitors. Clement agreed to this through pressure from the French king and his bishops, and it was the French bishops who now controlled the interrogations. What had started for Philip IV as a spiritual crusade with financial overtones had, by 1309, turned into a financial necessity with spiritual undertones. He needed to keep the Templars' revenues in his own hands, and they must be tried and found guilty. An ecclesiastical commission was convened at which Jacques de Molay asked that he and other officials of the Order be allowed to mount a defence. When he received the case papers he claimed that he was unlettered and did not understand them and asked that an attorney be appointed to plead for the brethren. Molay was able to read, as there is evidence that he read the documents given to him, but in asking for an attorney he was following the custom of the Order that generally used an attorney, even in minor disputes over land.

In February 1310, 532 Templars were in Paris to defend the Order. In March the list of articles was presented. The Templars were allowed attorneys to plead for them, but new witnesses were brought in to attest to their guilt and in the event of retractions to validate the original confessions. The defence continued until April, but was taking too long for Philip. He wanted a swift end to the proceedings, especially as it looked as if the commission might find the Templars not guilty. By coercion and manoeuvring, Philip managed to get 54 of the Templars, who had come to defend the Order and retracted their confessions, condemned to the stake. They died denying the charges. Those who remained to be examined quickly reverted to their original confessions, eager to agree to anything to save themselves. The fate of the Grand Master was to come later.

ARRESTS AND TRIALS IN THE BRITISH ISLES

Edward II was still reluctant to act against the Templars, despite threats and blandishments from his future father-in-law. He even wrote to the Pope suggesting that the charges were the work of the evil minded, but when he received the papal bull *Pastoralis praeemienitiae* and instructions to arrest the Templars, his own soul was put in jeopardy and he acted. Parker writes that 'he turned against the Templars'.[8] There is no evidence that Edward had any personal, political or spiritual animosity towards the Order, and his subsequent actions indicate that he obeyed the Pope's instructions reluctantly and only because any further reluctance to act might lead to his excommunication and place the country under an interdict. But in arresting the Templars and allowing a papal inquisition into the country he was setting a precedent and creating a court that was outside his jurisdiction.

Like his French counterpart, Edward was short of funds, and the revenues from the Templars' lands would be a valuable asset for him. But the Order had a long history of loyal service to his family and this might have contributed to his unwillingness to act against it. Finally there was a psychological reason that may have made him reluctant to arrest and investigate the Templars. One of the charges against the Order was sodomy. Even taking into account the biased nature of the evidence, the contemporary consensus was that Edward was a homosexual and the charge could equally well apply to him. But this was the beginning of his reign and the propaganda against him had not started, although there were complaints about his extravagant gifts to his favourite Piers Gaveston.

The sequence of events surrounding the arrest of the Templars can be reconstructed from the Close Rolls and other official documents.

15 December 1307. An order was sent to all county sheriffs telling them to choose 24 men to attend them early in the morning on the next Sunday to hear what was contained in a sealed mandate addressed to them from the king and intended for the preservation of the peace.

30 December 1307. The sealed mandates were prepared and given to royal clerks to deliver to the sheriffs. Before opening the mandates the sheriffs had to swear an oath before the clerk that the contents would not be revealed until they were to be put into effect, and then they were to do this with all speed, taking with then the aforesaid 24 chosen men.

The order was addressed to all county sheriffs, the justiciar of Ireland, John de Breton, Earl of Richmond in Scotland and the justices of north and west Wales and Chester.

Mandate to attach on Wednesday next after the Feast of the Epiphany in the morning the brethren of the order of the Temple, and to take an inventory of their goods and muniments in the presence of the keeper of the place, to wit a brother. The sheriff is then to cause their bodies to be

Great Seal of Edward II.

Plate 10.1 The Great Seal of Edward II. This is an early version as it shows Edward without a beard, and would have been the seal used for the mandates to arrest the Templars.
From *Annals of England*, 1876

safely guarded elsewhere than in their own places, but not to place them in a hard or vile prison, and to find them sustenance. The sheriff is to certify to the treasurer and the barons of the exchequer when he has done this, and to send the names of the brothers arrested and of their lands.

26 December 1307. Edward wrote to the Pope telling him he had done what was required,[9] although the arrests did not take place until 9–10 January 1308.

Edward had done what he thought would satisfy the letter of the Pope's instructions, if not the intentions, and he had done it in such a manner that showed he was not entirely in favour of the instructions. He did it legally through a royal writ, he assured that an inventory was taken of the Templars' possessions that was witnessed by one of the Order, and he made sure they were not to be kept in close confinement. He allowed the brothers to take their own bedding and other possessions with them into prison, and made sure they were treated honourably.

The British Templars must have been expecting their arrest. They would have known by one means or another what had happened in France. Also, they were not entirely friendless at the papal court and would have been aware of the papal bull sent to Edward. But no resistance to arrest was recorded. Few weapons were found in the preceptories, and none of the fabled treasure. The paucity of the goods in the British preceptories and the absence of any gold or other wealth has led to speculation that the British Templars, forewarned as to what might happen, had hidden it or sent it out of the country. However, the French Templars were taken completely by surprise and no treasure was found in their houses, nor any of the idols mentioned in the confessions. The implication is that neither treasure nor idols existed, and that the Templars were living in poverty, as their vows required.

The English Templars were taken by the county sheriffs to the nearest royal castles at Newcastle upon Tyne, York, Lincoln, Cambridge, Oxford, Warwick and Canterbury. It was to the latter that William de la More, Master of the Templars in England, and other officers of the Order were taken, having been arrested at Temple Ewell. Only two Templars were arrested in Scotland, 15 in Ireland and 153 in England. Of those arrested only 15 were knights, the rest were sergeants and chaplains.

The estates were placed in the hands of keepers and a further inventory shows that some goods, especially food, had disappeared between the arrests and the keepers' arrival. The keepers had to make sure that the rents were paid and the labour services performed.

One response of the keepers was to rationalise the estates and sell off crops and livestock, and to bring the remaining beasts on to one manor.[10] The estates had to provide the living expenses for the brothers whilst they were in prison. This was set at a rate of 4d a day for ordinary members, but 2s a day for William de la More. Parker suggests that de la More was released on bail to the Bishop of Durham.[11]

The evidence shows that the other Templars were on open arrest as shortly before the papal inquisitors arrived Edward sent a hurried notice to his sheriffs telling them to re-arrest all Templars still at large, and send them to the Tower of London, York or Lincoln Castles. Despite this, his orders were not complied with with any enthusiasm and in December 1309 he sent an order to the sheriff of Kent telling him 'to arrest all Templars wandering about in your bailiwick and send them to London as the king understands that divers Templars are wandering about in secular habits committing apostasy'. Another order was sent to the sheriff of York in March 1310 telling him to keep the Templars in his charge in safe custody so that he could answer to the king for them as the king understands they are allowed to wander about.[12]

This laxity must have been shocking to the papal inquisitors fresh from the harsh regime meted out to the Templars in France. A second shock was in store for them, as English law did not permit torture, so no confessions had been arranged for them in advance, and they could not extract these by physical means.

The papal inquisitors were the Abbot of Lagny and Sicard de Vaur, a French notary. Also present on the commission of inquiry were the Archbishops of Canterbury and York, and the Bishops of Chester, Durham, Lincoln, London and Orléans. The articles against the British Templars were broadly the same as those against the French, but the examinations show that the questioners concentrated on four areas: reception into the Order; whether the Master gave absolution from sin; secret meetings; and the death of Walter

Bachelor, the Irish knight who was assumed to have died whilst undergoing punishment in the New Temple. The latter was a civil matter and its appearance among the questions to the Templars may have been an attempt by the English authorities to find out the truth of the affair, or it could have been an attempt to convert the inquisition of the Templars into criminal proceedings and wrest the trial back into the King's Bench, and under the control of the king.

The proceedings against the Templars in the British Isles exist in summary form in a manuscript in the Bodleian Library. A printed version of this was produced in the eighteenth century.

The inquisition of the Templars in the Tower of London was held in the Priory of the Holy Trinity, and they were examined in Latin, English and French. The proceedings started with the articles against them being read out, and then each brother fit enough to be questioned was examined separately. They were asked how long they had been in the Order, where they were received, by whom and in what manner. They answered simply and honestly, saying nothing that would condemn them. For example, William Raven, when questioned about his reception into the Order, said he had been received into the Order by William de la More in the chapel at Temple Combe, and that there had been about one hundred people present, brothers and lay persons. He had vowed to serve God and the Blessed Virgin Mary to the end of his life, and had been asked if he entered the Order voluntarily. The Rule had been explained to him, and he had vowed to keep it, to obey his superiors, and never to lay violent hands on any Christian. Hugh de Tadcaster and Thomas Chamberlain had been received in the choir of the chapel at Faxfleet. No secular persons had been present, but other brothers were there. The Rule had been explained to them, and they had taken vows of poverty, chastity and obedience.[13]

One after another the brothers denied that any carnal kissing or other obscenities had taken place at their receptions. None admitted to denying Christ or desecrating the cross and only two said that the reception was held in secret. Ralph de Barton said he had been received at a secret court at Strood, but he had not denied Christ or spat on the cross. As he had admitted to secrecy, he was examined for three days and each article was put to him. In answer to most of them he replied no or that he did not know, but he admitted that the brothers wore cords under their habits, but knew nothing about any idols. William de Scotho agreed they wore cords, but denied all other charges. However, he had been received in the dormitory of the New Temple rather than the church.[14] Most gave a list of the brothers alive and dead who were present at their receptions. All said they did not know how receptions were done elsewhere.

One of those interrogated in England was Himbert Blank, the preceptor of the Auvergne, who had either happened to be in England or had fled there when the French Templars were arrested. He had been received into the Order in Syria 38 years previously in the presence of 30 brothers now all dead. He was taken through the articles one by one, and denied each. But when asked why the chapters were conducted in secrecy, he replied because they had been stupid and that their secrecy was their biggest mistake. He pointed out that the confessions of the French Templars had been obtained by torture, and were not true.[15]

There were no sensational revelations forthcoming in London, but the inquisitors managed to get some evidence against the Templars on the question of absolution. This was because many of those questioned did not understand the difference between absolution as a sacrament and absolution for errors against the Order and its Rule. When the Master or preceptor gave them absolution, they assumed it was as a sacrament. As this was absolution given by a person who was not an ordained priest, this could be seen as a heresy.

This was a small victory, and by December 1309 the commission had achieved very little and the papal inquisitors applied to

Edward for permission to use torture to get confessions. Edward prevaricated and the trial continued until March 1310 when there was a change in the way in which the Templars were being treated. Until then they had been kept in relative comfort in the Tower of London with access to each other. In April 1310 they were placed in solitary confinement and chained up. Even this hardship did not produce the desired results. The inquisitors told Edward to publish the French confessions to raise public opinion against the Templars and bring about a demand for them to be tortured. They also demanded that he place the bodies of the Templars under their jurisdiction rather than his gaolers, and suggested that as a last resort the British Templars should be taken to Edward's lands in France and tried there.

Still Edward would not agree to the torture of the Templars until he received another letter from the Pope. On the receipt of that he transferred the Templars in the Tower of London into the hands of the sheriff of London and told him to place them in the prisons within the city gates, and to permit the inquisitors to do what they would with them according to ecclesiastical law. This was a clever move by Edward as it meant that the Templars were no longer his responsibility, but the responsibility of the city of London and the Church. Similar orders were sent to the sheriffs of York and Lincoln Castles. The sheriffs were slow to comply with Edward's orders. His first was sent out in August, but by October nothing had happened and he had to send out a second order.[16]

The Templars at Lincoln were examined between March and April 1310. They included brethren from Keele and Lydley as well as those from the Lincolnshire preceptories. Twenty-one brothers were originally imprisoned in Lincoln Castle, three of these died there, and eventually only 11 were interrogated. One of these, Henry de la Wold, agreed that the Master had kissed him on the mouth when he was received, but this kiss was part of the ritual described in the Rule Book. Robert de Hamilton admitted to wearing a girdle that he thought might have touched a column in Nazareth. As in London those interrogated were unclear as to what type of absolution the Master or preceptor could give, and three brothers thought that two brethren they saw punished at Balsall may have committed sodomy, but they were not sure.[17] The Lincoln Templars were transferred to London in March 1311.

The Templars in York Castle were questioned in April 1310. All protested their innocence and denied the articles, but William de Grafton and Stephen de Radenach said they had been received in secret in the Master's room at the New Temple, and William de la Fenne said he had been received in the dormitory at Shipley. The York Templars were also transferred to London to be imprisoned separately and in chains.[18]

WITNESSES AGAINST THE TEMPLARS

The inquisitors had failed in their attempts to get the British Templars to confess, but they had a number of hostile witnesses they could call on. Many of these came from other religious orders eager to condemn the Templars and jealous of their lands. Others were probably paid, such as the 'loose women' who appeared in London. Some were former employees of the Order, such as the three London notaries, Adam, Robert and William le Dorturer. Robert said he had never seen any magic but he knew that receptions took place at night and in secret. Sometimes he had seen the brothers walk together in the New Temple gardens, and he had 'suspicions' about Guy de Foresta because he had enticed him into a room and tried to commit sodomy on him, but he had evaded this and escaped. Adam le Dorturer said receptions were held in the day, but chapters were held at night. The Rector of St Mary in the Strand said he did not know if they worshipped idols or denied Christ, but the mode of reception came from the occult, and would give the Templars powers over other men.

Master John of Warrington, an official of York, said that Milo of Stapelton and Adam of Everingham, knights, had been to a great feast at Temple Hirst where a calf was worshipped. John de Eure said that William de la Fenne had dined with him and had given his wife a book in which there was a slip with heretical doctrines on it that said Christ was not the son of God and had not been crucified. De la Fenne agreed he had given Lady Eure a book, but denied any knowledge of any inclusions of a heretical nature. He pointed out that the Eures had waited six years to make this accusation.

The Rector of Crofton in Yorkshire said that he was told by William de Reynbar, an Augustinian now dead, that the Templar Patrick of Ripon had said that when he was received into the Order he was clad only in his shirt and was led to the reception down a long passage to a secret chamber where he had been made to spit on the cross, deny God and kiss the image of a calf. But the rector added he had only heard these things after the arrests.

Robert of Oteringham, a Minorite friar, said that whilst he was staying at Ferriby he had woken in the night and had spied on a midnight gathering. The next morning, when he had asked what saint was being celebrated, he was told never to speak of it again on pain of death. Another Minorite said that a Templar's son had peeped through a chink at a preceptory and had seen a man slain when he refused to deny Christ. Others had heard of a boy who had hidden in a chest and heard the Master preach on how the Templars could enrich themselves.

Tales of idols, probably culled from the French articles, were reported. John de Gertin, a Minorite, had heard from a woman that one of the New Temple servants had hidden during a chapter meeting and had seen a black figure with shining eyes jump from a chest, and seen everyone present spit on the cross. John Walby heard John de Dingeston say that he had heard that there was a secret hiding place in the New Temple where a gilded head was kept. John de Dorrington said that an elderly Templar had told him there were four idols in England, at London, Bisham, Bruer, and a place he forgot, and that these had been introduced by William de la More. The 'loose' women gave evidence of disgusting abominations concerning a black cat and a stone.[19]

The depositions were read out to the Templars on 22 April 1311. Well aware of the fate of the French Templars, they asked for time to read the depositions and prepare a defence. When the documents were made available to them they realised the impossibility of laymen sifting through these, and asked instead for a legal counsel and the chance to state their innocence publicly. They were allowed to do this on 29 April 1311 at the church of All Hallows, Barking. When speaking in Norman French, William de la More declared that they were innocent of the crimes of which they were accused, and were true Christians, members of a noble order and obeyed the precepts of the Holy Church. Any mistakes they may have made were due to their ignorance.[20] Twenty-five Templars were present. They were returned to the London gates in fetters. Gooder suggests that torture was now applied in earnest to force confessions from them, but her evidence for this is drawn from Addison who in turn used the compilation in Rymer's *Foedera*.[21] There is no actual evidence that the English Templars were tortured, and Edward II had stipulated that any methods used should not draw blood. Only three confessions were ever obtained and these were from apostates who had fled from the Order. It is possible that they were tortured, or at least threatened with torture.

Stephen of Stapelbridge had fled during the arrests and had been captured later at Salisbury and put into gaol at Newgate. At the inquisition he showed himself eager to please the inquisitors, but at the same time to mollify his brethren. He described two types of reception, a good and a bad. A good one based on Christian principles and a bad one on evil. He claimed to have undergone both. The first in the good way, the second a year later at

Dinsley in the presence of Brian de Jay when he had been told to spit on the cross and deny God. He said he did this because he was surrounded by brethren with drawn swords. He claimed all brothers were received in this way. One of the brethren that Stapelbridge said was present at his second reception was Thomas de Tocci. He too was an apostate and although when first questioned he denied the existence of a second reception, he later agreed that this happened and that his second reception had been the same as Stapelbridge's. He also claimed that he had heard de Jay deny that Jesus was the true son of God many times. The third apostate, John de Stoke, said that his second reception, at which he had denied Christ, was before Jacques de Molay.[22]

The question has been asked whether the dual receptions were normal, or whether they were a compromise, with the words put into the mouths of the apostates by the inquisitors. The dual good and evil receptions would have been in line with a Manichean dualist philosophy sometimes claimed for the Templars, and with Cathar beliefs. Confessions about the dual receptions helped to bolster the accusations of heresy against the Order. The three apostates confessed their heresy in public at St Paul's Cathedral, were given a penance, absolved and reconciled into the Church.

PENANCE AND ABSOLUTION

Perhaps it was the treatment of the apostates that convinced the others that it was better to submit in this way. It was a better fate than had befallen their brothers in France. All but two of those remaining in prison confessed publicly that they abjured all heresies, they asked for penances, forgiveness and absolution and for reconciliation with the Church. Those who were able did this on the steps of St Paul's Cathedral, and the elderly and infirm in the chapel of St Mary, Barking. They were given a pension of 4d a day and sent to monasteries across the country to fulfil their penances. Only William de la More and Himbert Blanke refused to submit. De la More said he would not ask for absolution for something he had not done. He died in the Tower of London in February 1311, possessing goods worth £4 19s 11d. Blanke also died in prison.

Considering the fate in store for Jacques de Molay and other French officials, their deaths were peaceful. De Molay was still in prison in 1314, clinging to what Barber describes as the 'pathetic hope' that the Pope would save him. When brought before yet another commission of inquiry in Paris, he and three others revoked their confessions. They were handed over to the provost of Paris who was ordered by the king and his council to burn them as heretics on the same day.

SCOTLAND

Only two Templars were arrested in Scotland. Both of these were English. Walter Clifton had been in the Order ten years and was preceptor of Balantrodoch, and William Middleton had been at Balantrodoch but was then the preceptor of Culter. They were called to answer the articles against them on 17 November 1309 in front of the Bishop of St Andrews and the papal nuncio John de Solerio. Both said that their receptions had been according to the Rule. They had answered questions about their health, debts and marriage, and had knelt and placed their hands between the Master's and sworn to defend the Holy Land, God and the Blessed St Mary. The mantle was laid over their heads, and the cords tied round their waists. They said they thought all receptions were like this. They thought that the Grand Master could absolve brothers and had done so at a chapter held at Temple Dinsley.[23]

Fifty hostile witnesses were called, including a number of heads of religious houses, friars and rectors. Hugh, the Abbot of

Dunfermline, said he had heard of the clandestine reception of brothers. Patrick, the Prior of Holyrood, said that he had heard this as well. Servants from Balantrodoch said they knew of secret meetings at night. A number of the Scottish nobility, including Henry and William St Clair, said they heard things against the brothers' secret receptions, and that their fathers said that the Templars had lost the Holy Land.

The Scottish Templars were absolved and sent to Cistercian monasteries on the borders.[24]

IRELAND

The Templars arrested in Ireland were sent to Dublin Castle. Their names show them to be mostly English. The inquisitors arrived in Ireland in September 1309, but the trial did not start until January 1310. By this time one renegade Irish Templar, Henry Tanet, had been sent to England to give evidence that the Templars had made treaties with the Saracens. Fourteen brothers gave evidence in Ireland. Most of them had been in the Order for over 30 years, and all denied the articles against them. Hostile witnesses included members of the minor canons in Dublin. One, Hugh de Lummour, said he knew the Templars were guilty, but did not say how he knew. Another, Walter de Prendergast, said that the Templars made a scandal in the Church. Thomas, the Abbot of St Thomas the Martyr in Dublin, said that they denied Christ and his prior and seven of his monks agreed with this. Others accused them of being inattentive when the Gospels were read, and refusing to look at the host when it was raised in the mass.[25]

None of the witnesses could give concrete evidence, and, like the rest of the British Isles, the evidence against the Templars in Ireland was hearsay and lacking in proof. The Templars in Ireland did penance, were absolved and sent to Irish monasteries to repent.

SUPPRESSION OF THE ORDER AND DISPOSAL OF THE LANDS

By fair means or foul the Templars had been found guilty. The Pope removed his protection from the Order and disbanded it in *Vox in Excelsio*, a bull dated 22 March 1312. In biblical rhetoric, the bull accuses the Templars of 'impious apostasy, the abominable vice of idolatry, the deadly crime of the Sodomites, and various heresies'. It recounts how Clement had refused to believe such slanders against men so devout and heroic, until his 'dearest son in Christ, Philip of France, reported the crimes and brought him evidence', which he has shown to the Council of Vienne, and with their approval the Order of the Templars, its Rule, habit and name were suppressed.

What Clement failed to mention was that when he published the bull he was surrounded by armed Frenchmen, and that not all of the Council wanted the Order suppressed. There were those on the Council who thought that the Templars should be given the opportunity to defend themselves, and Clement had invited them to do so, thinking that the punishment meted out already would deter any Templar. He was more than a little shocked when seven knights arrived claiming that a further 2,000 of their armed brethren had surrounded the area. The seven were clapped in gaol and Clement's mind was concentrated on his personal safety and the possibility of an armed Templar uprising. His panic helped to force through the suppression, although by that time even Clement must have realised that there could not possibly be 2,000 Templars still at liberty. An Englishman present at the Council, Walter of Hemingburgh, commented that it could hardly be called a council when the Pope took all the decisions himself.[26]

There remained the question of the Templars' property. This had been given to them for the purpose of defending the Holy Land. That purpose no longer existed and the revenues were going into the coffers of secular princes. Clement wanted to grant the

Templars' property either to a new order founded by him, or to the Hospitallers. After much discussion he choose the latter. The bull *Ad providam*, issued on 2 May 1312, did this, but reserved the right for Clement to dispose of the properties in Aragon, Castile, Majorca and Portugal as he thought fit. The Hospitallers were to cancel all the King of France's debts to the Templars and to pay him compensation. It was a triumph for the Hospitallers, who increased their possessions and revenues.

In England there were some problems in handing the estates over to the Hospitallers. Edward II had not only put keepers into the manors, but had also given some manors away and allocated the revenues of others, and the descendants of those who had made the grants in the first place now wanted the properties back. Even when the Hospitallers did at last acquire some of the Templar properties, they found heavy outgoings on these. There were the corrodians whose pensions had been agreed with the Templars and allowed by the royal commissioners. There was the 4d a day maintenance for the Templars now in monasteries that had to be paid from the estates. Many of the estates were derelict with mills no longer working and buildings in disrepair. Edward had sold off grain, livestock and timber, including 1,000 trees from the Lincolnshire estates. His annual revenue had been boosted by about an extra £1,500 a year whilst he received the profits from the Templars lands, and he was reluctant to lose these. He did nothing when he received the bull giving the land to the Templars, referring the matter to Parliament and refusing the Prior of the Hospitallers permission to take over the lands until Parliament agreed to this. Once more it was only the threat of excommunication that eventually made him concede the estates to the Hospitallers. They had to wait until 1324 before the title deeds and charters pertaining to the estates were handed over, which gave those lords who had reclaimed their patrimony. Lengthy litigation followed and the Hospitallers only acquired some of the lands by paying an annuity to the person holding it. In 1338 they took an inquest of their holdings. A separate section gave the valuation of the Templars' lands, and at the end a list of the Templars' lands they had not received.

Templar lands not given to the Hospitallers, 1338

Estate	Owner	Value per annum
Strood, Kent	Earl of Pembroke	75 marks
Denny	Earl of Pembroke	100 marks
Temple Hirst and		
Temple Newsam	Earl of Pembroke	124 marks
Faxfleet with Cave	Lord Ralph Neville	150 marks
York water mills	Lord Ralph Neville	20 marks
Carleton	Lord Hugh Despencer	20 marks
Normanton	Lord de Ros	15 marks
Lydley estate	Earl of Arundel	100 marks
Penkerne	Earl of Gloucester	300 marks
Guyting and		
Bradewell	Master Panicum	200 marks
Bisham	Earl of Salisbury	100 marks
Sadlescombe	Earl de Warrenne	100 marks
Bulstrode	Burnham Abbey	75 marks

The Templars were disbanded and dispersed, but their name remained in the British countryside, showing where they had once been. Their presence can be seen in ruins and churches, and they appear in myths and legends, whilst the Temple Church is a lasting monument to their political presence in the British Isles.

WERE THE TEMPLARS GUILTY?

Contemporary opinion

Philip IV of France and his ministers believed the Templars to be guilty, and their propaganda helped to convince France of this.

Pope Clement was not so sure, and Edward of England was un-convinced. Of popular opinion we know little. Occasionally there are hints in papal bulls and official documents that the Templars were unpopular in some areas, but no more so than other land-owners. What their tenants felt will never be known.

There were some contemporary defenders of the Order, who doubted the veracity of confessions obtained by torture and were not afraid to say so. Jacques de Therines, professor of theology at the University of Paris, wrote a tract, *Contra Impugnatores Exemptionum*, that was not a defence of the Order, but made his own position clear. He accepted that the crimes described in the confessions were horrible, and against all Christian teaching, but he could not accept that the Templars were guilty of them. He pointed out that these were men of honour from good families who had taken religious vows and lived by a Rule Book drawn up and approved by the Pope. How and why did these perversions infiltrate the Order, and why had some retracted their confessions in the certain knowledge of death in the lake of fire?

No British academician came forward in the Templars' defence, but there is a letter by an anonymous Frenchman written in 1308 that was copied by a royal clerk. It condemns the proceedings against the Templars as designed to convict rather than discover the truth. *Lament for the Templars* is addressed to the doctors and scholars of the University of Paris. It expresses the writer's surprise and horror of the accusations made by the Gascons against the Templars. It describes the process against the Order as a cruel and unjust. It points out the Order's valour, their profound religious faith, and their adherence to their Rule Book. The 36 Templars who died under torture are mentioned, and there is a plea that the trial should reveal the truth.[27]

An eyewitness observer of de Molay's death was the father of Giovanni Boccaccio. He noted that the populace were amazed and perplexed at his constancy at the stake, and that many believed him to be innocent, but dared not say so.[28] Contemporary chronicles recounted the events without comment, leaving the readers to make up their own minds, although the St Albans chronicler wrote that Clement had once said that the Templars were of good repute.

Most of their contemporaries accepted the verdict. The Templars had condemned themselves and the articles were believable to the medieval mind. They had met their just desserts and evil had been rooted out.

The verdict of history

It is easy to see the Templars in black or white terms. Either they were guilty or they were innocent. If the latter, then Philip IV was the villain, Pope Clement his henchman and Jacques de Molay a martyr. The debate on this has continued since the fourteenth century. Some of the arguments will be discussed in the final chapter of this book, but this short conclusion will summarise some of the verdicts from nineteenth- and twentieth-century historians. H.C. Lea, writing in the late nineteenth century, was convinced of the Templars' innocence. He saw the manipulative rulers fabricating accusations and influencing public opinion. To him the Templars were victims of the secular and ecclesiastical hierarchy. He refutes views that the Templars were guilty by two German authors, Hammer-Pugstall and Prutz. The first claimed to have identified the whereabouts of 30 Templar idols, and the second thought that the Templars were guilty of a Manichean heresy that had infiltrated the inner chapter.[29]

Two English lawyers took diametrically opposed views. In the 1840s, C.G. Addison, who wrote a history of the Templars and an account of their trial, was unequivocal in his belief that the Templars were innocent. He described the trial as one of the greatest crimes of the Middle Ages. The accusations were 'monstrous and ridiculous . . . a monument of human folly, superstition, and credulity'.[30] G.J. Morshead, writing under the pseudonym of Justice Shallow in 1888, reviews the evidence with a lawyer's eye, and has left typewritten notes on this in Cambridge University Library. He points out that there are over 2,000 depositions and many of these coincide, and he suggests that the different versions of the reception reflect the international nature of the Order. He thought that the details about spitting on the cross, the idols and the heresies were correct, but had appeared because the Order in France had been taken over by fanatics who had never been on a crusade. The fall of the Templars, he felt, was inevitable. They were a failing aristocracy with a hopeless outlook. Finally, he suggests that Philip IV, de Nogaret, Clement V and de Molay were bent on self-aggrandisement; the king for his reputation, the Pope for his authority and the Templars for their plunder.[31] E.J. Martin, writing in the 1920s, suggested that the Templars had been infiltrated by criminals who dabbled in the occult brought in from the east. Norman Cohn saw them as victims of propaganda and inner fears of magic and sorcery, and scapegoats for the loss of Acre.[32]

Mid-twentieth-century modernists looked for a rational reason for the fall of the Templars and dismissed the charges of magic in favour of economics and the jealous eyes of European princes. A move away from this to a cultural-social approach came with Peter Partner's *The Murdered Magicians* (1982).[33] Partner describes the Templars as ordinary people caught up in extraordinary events. The evidence from the British trials suggests that the Templars were very ordinary men who told the truth as they experienced it. As individuals they were innocent, but they were a lost cause. The main reason for their existence had gone, and with it lethargy set in. The disrepair of their estates described in 1308 is evidence of this, and the small number of Templars arrested shows they did not have the personnel to maintain these. Many were elderly and infirm, and this sums up the whole Order by 1308 – elderly and infirm.

CHAPTER ELEVEN

THE TEMPLARS IN FACT AND FICTION: DEBATES, MYTHS AND LEGENDS

The charges brought against the Order at their arrest and the subsequent inquisition and trials have given rise to considerable speculation as to whether there was any truth in the accusations, and what actually went on behind the closed doors of the Templar preceptory, whilst interpretation of the evidence from the trials has led to a number of theories on what the Templars believed. The burning for heresy in 1314 of Jacques de Molay, the last Grand Master, and the suppression of the Order have been seen not as the end of the Templars, but as part of a continuum that links the fourteenth century with today, with an unbroken line of Grand Masters stretching from de Molay into the twenty-first century.

THE TEMPLARS AND HISTORY

The bias that exists in medieval chronicles when their compilers allowed their personal prejudices to intervene in their interpretation of events has already been discussed. It is a bias we must recognise in much that has been written about the Templars after their suppression. Again, this often represents the concerns of the writer and the attitudes of the day. A good example of this is to compare two fourteenth-century authors. In *The Chronicles of France* the Spanish writer, Ramon Lull, wanted to promote the unification of the military orders and so emphasised the Templars' guilt. In *The Divine Comedy* Dante, who was being oppressed by a Florentine French-backed party, wrote that the charges brought against the Templars were false, brought by a French king who wanted their wealth for himself.

In Germany the systematic persecution of social misfits dubbed witches led to Henry Cornelius Agrippa using the Templars as an example of the malevolent use of magic. His book, *De Occulta Philosophia*, first published in 1531, went through many editions and was extremely popular. Its lurid account of the Templars' depravity became firmly lodged in the public mind for centuries, so firmly lodged indeed that it led to the fabrication of an archaeological report in nineteenth-century England when Dr Oliver described how he had found a 'dreadful chamber' at Temple Bruer containing burnt and mutilated skeletons, which could not be located in a subsequent excavation.[1] A more rational approach to the accusations against the Templars came from Jean Bodin in *The Six Books of the Commonwealth*, first published in 1583. He suggested that what happened to the Templars was an example of the ability of those with power to persecute minorities.

The Reformation put Protestant writers in a difficult position with regard to commenting on the Templars. On the one hand they wanted to point out that they were an example of the corruption of the Roman Church, but on the other the Templars were branded heretics and persecuted by the Catholics. Thomas Fuller, a clergyman writing in the 1640s–60s, chose the first option, showing the Templars as an example of a corrupt Church. Sir George Buc, writing at the start of the seventeenth century, portrayed the Order as victims of the Catholic Church and praised their piety. Similarly, Elias Ashmole and fellow members of the Royal Society blamed the Pope for the Templars' downfall, rather than their guilt.

Using documents from the trial, at the start of the eighteenth century, the French Dupuy brothers showed to their own satisfaction that the Templars were a corrupt institution, and had been corrupt for at least a century before their suppression. The Dupuys wrote on the eve of the Enlightenment when tolerance, reason and the encouragement of scientific inquiry should have led to a rational discussion on the Order. But the growth of scientific inquiry also led to a renewed interest in the occult and pseudo-scientific theories. The Templars were ideal subjects for this, and it is in the eighteenth century that the link between the Templars and the Freemasons was formed. The development in the nineteenth century of history based on scientific principles and the rigorous examination of primary sources led to a number of original documents being printed. In England the Rolls Series was started. This printed edited but untranslated versions of medieval chronicles, drawing attention to the wealth of material available. Similarly, national records began to be exposed with the first survey and report in 1800. Public records were removed from the Tower of London and the collection of manuscripts in the British Museum became better known.

Two major reconstructions of the Temple Church in London, and the fact that it seems lawyers belonging to the Inner and Middle Temple Societies in the nineteenth century had time on their hands, led to a number of histories of the Order being written by lawyers. The best of these was by C.G. Addison, published in 1840 with a second edition in 1842. Addison used primary sources and quoted freely from them. He brought a lawyer's mind to bear on the evidence, but in the introduction to the second edition he unashamedly admitted his bias: 'I have been accused of writing a flattering and partial account of the order, and some surprise has been expressed to see the Knights Templar not merely finding an apologist, but an enthusiastic champion in modern times.'[2]

Later nineteenth-century books on the Templars have relied heavily on Addison. Often these avoided the Order's downfall and concentrated on their chivalric aspect. For example, F.C.

Woodhouse's *Military Religious Orders* was a Protestant tract that blamed France and the Catholics for the Order's fall. J.A. Froude's chapter on the Templars in *The Spanish Story of the Armada* describes the Templars as 'mounted police on the pilgrims' roads'.[3] As well as Addison's book, at least six full-length histories of the Order were published between 1837 and 1888.[4] In 1841 the French trial documents had been published by P. Michelet. This was followed in 1913 by the publication of the general cartulary of grants to the Order.[5] The definitive collection of English documents on the Templars, the 1185 Inquest, was edited by Beatrice Lees and published in 1935.[6]

A considerable number of works on the Templars in general appeared in the twentieth century. Some were by academics, based on the interpretation of primary source material. Others were syntheses of secondary sources accessible to the general reader. Malcolm Barber's *The New Knighthood* stands out among the first and Piers Paul Read's *The Templars* is an exemplar of the second.[7] In 1965 Professor Parker published *The Knights Templar in England*, and there have been papers and articles on separate sites.

THE TEMPLARS AND MEDIEVAL LITERATURE

Although Jacques de Molay claimed that he could neither read nor write, there was at least one literate Templar, who resided at Temple Bruer and was able to compose blank verse in Anglo-Norman French. Once he was thought to be Henry D'Arci, but M.D. Legge suggests that the poems were not written by him but dedicated to him in about 1240.

> *Henry D'Arci, brother of the Temple of Solomon*
> *For the love of God I have made you this sermon*
> *I offer it to you and the brothers of the house*
> *I do not seek reward from you, save good-will*
> *But now, by your leave I will stop writing.*[8]

Four poems have survived. All are didactic and written not to entertain but to teach and warn. These included *The Lives of the Fathers*, *Thais*, *The Anti-Christ* and *St Paul's Descent into Hell*.

It is not surprising to find an order with such a high profile as the Templars appearing in the pages of medieval tales and romances. These can be divided into those in which the Templars are part of the *dramatis personae* and those in which the Templars are referred to and play a part but do not actually appear. An example of the latter is the distasteful tale of *The Count of Ponthieu's Daughter*, written in about 1200. The story hinges on the remorse felt by the count for his treatment of his daughter. On a pilgrimage with her husband they were set upon and she was gang-raped. When set free she tried to kill her husband, and on hearing this the count sets her afloat in a barrel. Eventually, to salve their consciences, the count and his son-in-law take a pilgrimage to the Holy Land where they join the Templars as associates for a year. On the way back to France they fall into the hands of the Sultan of Almeira, now the count's daughter's husband. She rescues her family and escapes with them to Brindisi where 'the count fitted himself out, procuring the wherewithal from merchants and from the Templars who gladly made him advances out their funds'.[9]

The role of the Templars in providing an avenue for redemption appears in other twelfth-century tales such as *Orson of Beauvais* and *Raoul de Cambrai*. The first of these is a putative royal assassin and the second a mass murderer, unsavoury characters who can have done the Order's image no good. A theme that mirrored real life was that of a knight joining the Order on his deathbed. William Marshal did this and was buried in the New Temple. Two fictional characters, *L'Escoufle* and *Bevis of Hampton*, do the same. Troubadours sang of love, and they portrayed the Order as a place where an unrequited lover could find refuge or could act as a go-between for lovers.

The most important appearance of Templars in medieval tales is in the grail stories. The original written version by Wolfram von

Eschenbach appeared in about 1210. In this the grail is guarded by a group of men described as *Templeisen*. This has been assumed by later writers to mean that the grail's guard were Templars, and this gave rise to the legend that the Templars had hidden the grail to keep it safe. Eschenbach's text suggests that Templars might have been used as a model for the grail knights, but they are not Templars or their badge would have been the red cross rather than the turtle dove worn by the grail knights. There is another grail text, the *Perlesraus*, where the grail knights do bear the red cross, suggesting that there was some connection in the minds of medieval writers between the purity of the grail knights and the Templars.

As the Templars fell from grace so they also fell out of medieval tales. In Britain, the Arthurian knights of *Morte D'Arthur* took their place. Helen Nicholson suggests that in the later period there is little evidence of the Order's unpopularity in the literature. She thinks they disappear because of a change in literary fashions, and to seek the Templars in their later years we must return to the chronicles.[10]

IVANHOE AND OTHERS: THE TEMPLARS IN NINETEENTH-CENTURY LITERATURE

Ivanhoe was published in December 1819. It is a tale of a disinherited Saxon knight fighting against the Norman conquerors. It pits Saxon justice and honesty against the corruption and greed of the Normans, as personified by the Templar, Sir Brian de Bois-Guilbert. The idea that the Normans had changed and spoilt an admirable legal system and stolen the land for themselves gained ground in the nineteenth century, and Sir Walter Scott, *Ivanhoe*'s author, was in the vanguard of this movement. Although the great nineteenth-century legal historians such as F.W. Maitland gave this movement its academic credibility, it was Scott who gave it dramatic impetus, and it was Scott who implanted in public minds the image of the proud, cruel and corrupt Templar.

The cast of characters in the novel includes Sir Wilfred of Ivanhoe, a Saxon crusader returning home in disguise, with Richard I also in disguise to fool his wicked brother Prince John. There is a Saxon noblewoman Rowena, and a beautiful Jewess, Rebecca, and her father, Robin Hood in the guise of Robin of Locksley, Friar Tuck and Athelstan, a Saxon prince, pass through the pages, as do various comic Saxons, corrupt clerics and ruthless Norman knights, and most corrupt of all are the Templar Grand Master and Sir Brian.

Sir Brian had broken most of the Templar Rule. He wore rich clothing, black velvet with a red cross, or scarlet silk with a white cross. He arrived at the Saxon's hall with Saracen slaves and Cedric the Saxon says of him: 'They say he is valiant as the bravest of the order; but stained with their usual vices – pride, arrogance, cruelty and voluptuousness – a hard hearted man who knows neither fear of earth nor awe of heaven.'[11] Worse yet, Sir Brian had broken the vow of chastity and lusted after the beautiful Rebecca. When she rejected his advances he abducted her and took her to Torquilstone Castle where, against the background of a siege and fire, she again rejected him. He then carried her to the preceptory at Templestowe where the Grand Master visiting England accused her of bewitching Sir Brian. The Grand Master 'was a man advanced in age, as was testified by his long grey beard. . . . A formidable warrior, his thin and severe features retained the soldier's fierceness of expression, an ascetic bigot, they were no less marked by the emaciation of abstinence, and the spiritual self-satisfied devotee.'[12] The climax is a trial by combat between Rebecca's champion, an unknown knight (Ivanhoe) and Sir Brian. Sir Brian died of remorse before he had struck a blow and the newly revealed Richard I dissolves the Templars' chapter and sends them on their way.

Ivanhoe is discussed in some detail because of its importance in the lineage of Templar images. Although Ivanhoe and the Saxons are the nominal heroes of the book, it is the Templar and Rebecca who are the strongest characters, both representing different facets of the east; one an innocent but an outcast, the other a member of an accepted society but evil.

Why did Scott show the Templars in such an unfavourable light? It is partly through Protestant righteousness, and for this book Richard I becomes an honorary Protestant. When the Grand Master says he will appeal to the Pope, Richard, foreshadowing Henry VIII, tells him to do so, but he does not want such treasonable conspiracies in his kingdom.[13] Scott was writing at a time when there was a renewed interest in the occult, and a plethora of secret societies. He wanted to show the danger of these through the medium of the Templar knights. Finally, his characterisation of Sir Brian was influenced by the narrative of the Templars and Christiane of Esperston.

Ivanhoe was an instant success. Its dramatic potential was quickly seized on, and by 20 January 1820 it had been turned into a play by T.J. Dibdin and performed at the Surrey Theatre. Dibdin made the three dramatic events in the novel – a tournament at Ashby de la Zouche, the siege and burning of Torquilstone Castle, and the trial by combat – into his three acts. In each of these Sir Brian played a major part, and he became the archetypical stage villain that the audience loved to boo. The dramatisation introduced him to a wider public. Dibdin's play set the mould. Four days later another version appeared at the Coburg Theatre, called *Ivanhoe or the Jew of York*, and on 27 January 1820 an anonymous play, *Ivanhoe or the Knight Templar*, was performed. New productions appeared throughout the 1830s and 1840s, and in 1846 the story was given a new twist and introduced to another audience by turning it into a burlesque. By 1862 it was a pantomime and at the end of the nineteenth century satirical versions were being played, such as *Ivanhoe a la Carte*, performed by the Cambridge Amateur Dramatic Club in 1891, and *All My Eye Vanhoe*, performed at the Trafalgar Theatre in 1894. Dramatic versions continued to appear in the 1900s, and the novel lent itself to the cinema, appearing in various guises and more recently as a television serial.

The novel was also seized upon by composers and their librettists. Between 1826 and 1891 seven operas appeared using *Ivanhoe* as their story line. Rossini's opera opened in Paris in September 1826 and was seen by Sir Walter Scott on 31 October. An English version by M.R. Lacy, *The Maid of Judah*, was shown at Covent Garden in March 1829. This version shows Sir Brian in a better light, actually defending Rebecca's honour. A German opera by A. Marschner also concentrates on Sir Brian. In this version he claims that he joined the Templars because he had been rejected in love and had killed his beloved's bridegroom on their wedding day. In Britain the most important production was Sir Arthur Sullivan's *Ivanhoe* with libretto by R. Sturges. This was the only serious opera Sullivan was to complete. It was dedicated to the Queen and enthusiastically received at its first night, on 31 January 1891, by all critics except George Bernard Shaw. The opera includes a Templar chorus who sing in Latin, and Sir Brian is shown to be a victim of his own pride. A revival in 1910 included real horses galloping across the stage, which detracted from the music somewhat.[14]

Scott's involvement with the Templars did not end with *Ivanhoe*. They reappear in *The Talisman*, *The Betrothed* and *Count Robert of Paris*. *The Talisman* is set in the Holy Land with a Scottish knight, Sir Kenneth, as its hero. It shows the Order double-dealing between Christians and Saracens and plotting to bring about the downfall of Richard I. The Grand Master is described as 'seeking the advancement of his power even at the hazard of that very religion which the fraternity was originally formed to protect'.[15] Richard, in a speech pre-figuring later accusations, charges the Grand Master with being an idolator, a devil-worshipper and a necromancer, to be found in secret places of abomination and darkness.

The novel was published in early June 1825 and by 22 June a version by W.H. Murray was performed at the Theatre Royal in

Plate 11.1 Leon Coquiet *Rebecca and Sir Brian de Bois-Guilbert*
Reproduced by permission of the Trustees of the Wallace Collection, London

Edinburgh with Sarah Siddons as Edith Plantagenet. Stage portrayals of the Templars in Scott's novels, and the illustrations and paintings based on the books, added to the image of the Templars as a cruel and ruthless spirit of darkness. Lee Coquiet's painting *Rebecca and Brian de Bois-Guilbert,* now in the Wallace collection, shows Rebecca clasped on the saddle of one of his Saracen slaves whilst he is in darkness with a ray of light illuminating the red cross on his mantle. Illustrations to the Waverley edition of Scott's novel show him grim-visaged with Rebecca thrown over his shoulder like a sack of potatoes. The counter-balance to this came from the lawyers of the Temple in London. An unusual example of their work is an anonymous poem published by a 'Templar' in 1822 and dedicated to the Temple students. The original inhabitants of the Temple appear in Canto II.

> *'Hail, Templar Knights! Jerusalem crusaders*
> *Ye pilgrim friends, who bang'd their rash invaders*
> *Ye who, to keep your chastity from rusting*
> *Swore that "you never to your will would yield*
> *Ye disciplined disciples of Augustine*
> *Who built your creed upon your sword and shield*
> *On alms subsisting, and your bodies trusting*
> *Two on one horse, you rush'd into the field*
> *A vagrant crew – without a habitation*
> *A name, fame, or fortune, rank or station".'*

The author claimed it had taken him six weeks to write, and in between sucking his pen he had looked out of his window in the Middle Temple to see the Surrey Hills in the distance![16]

TEMPLARS AND FREEMASONS

The connection between the Templars and the Freemasons takes us back across the Scottish border as the relationship between the two had a Scottish origin that came as the result of Freemasons formalising their institution and giving it an ancient lineage. Freemasonry emerged as a secret society in the latter years of the seventeenth century. It was an upper- and middle-class organisation overlaid with ritual and mystery based on the building of the Temple of Solomon. As is the custom with organisations, it was to splinter into different groups with different Rules, and it was an anxiety to prove the validity of the one brand of Masonry that led to Andrew Ramsey, a Jacobite Scot in exile, suggesting that the Masons were descended from the crusaders. Ramsey did not go so far as to suggest that these were Templars, but once he had sown the seed of the idea it did not take long for it to germinate. It seemed a logical progression to name the Templars as the ancestors of the Masons as the Temple of Solomon was sacred to Masonic ritual.

A Scot planted the seed but it was in Germany that it grew, and a brand of Templar Masonry developed using rituals it claimed it had inherited from the military order. Its publicists, Simon Rosa and George Johnson, proved to their own satisfaction that there was a link from the Masons to Jacques de Molay. In France this link seemed to become fact with the discovery in 1804 of the *Larmenius Charter*. This demonstrated that de Molay had handed on the Grand Mastership to John Larmenius, and from him an unbroken line of Grand Masters had signed the charter. Despite being a poor forgery with little acknowledgement of medieval scriptural conventions, it gave the Templar Masonic lodges their historical justification, and *carte blanche* to parade in opulent medieval robes of white robes with red crosses, silken yellow pantaloons and white and gold boots with red heels. H. Lucas proudly proclaimed at the start of his book, 'the order of the Templars never ceased to exist'. He added that other orders of Freemasonry were counterfeits and that Hugh of the Pagans (*sic*) had been given the secret of the dogmas and mortality of the God-Man.[17]

The French Templar Masons were now a rival body to the Scottish Masons who claimed that they too had an unbroken line coming from refugee Templars who had fled to Scotland after the arrests and joined Masonic craft guilds. An English admiral, Sir William Sydney Smith, also became connected with the Templar Masons. In 1840 James Burnes dedicated his book on Templars to the Admiral. This book shows how the medieval vows of poverty, chastity and obedience were interpreted in the nineteenth century as a readiness to share with brothers of the Order, suppression of vicious propensities and obedience to the Grand Master and to the state as a citizen.[18] The Templar Masonic lodges quickly spread across the world, becoming very popular in North America, so that although 'More than six hundred years have passed since the suppression of the Knights Templar . . . their heritage lives on in the largest fraternal organisation ever known.'[19]

John Robinson proposes a different chronological link between the Templars and the Masons. He claims that when the Templars were arrested in 1308 in England a large number went underground and reorganised into a secret society, which in 1381 was responsible for the organisation of the Peasants' Revolt.[20] Baigent and Leigh (1998) have an alternative theory linking the Templars and the Masons that hinges on a group of burials at Kilmartin in Argyle. Their hypothesis is that a group of refugee Templars ended up there, and the Masonic form of Templarism was to emerge via their association with Scottish craft guilds.

It has to be pointed out that other forms of Masons do not accept that they date to before the eighteenth century, but it is clear from manuals such as that written by Lucas that the Knights Templar provided a useful model for some lodges to follow and it was useful to be able to give Masonry a long pedigree. In the British Isles this was made possible by a providential series of coincidences that lead us to that strange building, Roslin Chapel.

1. The hereditary Grand Masters of the Masons in Scotland are the Sinclair family. Traditionally Hugh de Payens was supposed to have married Katherine St Clair.
2. Roslin Chapel with its mysterious and copious carving was built and is still owned by the Sinclair family.
3. It contains within it the burial stone of William Sinclair who died fighting the Moors in Spain whilst taking the heart of Robert the Bruce to be buried in the Holy Land. The grave slab has a foliated sword on it that is presumed to represent the Templars.

Roslin Chapel and the Templar legends are inexorably mixed, even though the chapel was founded over a hundred years after the Order's suppression. It figures largely in many theories about the Templars, their purpose and survival.

THE TEMPLARS, BAPHOMET AND THE HEAD OF GOD

Masonic Templars act out the rituals of the medieval knights in a contemporary setting. This helps to give their institution form and context, even though these are based on a structure for which there is no firm evidence. Other theories about the Templars have taken tales and legends, with evidence from the trials, to build up elaborate plots that demonstrate that the Templars hold the key to life and wisdom.

The books that contain these theories have much in common, and could be said to form a Templar genre of literature. Many take the evidence from the trial and descriptions in medieval romances as literal truth and work from there. There is a pervading anti-academic tone about the works, or an 'anonymous' academic will be said to agree with the theories being discussed. The style of writing is subjective and includes details of journeys by car and motorcycle, meals eaten and hospitality given. Often the mystery is heightened by events

Plate 11.2 Magical Head as allegedly worshipped by the Templars
From Levi, E. *The History of Magic*, 1855

that hinder the investigation, pictures missing from galleries, books
from libraries, access to building denied, locals refusing to talk about
the Templars. The sources used by these books include cathedrals,
paintings, the landscape, geometry and of course Roslin Chapel.

The first of these theories, the 'head of God', takes as its starting point the evidence from the French trials that some Templars reported that they worshipped a mysterious idol in the form of a head, sometimes referred to as Baphomet and sometimes appearing as a mummified human head, sometimes as an image in gold and silver. The head, it was said, could make the land fertile. The idea of Baphomet as a magic figure surfaced in 1818 with the publication of Joseph Hammer-Purgstall's *Mysterium Baphometi, Revelation*. He saw the head as the symbol of the renunciation of Christ and the symbol of wisdom inherited from the Egyptians. Over the next hundred years others were to develop this theory and speculations on Baphomet continued through the twentieth century.

The most up-to-date exposition on this is in *The Head of God* by K. Laidler, published in 1998. Laidler asks an obvious question which former writers had ignored. If the heads existed, why were none found at the time of the arrests? The answer he gives is that following a prior warning they had been spirited away. He suggests that the head or heads had come to the Templars via the heretic pharaoh Akenaten who was the same person as Moses. A group of his followers travelled to the British Isles bringing with them Jacob's Pillow (the stone of Bethel) which became the Scottish Stone of Destiny or Stone of Scone.

The head itself was one of the items that the Templars sought during their early years in the Temple of Solomon. It was an embalmed head and this head was also the grail of the legends. Whose head was it? It was the Head of God, and it was dangerous as it showed that God was a Man. It had come into the Templars' possession not from their excavations in the Temple but from the Cathars, the French heretics. They had received it from Mary Magdalene who had brought it with her when she fled to Marseilles to found a Jewish colony.

Where did it go after the arrests? To Roslin Chapel is the answer. The exuberant carvings include many bodiless heads, and bodies with heads removed. Clues to where the head can be found are placed throughout the chapel, and the head lies beneath the chapel vaults.[21]

Other theories have emerged about the heads referred to at the trial. Noel Currer-Briggs points out that Hugh de Peraud claimed that he had touched the idol and that it had four feet. This could be a description of the Turin Shroud when it is hung suspended, and thus the Templars' head could be the Turin Shroud.[22] Evidence that suggests that the Templars did worship a head are so-called Masonic gravestones showing a skull and cross-bones, but this was a common motif on eighteenth-century gravestones, reminding Mankind of mortality, and not indicative of a Mason's burial. The contents of William Sinclair's tomb at Roslin showed that the head had been removed from the body. But he died in Spain, and it was customary practice to boil the flesh from the bones and disarticulate these for transport home.

THE TEMPLARS AND THE TURIN SHROUD

There is no evidence for the whereabouts of the Turin Shroud between 1204 and 1389 when it was displayed by the de Charney family. Again coincidence plays a part as one of the knights burnt with Jacques de Molay was Geoffrey de Charney, the preceptor of Normandy. It is assumed that he gave the shroud to other members of his family for safe-keeping at the time of the arrests and they hid it, later refusing to say where it came from for fear of reprisals from the French king.

How did the Templars obtain the shroud? The earliest documentary evidence of anything resembling the shroud comes from Constantinople. It is thought that when that city fell to the Latins in 1204 the shroud became part of the Templars' loot. Neither the theory of the way in which the de Charneys obtained the shroud nor the way in which it came into the Templars' hands can be proved. There is no genealogical link that can be shown between the de Charneys and there is no evidence of any Templars being present at the Siege of Constantinople. Barber asks why, if the Templars had the shroud, had they not put it on display for pilgrims visiting Jerusalem to pay for the privilege of seeing it?[23]

It has been suggested that copies of the image on the shroud were made and distributed to Templar houses. The discovery at Temple Combe in Somerset of a painting of a bearded face which bears a resemblance to the image on the shroud could be evidence for this.[24] However, despite being found in a village with Templar connections, the painting was found in a cottage, and the image is a familiar one in medieval paintings and icons.

Another theory is that the image on the shroud is not Christ but Jacques de Molay. According to Knight and Lomas, he was crucified on a wooden door before being burnt and this is his image, kept and revered by the Templars before being passed on to the de Charney family. There is no evidence for this provenance and none that links the Templars with the shroud as fact.[25]

THE TEMPLARS, THE GRAIL, TAROT CARDS, THE CABALA AND TREASURE

Legends associating the Templars with the Holy Grail date back to the thirteenth century. Traditionally the grail was the chalice used in the last supper containing the wine that Christ used as an analogy for his blood. But the grail could equally well be a stone, or a platter bearing a severed head.[26] Although in the thirteenth-century tales the grail is a Christian symbol, it has been suggested that the idea of a quest for a relic is connected to pre-Christian ideas about the fertility of the land and its ruler. This can be connected to the evidence in the trial that the idol worshipped by the Templars could make the land fertile and the trees bloom. The hypothesis is that the pre-Christian beliefs survived in a sect in Palestine known as the Naassenes, a Gnostic sect claiming special mystical knowledge. The Templars became the guardians of this sect and of the grail that was the source of the knowledge.[27] Intermixed with this is the legend that the grail was brought to England by Joseph of Aramethia and it was hidden in an English preceptory. Before the arrests it was taken to Scotland where it was hidden with other Templar relics in Roslin Chapel, guarded by the grail knights who are assumed to be buried in its vaults.

Charges of magic and witchcraft were also levelled at the Templars. Connected to this was necromancy or foretelling the future. Knight and Lomas suggest that the Tarot cards used by fortune-tellers came into the west with the Templars. At first these cards were used as story cards, a device borrowed from the Saracens. The fool represents the novice of the Order, the hanged man with crossed legs the Templar knight, and so on. When the Order was suppressed the cards passed into other hands and were used as fortune-telling aids by gypsies and other travellers. By another quirk of coincidence, the Sinclairs were known to welcome and support gypsies at Roslin. Knight and Lomas return to Roslin Chapel and look at its ground plan. This they claim is based on the triple T or Tau which is identical to the Temple of Solomon in Jerusalem.[28]

Calculations based on the measurements of the Templar buildings have been used to show that the Templars were familiar with and used the cabbalistic mystical geometric system to plan their churches, and that these structures can be used to read the truth about the mystery of the Templars. In the eighteenth century John Byrom took measurements of the Temple Church in London and demonstrated that, like Roslin, it too was based on the Tau cross.[29] Baigent, Leigh and Lincoln point out that Troyes, the epicentre of the Templar foundation, had been noted for its cabbalistic school of philosophy since 1070.[30] As the Templars had strong connections with Troyes, it was likely that they were familiar with this, and applied its tenets to the plans of their churches and chapels, leaving

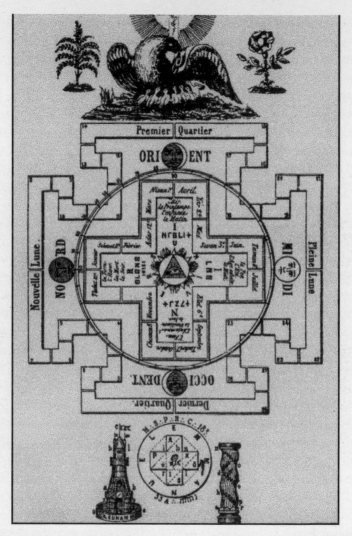

Plate 11.3 The Philosophical Cross or the plan of the third Temple as prophesied by Ezekiel and illustrated in the building schemes of the Knights Templars
From Levi, E. *The History of Magic*, 1855

a story in stone for others to follow. French writers have carried an obsession with geometrical secrets into buildings not known to have been built by the Templars, such as Chartres Cathedral where, hidden within a seven-pointed star that can be read from the architecture, the Ark of Moses can be found. Picknett and Prince go further, interpreting the characteristic round churches of the Templars as not only imitations of the Temple or the Dome of the Rock but as symbolic of the feminine side of nature.[31]

Numbers may also hold the key to the whereabouts of the Templars' treasure. The inventories show that at the time of the arrests little of value was found, although the Templars were rumoured to be fabulously wealthy. If it existed, where had it gone? Everyone loves a treasure hunt, and the search was stimulated when Henry Lincoln uncovered the story of a nineteenth-century priest who was supposed to have found buried treasure at Rennes le Chateau in the Pyrenees, a few miles from a Templar preceptory. Where the treasure was found and what happened to it was the key to unravelling what it was. A painting by Poussin shows the area in which it was found, and leads to a geometric translation of the landscape.[32] A similar geometric method has been applied to the Danish island of Bornholm in the Baltic, a remarkable place with 15 stone medieval churches. These churches, the distance between them and the shapes they make may hold the key to the Templars' treasure, but as the authors point out, this is not a treasure of gold and silver, but the treasure of knowledge and wisdom.[33]

THE TEMPLARS AND TWENTIETH-CENTURY FICTION

Fascinating as these theories are, they have attracted critics. Perhaps the most forceful of these is Umberto Eco's *Foucault's Pendulum* (1989), in which the Templars are central to the book's theme of bogus scholarship and the power of suggestion. A scholar, Casaubon, whose dissertation was on the Templars, and two publishing colleagues set out to create a book on the occult using a computer to write a secret history of the world based on Casaubon's work on the Templars. Their aim is to create a spurious chapter in the history of the occult. In the end they come to believe their own fantasies and, pursued by those whose lives and livelihoods depend on the Templars' myths, are destroyed.

A fictional Templar appears in Michael Jecks's medieval mystery story, *The Last Templar* (1995). The Templar is a survivor of the suppression and exacts vengeance on one of the persecutors by burning him to death in a Somerset wood. In *The Knights of the Cross* (1998), Piers Paul Read translates incidents recounted in the trial into the setting of a twentieth-century spy story, and Roslin Chapel appears in *Set in Darkness* by Ian Rankin, which includes a visit and description of the chapel (2000). Roslin Chapel reappears in Rankin's novel *The Falls*, published in 2001.

The mysteries surrounding the Templars continue to attract novelists. Their latest appearance is in Don Brown's *The Da Vinci Code* published in 2003. There are a growing number of websites dedicated to the order, showing that the hold the Templars have over modern minds is by no means diminished in the electronic age.

NOTES

CHAPTER ONE *The Knights Templar: Knightly Monks or Monkish Knights?*

1. Garmonsway, G., ed. (1986) *The Anglo-Saxon Chronicle*, London: Dent, 259.

2. Barber, M. (1970) 'The Origins of the Order of the Temple', *Studia Monastica* (XII), 214.

3. William of Tyre (1943) *A History of Deeds Done Beyond the Sea*, trans. Badcock, E.A. and A.C. Krey, New York: Columbia University Press (Vol. 1), 524.

4. Hartland, F.S., ed., James, M.R., trans. (1923) Walter Map, *De Nugis Curialium*, London: Cymmrodian Record Series (IX), 23 (hereafter Map).

5. Luard, H.S., ed. (1883) Matthew Paris, *Chronica Majora*, London: Rolls Series (57), 144. See also J.B. Chabal, *Chronicle de Michel le Syrian* (1909) Paris.

6. Map, 1.

7. Addison, C.G. (1842) *The Knights Templars*, London: Longman, xiv; Menarche, S. (1995) 'Re-writing the History of the Templars according to Matthew Paris', in M.S. Goodich, S. Menarche and S. Schein, eds, *Cross-Cultural Convergance in the Crusader Period*, New York: Peter Lang, 183–213; Nicholson, H. (1992) 'Steamy Syrian Scandals. Matthew Paris and the Templars and Hospitallers', *Medieval History* (Vol. 2, No. 2), 68–85.

8. Nicholson, H. (1993) *Templars, Hospitallers and Teutonic Knights: Images of Military Orders, 1128–1291*, Leicester: Leicester University Press, 2; Barber, 'Origins', 224, 226.

9. William of Tyre, 525.

10. Partner, P. (1982) *The Murdered Magicians*, Oxford: Oxford University Press, 4.

11. Bloch, M. (1989) *Feudal Society*, London: Routledge, 443.

12. Riley-Smith, J. (1997) *The First Crusaders, 1095–1131*, Cambridge: Cambridge University Press, 160.

13. Wilkinson J., with J. Hill and W.F. Ryan, eds (1988) *Jerusalem Pilgrimages 1099–1185*, London: The Hakluyt Society, 2nd Series, 293–4.

14. Riley-Smith, J. (1993) *The First Crusade and the Idea of Crusading*, London: The Athlone Press, 5, 16; St Bernard of Clairvaux (1963) *De Laude Novae Militae*, S. Bernardi Opera. Rome: Editiones Cisterciensis (Vol. 111), 217.

15. Cerrini, S. (1992) 'A New Edition of the Latin and French Rule of the Temple', in H. Nicholson, ed., *The Military Orders*, Andover: Ashgate (Vol. 2), 207; Upton-Ward, J. trans. (1992) *The Rule of the Templars*, Woodbridge: The Boydell Press, 11–16.

16. Upton-Ward, 22, Clause 10.

17. Ibid., 82–105, Clauses 279–385.

18. Ibid., 142–67, Clauses 544–656.

19. Ibid., 168–74, Clauses 657–86.

20. Ibid., 61, Clause 169.

21. Sayers, J.E. (1999) *Original Papal Documents in England and Wales from the Accession of Innocent III to the Death of Pope Benedict XI (1198–1304)*, Oxford: Oxford University Press.

22. William of Tyre, 526.

23. Lunt, W.E. (1915) 'Papal Taxation in England in the Reign of Edward I', *The English Historical Review* CXIX, 398–417.

24. Upton-Ward, 24–8, Clause 17.

25. William of Tyre, 527.

26. Upton-Ward, 53, Clause 138.

27. Barber, M. (1994) *The New Knighthood*, Cambridge: Canto, 45.

28. *De Laudae Novae Militae*, S. Bernardi, 213–39.

29. William of Tyre, 202.

30. Theoderic, Wilkinson, 303, 313.

31. For further information on events in the Holy Land, see the chronology supplied, p. xxii.
32. Luard, H. ed. (1864) *Annales Monastici de Burton*, London: HMSO
(Vol. 1), 285–90, 203, 491.
33. Thorpe, L. trans. (1978) *Gerald of Wales, Journey Through Wales*, London:
Penguin, 204.

CHAPTER TWO *The Templars in the British Isles: London and its Suburbs*

1. Riley-Smith, J. (2001) *The Origins of the Commandery in the Temple and the
Hospital*, Proceedings, Larzac Conference, 2000, 1, 4.
2. Wilkins, D. (1737) *Concilae Magnae Britanniae et Hiberniae*, London
(Vol. 2), 240.
3. *Calendar of Close Rolls, 1235–1237* (1908), London: HMSO, 88, 94; *1237–
1242*, 426.
4. Parker, T.W. (1965) *The Knights Templar in England*, Tucson: University
of Arizona Press, 125.
5. Lees, B. (1935) *The Records of the Templars in England in the Twelfth
Century. The 1185 Inquest*, London: British Academy, 1, 13, 17, 26, 41,
63, 78, 104, 106, 107, 108, 112, 116, 117.
6. Riley-Smith, 3.
7. Christie, R.M. and J.G. Coad (1980) 'Excavations at Denny', *Archaeological Journal*, 137.
8. Wilkins, 347.
9. PRO E164/16.
10. For a description of London at this time, see Butler, H.E. (1934)
A Description of London by William Fitz-Stephen, London: Historical
Association; Clark, P. and P. Slack (1976) *English Towns in Transition,
1500–1700*, Oxford: Oxford University Press, 1–16.
11. Ekwall, E. (1951) *Two Early London Subsidy Rolls*, Lund: Humanist
Vet.Samfundet, 43–5, 306–11.
12. Lees, xxxiii–xxxix, 156.
13. Addison, C.G. (1842) *The Knights Templar*, London: Longman, 90; Lees,
159; Stow, J. (1971) *The Survey of London*, Oxford: Kingsford, 47–51;
Sachs, J. (1904) 'Discoveries made during the Excavations for the
Foundation of the Safe Deposit Bank, Chancery Lane', *London and*

Middlesex Archaeological Society Transactions (New Series 1), 256–9; St John Hope, W. (1908) 'The Round Church of the Templars at Temple Bruer, Lincolnshire', *Archaeologia* (61), 177–98.

14. Lees, 158–60.

15. PRO E358/20; Godfrey, W. (1951) 'Recent Discoveries at the Temple and Notes on the Topography of the Site', *Archaeologia* (XIV), 130.

16. Dove, W. (1967) 'The Temple Church and its Restoration', *London and Middlesex Archaeological Society Transactions* (Vol. 21, No. 3), 164–71.

17. Addison, C.G. (1843) *The Temple Church*, London: Longman, 46; Mordaunt-Crook, J. (1965) 'The Restoration of the Temple Church. Ecclesiosology and Recrimination', *Architectural History* (8), 39–46.

18. Zarnecki, G. (1979) *Studies in Romanesque Sculpture*, London: The Dorian Press, 245–52.

19. Godfrey, 127–33.

20. Painter, S. (1982) *William Marshal*, Toronto: University of Toronto Press, 56, 282, 284, 289; Luard, H.S., ed. (1883) Matthew Paris, *Chronica Majora*, London: Rolls Series (IV), 203.

21. Lees, 157, 168.

22. Clew, H. and M. Weinbaum (1960) *The London Eyre of 1244*, London: London Record Society (VI), 138; William, E. (1927) *Early Holborn and the Legal Quarter*, London: Sweet & Maxwell (Vol. 1), 244, 248.

23. Lees, 14–17.

24. Thomas, A.D., ed. (1924) *Calendar of the Mayor's Court Rolls*, Cambridge: Cambridge University Press; Thomas, A.D. (1938) *The Great Chronicle of London*, Cambridge: Cambridge University Press; Weinbaum, M. (1976) *The London Eyre, 1276*, London: London Record Society (Vol. XII).

25. Cole, H. (1844) *Documents Illustrative of English History in the 13th and 14th Centuries*, London: Eyre & Spottiswood, 142.

26. Carlin, M. (1996) *Medieval Southwark*, London: The Hambledon Press, 32–41; Lees, 171–2; Meynott, W.J. (1881) *An Historical Record of the Parish Church of Christ Church, Surrey, with a short history of the Manor of Old Paris Gardens*, London: privately printed by the author, 36–40; Page, W., ed. (1967) VCH, *Surrey*, Oxford: Oxford University Press (Vol. 4), 149.

27. Lees, B. (1933–37) 'The *Humbra* and *Quabba* of Hackney and Leyton', *London and Middlesex Archaeological Society, Transactions* (New Series 7), 229–33; Lees, *Records*, 16–17.
28. BL Cotton Nero E V1.165.
29. McDonald, K. (1968) *Medieval London Suburbs*, Chichester: Phillimore, 36.
30. Pugh, R.B. (1972) VCH, *Middlesex*, Oxford: Oxford University Press (Vol. 3), 178–81.
31. Baker, T. (1972) *The Victoria County History of England and Wales, Middlesex*, Oxford: Oxford University Press (Vol. 9), 102–13; Larking, L.B. (1857) *The Knights Hospitallers in England. The 1338 Inquest*, London: Camden Society (Vol. 65), 173.

CHAPTER THREE *The Templars and the Countryside: Eastern England*

1. Wilkinson, J., with J. Hill and W.F. Ryan, eds (1998) *Jerusalem Pilgrimages 1099–1185*, London: The Hakluyt Society, 2nd Series, 288.
2. Sayers, J.E. (1999) *Original Papal Documents in England and Wales from the Accession of Pope Innocent III to the Death of Pope Benedict XI (1198–1304)*, Oxford: Oxford University Press, 238.
3. Duby, G. (1968) *The Rural Economy and Country Life in the Medieval West*, Columbia: University of South Carolina Press, 506–7.
4. For the Postan thesis see, for example, Postan, M. (1975) *The Medieval Economy and Society*, Cambridge: Cambridge University Press.
5. Barber, M. (1994) *The New Knighthood*, Cambridge: Cambridge University Press, 237.
6. Miller, E. and J. Hatcher (1978) *Medieval England, Rural Society and Economic Change, 1086–1348*, London: Longman, 59.
7. Garmonsway, G.N., ed. (1986) *The Anglo-Saxon Chronicle*, London: Dent, 261.
8. Luard, H. (1972 repr.) *Annales Monastici*, London: HMSO, RS 36 (2), 189, 194, 199, 205, 210–11, 280, 283, 299, 305, 338, 370–1.
9. Britnell, R. (1983) 'Agriculture in a Region of Ancient Enclosure, 1185–1500', *Nottingham Medieval Studies* (XXVII), 317–55.
10. Ryan, P. (1993) 'Cressing Temple: Its History from Documents', and Hunter, J. (1993) 'Historic Landscape of Cressing and Its Environs',

in Andrews, D., ed. *Cressing Temple*, Chelmsford: Essex County Council.

11. Beaumont, G.F. (1925) 'The Manor of Borley, AD 1308', *Transactions Essex Archaeological Society* (18) 254–69; Newton, K. (1970) *The Manor of Writtle*, Chichester, Phillimore.

12. For Hewitt's conclusion on the barns see, for example, Hewitt, C. (1967) 'The Barns at Cressing Temple and their Significance in the History of English Carpentry', *Journal of the Society of Architectural History* (XXVI), 48–70. Essex County Record Office has a newspaper file of theories on the barns' date.

13. Andrews, 16.

14. Britnell, R. (1968) 'The Making of Witham', *History Studies* (1), 13–21.

15. Rodwell, W. (1993) *The Origins and Development of Witham, Essex*, Oxford: Oxbow Monograph, 26.

16. Britnell, 'Witham', 15–19.

17. Printed versions of the 1309 values for Essex can be found in Gervers, M. (1996) *The Cartulary of the Knights of St John of Jerusalem in England*, Oxford: The British Academy.

18. Lees, B. (1935) *The Records of the Templars in England in the Twelfth Century. The 1185 Inquest*, London: British Academy, 211–16. Table compiled by the author.

19. PRO E358/19.

20. Hine, R. (1927) *The History of Hitchin*, London: Allen and Unwin; Huyshe, W. (1906) *The Royal Manor of Hitchin*, London: Duckworth. Hildebrand of Hitchen is quoted in Beamon. She quotes a discussion on this by A. Fled in 1984. It is not mentioned in the VCH or Hine.

21. PRO E358/19.

22. Levett, A. (1938) *Studies in Manorial History*, Oxford: Clarendon Press, 181, 188–9, 350–1, 360, 362, 366.

23. Gooder, E. (1995) *Temple Balsall*, Chichester: Phillimore, 149.

24. Wilkins, D. (1737) *Concilia Magnae Britanniae et Hiberniae*, London, 339, 345, 347.

25. Cole, H. (1844) *Documents Illustrative of English History*, London: Eyre & Spottiswood.

26. PRO E358/18.
27. Christie, P.M. and J.G. Coad (1980) 'Excavations at Denny Abbey', *Archaeological Journal*.
28. Wilkins, 361.
29. PRO E142/112.

CHAPTER FOUR *The Templars in the Countryside: North-eastern England*

1. Riley-Smith, J. (2001) 'The Origins of the Commandery in the Temple and the Hospital', Proceedings, Larzac Conference, 2000, 1, 4.
2. Howlett, R. (1886) *Chronicles of Stephen, Henry II and Richard I*, London: HMSO (Vol. 111), 284.
3. Lees, B. (1935) *The Records of the Templars in England in the Twelfth Century. The 1185 Inquest*, London: British Academy, 94, 254.
4. *Calendar of Patent Rolls, 1298* (1894), London HMSO, 332; Owen, D. (1971) *Church and Society in Medieval Lincolnshire*, Lincoln: History of Lincolnshire (Vol. V), 57–63.
5. Toulmin-Smith, L. (1907) *The Itinerary of John Leland 1535–43*, London: Alexander, George Bell, 28; in the latest edition of the itinerary, John Chandler translates *champaign* as 'open'.
6. St John Hope, W. (1908) 'The Round Church of the Templars at Temple Bruer, Lincolnshire', *Archaelogia* (61), 177–98.
7. Coles, H. (1847) *Documents Illustrative of English History in the 13th and 14th centuries*, London: Eyre & Spottiswood, 148, 152, 154, 156.
8. Larking, L. (1857) *The Knights Hospitaller in England*, London: Camden Society, 154–5.
9. 'South Witham', *Current Archaeology* (1968), 232–7.
10. Wilkins, D. (1737) *Concilae Magnae Britanniae et Hiberniae*, London, 365–6.
11. Lees, cli–iii.
12. Platts, G. (1985) *Land and People in Medieval Lincolnshire*, Lincoln: History of Lincolnshire Committee, 58.
13. Ibid., 106, 116, 166.
14. Gooder, E. (1995) *Temple Balsall*, Chichester: Phillimore.
15. PRO E385/18; *The Gentleman's Magazine* (1857), (New Series 111), 519–27.

16. Parker adds Whitley to this list.
17. Chetwynd-Staplyton, A. (1887–89) 'The Templars at Temple Hirst', *Yorkshire Archaeological and Topographical Society Transactions* (X), 276–96.
18. PRO E358/19.
19. *Calendar of Patent Rolls, 1307–1313* (1894), London: HMSO.
20. Dyer, C. (1989) *The Standard of Living in the Later Middle Ages*, Cambridge: Cambridge University Press, 57, 64, 114, 133–5, 153–9, 221.
21. Braithwaite, W. (1909) 'Discovery of Ancient Foundations and Human Remains at Temple Newsam', *Thoresby Society Miscellany*, XV.
22. PRO E142/17.
23. Taylor, B.V. (1881–82) 'Ribston and the Knights Templar', *Yorkshire Archaeological and Topographical Journal* (11), 429–52.
24. Bogg, E. (1908) *Richmondshire*, Leeds: J. Miller, 641–2.
25. PRO E142/17.
26. Royal Commission for Historical Monuments (1987), *Houses of the North York Moors*, London: HMSO, 15, 203.
27. Wilkins, 371–2.
28. Hodgson, J. (1827) *Northumberland*, Newcastle upon Tyne: T. & J. Pigg (Part 2, Vol. 2), 311.
29. Wilkins, 377.
30. PRO E142/11; Hodgson, J. (1895) 'Temple Thornton Accounts, 1308', *Archaeologia Aeliana* (XVII), 40–53.

CHAPTER FIVE *The Templars in the Countryside: the Midlands, the Chilterns and Oxfordshire*

1. Gooder, E. (1995) *Temple Balsall*, Chichester: Phillimore, 52.
2. Clark, G.T. (1889) 'The Customary of the Manor and Soke of Rothley', *Archaeologia* (XLVII), 89–130; Nichols, J. (1804) *The History and Antiquities of the County of Leicester*, Leicester: Leicestershire County Council, facsimile edition; W.G. Hoskins (1969) VCH, Oxford: Oxford University Press (Vol. 2).
3. Hundred Rolls 324, 455; PRO E142/104–5; Larking, L. (1856–57) *The Knights Hospitallers in England*, London: Camden Society, 176–7. Fosbrooke, T.H. (1921–2) 'Rothley – the Preceptory', *Leicestershire Archaeological Society*, 2–32.

4. PRO E142/104–5.
5. Gooder, 33–5.
6. Dyer, C. (1989) *The Standard of Living in the Later Middle Ages*, Cambridge: Cambridge University Press, 55–71, 151–60.
7. Gooder, 64–80.
8. Gooder, 54–8.
9. Harrison, C. (1986) *Essays on the History of Keele*, Keele: Keele University Press, 6–14.
10. PRO E358/19.
11. Lees, B. (1935) *The Records of the Templars in England in the Twelfth Century. The 1185 Inquest*, London: British Academy, Records of the Social and Economic History of England and Wales (IX), 75–7.
12. Illingworth, W. and J. Caley (1818) *Rotuli Hundredorum in Turri Londensis*, London: Record Commission.
13. Fowler, G.H. (1919) *Calendar of Feet of Fines, Bedfordshire*, Bedford: Bedfordshire Record Society (Vol. 6).
14. Fowler, G.H. (1929) *Roll of the Justice of the Eyre in Bedfordshire, 1240*, Bedford: Bedfordshire Record Society (Vol. 9), 103, 139, 142; Fowler, G.H. (1935) *Roll of the Justice of the Eyre, in Bedfordshire 1247*, Bedford: Bedfordshire Record Society (Vol. 17), 39, 55, 85, 103–4, 123; Gaydon, A.J. (1958) *The Taxation Rolls of 1297*, Bedford: Bedfordshire Record Society, 39, 51.
15. PRO E358/19.
16. Leys, A. (1938) *The Sandford Cartulary*, Oxford: Oxford Record Society, numbers 19 and 22.
17. Lees, 43–4.
18. Leys, 48.
19. Roberts, E. (1963) 'The Boundary and Woodlands of Shotover Forest', *Oxoniensia* (23), 68–73.
20. Dunking, J. (1823) *The Hundred of Bollington*, Oxford: Harding, Mavor and Lepard, (Vol. 1), 95, 119.
21. Leys, 48; PRO E142/109–10; Larking, 190–1.
22. Lees, 44–5; Hundred Rolls 725–55; PRO E142/109/110; Larking, 190.
23. PRO E142/13; E358/18.
24. Ibid.

25. Postles, D. (1993) 'Some Difference between Seignorial Demesnes in Medieval Oxfordshire', *Oxoniensia* (58), 220–32.

CHAPTER SIX *The Templars in the Countryside: the Welsh Marches, Wales, the West and Southern England*

1. *Calendar of Patent Rolls, 1272–1281* (1901), London: HMSO, 435–6, 461.
2. Webb, J. (1844) 'Notes on the Preceptory of the Templars at Garway in the County of Hereford', *Archaeologia* (XXI), 182–97.
3. Rees, W. (1947) *A History of the Order of St John of Jerusalem in Wales and the Welsh Border, including an account of the Templars*, Cardiff: University of Wales, 32, 56.
4. Ibid., 58.
5. Forey, A. (1973) *The Templars in the Corona de Aragon*, Oxford: Oxford University Press, 189–204.
6. Ibid., 198–9.
7. Gaydon, A. (1973) *The Victoria County History of England and Wales, Shropshire*, Oxford: Oxford University Press (Vol. 2), 85.
8. PRO E358/19.
9. Baldwyne, R.C. and H. O'Neill (1958) 'A Medieval Site at Chalk Hill, Temple Guiting', *Transactions of the Bristol and Gloucestershire Archaeological Society* (VLXXXVII), 61–5.
10. Holt, R. and G. Rosser (1990) *The English Medieval Town 1200–1540*, London: Longman.
11. Pryor, J. (1982) 'Transportation of Horses by Sea during the Era of the Crusdades: Eighth Century to 1285 AD', *Mariners Mirror* (68), 9–27; Barber, M. (1992) 'Supplying the Crusader States', in B.Z. Kedar, ed., *The Horns of Hattin*, Jerusalem and London: Variorum.
12. Gavignan, J.J. ed. (1948) Oliver of Paderborn, *The Siege of Damietta*, Philadelphia: University of Pennsylvania Press, 66, 85.
13. Barber, 'Supplying the Crusader States', 322.
14. *Calendar of Patent Rolls, 1225–1232* (1903).
15. Hardy T.D., ed. (1844) *Rotuli Litterarum Clausam in Turri Londensis*, London: George Eyre (Vol. 2), 14, 39, 62, 94, 113–14, 122, 160, 167, 194.
16. PRO E142/15.

17. Wilson, A.E. (1961) 'Custumals of the Manors of Laughton, Willingdon and Goring', Lewes: Sussex Record Society, 1–19.

18. PRO E142/15.

19. McKinley, R. (1988) *The Surnames of Sussex*, Oxford: The Leopard's Head Press, 301–69.

20. BL Ms Cotton Nero VI, fol. 267.

21. Forey, A. (1987) 'Women and the Military Orders in 12th and 13th Centuries', *Studia Monastica* (29, 1), 63–85; Nicholson, H. (1991) 'Templar Attitudes Towards Women', *Medieval History* (1, 3), 74–80.

22. In the other palatine counties of Durham and Lancashire the Templars received a few shillings of rent, but had no property.

23. Gooder, E. (1995) *Temple Balsall*, Chichester: Phillimore, 145–6.

24. Forey, 'Women', 56–9; *Calendar of Patent Rolls, 1292–1301* (1895), 480, 592; Duby, G. (1968) *Rural Economy and Life in the Medieval West*, Columbia: University of South Carolina Press, 142–8.

25. Lloyd, S. (1986) 'Crusader Knights and the Land Market in the Thirteenth Century', in P. Coss and S. Lloyd, *Thirteenth Century England*, Woodbridge: The Boydell Press, 121–2.

CHAPTER SEVEN *The Knights Templar in Ireland and Scotland*

1. MacInery, M.H. (1913) 'The Templars in Ireland', *The Irish Ecclesiastical Review*, 5th series (11), 225–45.

2. Ibid., 230.

3. Smith, B. (1999) *Colonisation and Conquest in Medieval Ireland*, Cambridge: Cambridge University Press, 1–60.

4. Davies, R.R. (2000) *The First English Empire*, Oxford: Oxford University Press, 163–70.

5. Hore, P.H. (1904) *History of the Town and County of Wexford*, London: Eliot Stock (Vol. IV), 260–73.

6. Addison, C.G. (1842) *History of the Knights Templar*, London: Longman, 74.

7. Luard, H.S., ed. (1883) Matthew Paris, *Chronica Majora*, London: Rolls Series (III), 254.

8. MacNiociall, G. (1967) 'Documents relating to the Suppression of the Templars in Ireland', *Analecta Hibernica* (24), 183–226.

9. Wood, H. (1906) 'The Templars in Ireland', *Proceedings of the Royal Irish Academy* (XXV), Section C, 344. The Book of Howth is a sixteenth-century compilation of medieval texts.

10. National Archives of Scotland, GD160/112/4; RH 6/17.

11. Maidment, J. (1833) *A Rental of all the Annual Rents of Temple Lands throughout the Kingdom of Scotland*, Scottish National Library, Acc. 8090. This manuscript must be used with caution as many of the properties listed did not belong to the medieval Templars.

12. Cowan, I.B. and D. Eason (1976) *Medieval Religious Houses in Scotland*, London: Longman, 158.

13. Royal Commission on Ancient and Historical Monuments of Scotland (1929) *Mid and West Lothian*, Edinburgh: HMSO, 176–9; Sinclair, J., ed. (1771–99) *The Statistical Account of Scotland, The Lothians*, Edinburgh, 429–33; SNL Mss 26287.

14. *Calendar of Close Rolls, Edward 1, 1288–96* (1908), London: HMSO, 511.

15. Details of swearing fealty in Bain, J., ed. (1884) *Calendar of documents relating to Scotland in the PRO*, Edinburgh: HMSO. National Archives of Scotland, RH6/122.

16. 'Simple' could mean low born and not slow witted.

17. Barrow, G.W. (1978) 'The Aftermath of War: Scotland and England in the Late 13th and Early 14th Century', *Transactions of the Royal Historical Society*, 5th Series (28), 103–25; Edwards, J. (1909) 'The Templars in Scotland in the 13th Century', *Scottish Historical Review*, 7, 13–17.

18. For example, National Archives of Scotland, RH6/114–15; RH6/118.

19. Henderson, D. (1892) *Annals of Lower Deeside*, Aberdeen: D. Wylie; Walker, A. (1887) *The Knights Templar in and around Aberdeen*, Aberdeen: Aberdeen University Press, 20.

20. *Liber S. Marie de Calcho* (1846), Edinburgh: The Bannatyne Club, 182.

21. Henderson, 167–76.

22. National Archives of Scotland, RH11/23/1, *Charter Book of the Earl of Haddington*.

23. The village in which the chapel lies is Roslin. The chapel is referred to as Rosslyn in guide books, but the Royal Commission of Ancient and Historical monuments uses Roslin. This spelling will be used here.

24. Crowden, S. (1986) *Scottish Medieval Churches*, Edinburgh: John Donald, 188–9.
25. Ibid., 193–4.
26. Bain, J. (1884) *Calendar of Documents Relating to Scotland in the PRO*, Edinburgh: HMSO (Vol. 111), 17, 51, 60.
27. McKerrack, A. (1991) 'Bruce's Secret Weapon', *The Scots Magazine*, June, 261–8.

CHAPTER EIGHT *The Templars and the Plantagenets*

1. Forey, A. (1973) *The Templars in the Corona de Aragon*, Oxford: Oxford University Press, 344–6.
2. Forester, T., ed. (1858) *The Chronicle of Henry of Huntingdon*, London: HMSO, 254, 261 (hereafter Huntingdon).
3. Howlett, R., ed. (1886) *Gesta Stephani Regis Angolorum*, London: HMSO, 5; Hartland, F.S., ed., James, M.R., trans. (1923) Walter Map, *De Nugis Curialium*, Cymmrodian Record Series (IX), 260 (hereafter Map).
4. Huntingdon, 272.
5. Huntingdon, 289.
6. Map, 261.
7. Stubbs, W., ed. (1867) *Gesta Regis Henrici Secundi*, London: HMSO, 111, 169.
8. Barber, M. (1994) *The New Knighthood*, Cambridge: Cambridge University Press, 277.
9. The bridegroom was five, the bride three.
10. Stubbs, W., ed. (1868) *Chronica Magistri Rogeri de Hovedene*, London: HMSO, 5, 218.
11. This is discussed in Turner, R.N. and R. Heiser (2000) *The Reign of Richard Lionheart*, London: Longman, 1–16. Gillingham, J. (1994) *Richard Coeur de Lion* and Prestwich, J.O. 'Richard Coeur de Lion'.
12. Hewett, H., ed. (1887) *The Flowers of History by Roger Wendover*, London: HMSO, Rolls Series (82), 111, 68.
13. *Calendar of Charter Rolls, 1226–1257* (1903), London: HMSO, 135, 219.
14. Shirley, W., ed. (1862) *Rerum Britannia Medii Aevi Scriptori*, London: HMSO, (2), 31, 69.

15. Figures are taken from Tout, T.F. (1920) *Chapters in the Administrative History of Medieval England*, Manchester: Manchester University Press, 162, 244.

16. Ibid., 250–1.

17. Powicke, F.M. (1947) *Henry III and the Lord Edward*, Oxford: Clarendon Press, 2, 781–2.

18. *Calendar of Close Rolls, 1237–1242* (1911), London: HMSO, 18; *Calendar of Patent Rolls, 1238–1246* (1906), London: HMSO, 495.

19. For a full account of De Burgh's rise and fall, see Ellis, C. (1952) *Hubert de Burgh*, London: Phoenix House. Inventory of Hubert's treasure in *Calendar of Close Rolls*, 7 Feb 1233.

20. *Calendar of Patent Rolls, 1237–1247* (1906), 456–7.

21. Carpenter, D.A. (1988) 'The Gold Treasure of Henry II', in P.R. Cross and S. Lloyd, ed., *Thirteenth Century England*, Woodbridge: The Boydell Press, 61–88.

22. Treharne, R.F. (1971) *The Baronial Plan of Reform, 1258–1263*, Manchester: Manchester University Press, 107.

CHAPTER NINE *The Templars as Bankers*

1. The amount may have been £10,000.

2. Hughes, A., A. Gouge and C. Johnson, eds (1902) *Dialogus de Scaccarios*, Oxford: Oxford University Press (hereafter *Dialogus*).

3. *Calendar of Librate Rolls, 1226–1240* (1916), London: HMSO, 333.

4. Ibid., 230, 309.

5. *Dialogus*, 333–4.

6. Picquet, J. (1939) *Les Templiers. Etude de leurs Operations Financieres*, Paris: Librairie Hachette.

7. Ibid., 39–40.

8. Ibid., 3.

9. Metcalf, D.W. (1980) 'The Templars as Bankers and Monetary Transfers between West and East in the Twelfth Century', in P.W. Edbury and D.W. Metcalf, *Coinage in the Latin East*, Oxford: BAR International Series, 1–18.

10. *The Receipts and Issue Roll 1241–42* (1992), London: Pipe Roll Society, xxv.

11. Ebden, E.P. (1972) *The Great Roll of the Pipe, 1218*, London: Pipe Roll Society, xix.
12. Piquet, 215.
13. Spufford, P. (1988) *Money and Its Use in Medieval Europe*, Cambridge: Cambridge University Press, 161.
14. Hardy, T.D., ed. (1835) *Rotuli Litterarum Patenti in Turri Londensis asservati*, London: George Eyre (Vol. 1), 41–2.
15. Constable, G. (1982) 'The Financing of the Crusades in the Twelfth Century', in B.Z. Kedar, H. Mayer and R. Smail, *Outremer*, Jerusalem: Yad Izhak Ben-Zvi Institute, 72–6.
16. *Calendar of Patent Rolls, 1215–1225* (1901), London: HMSO, 453, 456, 497, 537, 612.
17. Ibid., 203.
18. *Calendar of Patent Rolls, 1272–1281* (1901), 52.
19. *Calendar of Patent Rolls, 1247–1254* (1908), 108, 326.
20. Forey, A. (1973) *The Templars in the Corona de Aragon*, London: Oxford University Press, 394.
21. *Calendar of Patent Rolls, 1292–1301* (1895), 332; *Calendar of Patent Rolls, 1307–1313* (1894), 210.
22. Other examples can be found in the *Calendar of Close Rolls, 1256–1259* (1932), London: HMSO, 115, 122, 317, etc.
23. *Calendar of Close Rolls, 1237–1242* (1911), 55.
24. *Calendar of Librate Rolls, 1226–1240*, 14, 213.
25. *Calendar of Librate Rolls, 1251–1260* (1959), 159, 168, 177, 201, 336; *Calendar of Patent Rolls, 1255–1265*, 3, 67.
26. *Calendar of Close Rolls, 1256–1259* (1932), 270.

CHAPTER TEN *The Trial and Fall of the Templars*

1. Barber, M. (1978) *The Trial of the Templars*, Cambridge: Canto, 15.
2. Parker, J. (1965) *The Knights Templars in England*, Tucson: University of Arizona Press, 85.
3. Cohn, N. (1993) *Europe's Inner Demons*, London: Pimilico, 84–5.
4. Ibid., 87–8.
5. Barber, 51.

6. Boswell, J. (1980) *Christianity, Social Tolerance and Homosexuality*, Chicago: University of Chicago Press, 92–4.

7. Barber, 101–2.

8. Parker, 92.

9. *Calendar of Close Rolls, 1307–1313* (1892), London: HMSO, 13, 48–9.

10. For an in-depth analysis of a keeper's management of a Templar estate, see Gooder, E. (1995) *Temple Balsall*, Chichester: Phillimore.

11. Parker, 93.

12. *Calendar of Close Rolls, 1307–1313* (1892), 179, 189, 206.

13. Ibid., 334–5.

14. Ibid., 335, 339.

15. Ibid., 337.

16. Ibid., 279, 285.

17. Wilkins, D. (1737) *Concilia Magnae Britanniae et Hiberniae*, London, 365–7.

18. Ibid., 372; *Calendar of Close Rolls, 1307–1313* (1892), 308.

19. Wilkins, 358–64, 378–84.

20. Ibid., 384.

21. Gooder, 114, 160.

22. Wilkins, 386–8.

23. *The Spottiswode Miscellany* (1845), Edinburgh: The Spottiswode Society, 2, 8–11.

24. Wilkins, 380–2.

25. Ibid., 373–8.

26. Walter of Hemingburgh, *Chronica Domum Walteri de Hemingburgh, De Gesta Regum Angliae*, Hamilton, H.C., ed. (1865) London: HMSO (RS 82).

27. Corpus Christi College, Cambridge, Mss 250, p. 169; the whole text is published in Cheney, C.R. (1973) *Medieval Texts and Studies*, Oxford: Clarendon Press, 322–7.

28. Cheney, 317.

29. Lea, H.C. (1888) *The History of the Inquisition in the Middle Ages*, London: Sampson Low, 238–334. Hammer-Purgstall, J. von (1853) *Die Schuld der Templier*, Vienna: Aked der Wissenchaft; Prutz, H. (1887) *Entwicklung und Untergang der Tempelhenenorden*, Berlin: G. Groeriche Verlagbuch.

30. Addison, C.G. (1842) *The History of the Knights Templar*, London: Longman, 470.

31. Morshead, G.J. (1888) *The Templars Trials*, London: Stevens and Sons, 47–73.

32. Cohn, 79–99; Martin, E.J. (1928) *The Trial of the Templars*, London: Allan and Unwin, 61–2; Peters, E. (1978) *The Magician, the Witch and the Law*, Philadelphia: University of Pennsylvania Press, 128.

33. For a full discussion on late twentieth-century ideas on the fall of the Templars, see Ward, J.O. (1983) 'The Fall of the Templars, a Review Article', *The Journal of Religious History* (13), 92–113.

CHAPTER ELEVEN *The Templars in Fact and Fiction: Debates, Myths and Legends*

1. St John Hope, W. (1908) 'The Round Church of the Templars at Temple Bruer, Lincolnshire', *Archaeologia* (61), 182.

2. Addison, C.G. (1842) *The Knights Templar*, London: Longman, xiii; Ashmole, E. (1672) *Institution, Laws and Ceremonies of the most noble order of the Garter*, London; Buc, G. (1631) 'The Third University of England' in J. Stow, *Annales or a General Chronicle of England*, London; Fuller, T. (1647) *The History of the Holy War*, London: J. Williams.

3. Froude, J.A. (1892) *The Spanish Story of the Armada and other essays*, London: Longman, 216–17; Woodhouse, F.C. (1879) *Military Religious Orders*, London: SPCK.

4. Nineteenth-century histories of the Order in English: Burnes, J. (1837) *A History of the Knights Templar*; Cunningham, H. (1845) *The Templars*; O'Neal Haye, A. (1865) *The Persecution of the Templars*; Lambert, G. (1887) *The Templars*; Walker, A. (1887) *The Knights Templar*; Morshead, J.C. (1888) *The Templars' Trials*.

5. Marquis D'Albon, ed. (1913) *Cartulaire General de l'Ordre du Temple 1119?[sic]–1150*, Paris.

6. Lees, B.A. (1935) *Records of the Templars in England in the Twelfth Century*, London: British Academy.

7. Examples of twentieth-century works on the Templars in English: Bothwell-Gosse, A. (1918) *The Templars*; Campbell, G.A. (1937) *The*

Knights Templar: Their Rise and Fall, London: Duckworth; Simon, E. (1959) *The Piebald Standard*; Howarth, S. (1982) *The Knights Templar*; Partner, P. (1982) *The Murdered Magicians*, Oxford: Oxford University Press; Burman, E. (1986) *The Templar Knights of God*; Hugh, A.R. *The Champions of the Cross*; Barber, M. (1994) *The New Knighthood*, Cambridge: Canto; Read, P.P. (1999) *The Templars*, London: Weidenfeld and Nicolson.

8. Legge, M.D. (1963) *Anglo-Norman Literature and Its Background*, Oxford: Oleander Press, 191.

9. Matarasso, P. (1971) *Aucassin and Nicolette and other tales*, London: Penguin.

10. Nicholson, H. (1993) *Templars, Hospitallers and Teutonic Knights: Images of the Military Orders 1128–1291*, Leicester: Leicester University Press, Chapter 5.

11. Scott, W. (1994) *Ivanhoe*, London: Penguin, 31.

12. Ibid., 391.

13. Ibid., 508.

14. *The Pall Mall Gazette* (1910), 5th March.

15. Scott, W. (1825 repr. 1968) *The Talisman*, Ipswich, 114.

16. Anon (1822) *The Templar*, London: T. & G. Woodward.

17. Lucas, H. (1830) *Manual of the Order at the Temple*, English translation, Liverpool: David Marple, 9, 12, 16.

18. Burnes, J. (1840) *Sketch of the History of the Knights Templar* (2nd edition), Edinburgh, 48, 51.

19. Robinson, J.J. (1989) *Born in Blood – The Lost Secrets of Freemasonry*, London: Century Books, xix.

20. Ibid., 50–1. Baigent, M. and R. Leigh, *The Temple and the Lodge*, London: Arrow, 125–7.

21. Laidler, K. (1998) *The Head of God*, London: Weidenfeld and Nicolson, 26, 53–4, 256–71, 273.

22. Currer-Briggs, N. (1987) *The Shroud and the Grail*, London: Weidenfeld and Nicolson, 90.

23. Wilson, I. (1998) *The Blood and the Shroud*, London: Weidenfeld and Nicolson; Barber, M. (1982) 'The Templars and the Turin Shroud', *The Catholic Historical Review* (LXVIII, No. 2), 206–25.

NOTES

24. Wilson, p. 136.
25. Knight, C. and R. Lomas (1997) *The Second Messiah, Templars, the Turin Shroud and the Great Secret of Freemasonry*, London: Arrow, 200–10.
26. Sinclair, A. (1995) *The Sword and the Grail*, London: Century, 64.
27. Weston, J.L. (1913) *The Quest for the Holy Grail*, London: G. Bell & Sons, 10, 12, 136.
28. Knight and Lomas, 117–34.
29. Hancox, J. (1992) *The Byrom Collection*, London: Cape, 139.
30. Baigent, M., K. Leigh and H. Lincoln (1982) *The Holy Blood and the Holy Grail*, London: Cape, 52.
31. Picknett, L. and C. Prince (1997) *The Templar Revelation*, London: Bantam Press, 110.
32. Lincoln, H. (1997) *Key to the Sacred Pattern*, Moreton in the Marsh: The Windrush Press.
33. Haagenson, E. and H. Lincoln (2000) *The Templars Secret*, Moreton in the Marsh: The Windrush Press.

TEMPLAR RECORDS IN THE
NATIONAL ARCHIVES

The majority of surviving Templar records in England can be found in The National Archives under class E. The 1185 Inquest is at E164/16, but this is a 'secure document' that needs special permission before it can be consulted. This is because it is in its original twelfth-century binding of reddish-brown leather over beech boards. Stamped decoration is found on both covers consisting of shields and a daisy motif as well as fishes, birds, griffins, trefoils, David and his harp, fantastic birds and trees. The book was once held together by clasps and there is a note inside that the end sheets were removed and replaced in what was thought to be their original position in 1948. The script is clear with the capital letters in red or green. At least three different hands can be observed, and the final entry on fol. 65r for Dunwich appears to be in a later script. The pages following this entry are pricked and ruled ready for use but have no entries. Some passages appear to be crossed out, but this was a method of emphasising passages that can also be seen in the Domesday Book. There is some marginalia and the occasional addition in a later hand such as fol. 6 in which an addition reads 'In Deptford a gift of Henry the king, a carucate of land worth 6 marks'. Lees's printed version is a faithful transcription and can be used with impunity.

E142/9 contains enrolled inquisitions taken on behalf of those claiming corrodies and dating from 1308 to 1314. These documents illustrative of English History in the Thirteenth Century are printed in Cole. E142/19–20 also deal with corrodies, and include the writs sent out by the king setting up the inquisitions.

E142/10–19 are the extents and inquisition of the Templars' lands and goods in 1308. Unfortunately some of these have suffered severe rodent damage to the top of the document in exactly the position that tells us which manor is being referred to in the inquisition. E142/10 for Essex is in reasonable condition but /11 for Northumberland and Cumberland is severely damaged, and /12, Nottinghamshire, is damaged on the side. The name of the manor is visible on the rest, and these are mainly intact, but not all counties are covered in this series.

E142/89–118 are also extents and inquisitions and are in better condition. These show which manors were being charged for the maintenance of the Templars whilst they were in prison. There are good inventories for Bedfordshire and Cambridgeshire, but that for Essex is damaged and includes the Hertfordshire manor of Preston. Some, for example /107 for London, show that a jury agreed that a Templar should have maintenance but few other details. Others give good details. There are good extents for Huntingdonshire, Northamptonshire and Suffolk. Damage has occurred to the Dorset and Somerset returns, but Wiltshire, Lincolnshire and Yorkshire are in fair condition.

E142/119–20 are inquisitions on debts due to the Templars, including the writ, and sometimes only the writ has survived. These give jury lists and what they swore on oath. For example in E142/ 119 the jury declared that John Godkyne and Ralph Kimball owed £4 8s to Brother Michael for cows purchased at Wycombe.

E358/18–20 are the accounts from 1308 to 1314 kept by the keepers of the land put in by the king after the Templars' arrest. These are in large rolls some two-and-a-half feet wide and eight feet long with entries on both sides of the roll. Handling these is difficult and there is no order to the entries. PRO Ind 1/7029 is a list of the manors in the rolls, but does not give the order in which they appear.

Each entry starts by giving the names of the keepers rendering the accounts and the name of the place. The entry includes rents received, sales of produce, crops sown, livestock movements, expenditure on repairs, and a final inventory before the manor was handed over to the Hospitallers. As these cover a number of different farming districts, as a record of fourteenth-century farming they are unique, but each section takes many hours to read. To a historian working on a particular place this would be manageable.

The accounts and inventories of the Templars' Irish estates can be found in E101/239/11 and E101/239/13. These were sent to England in 1328 after frequent requests from the king.

All of these documents are in Latin. The original Close, Charter, Librate, Patent and Pipe Rolls are also in the NA, but there are printed calendars of these covering most of the Templars' period.

Evidence from Scotland is sparse and confined to deeds in the National Archives of Scotland that are listed in the bibliography.

GAZETTEER OF TEMPLAR SITES

Standing Templar remains are rare and those that have survived are often on private property and not always accessible. Where possible information on access is included. Places associated with the Templars are also listed. Although in many areas all physical traces of the Order have disappeared, it is still possible to trace where their preceptory or manor may have been by looking at modern place-names. For example, Templar Place, Templar Court and Templars Avenue mark the site of the Templars' estate in Hampstead. The fourth edition of the *Ordnance Survey Gazetteer of Great Britain* lists 150 examples of Temple used as a place-name.

Bristol ST 593792

Temple Church. Ruined tower and walls set in a public garden. In Temple Street, off Victoria Street. Open on Heritage Days only.

Cambridgeshire

Cambridge Castle. The castle mound still stands on Shire Hill above the River Cam in the grounds of Shire Hall. This was where the

Templars arrested in the eastern counties were imprisoned in 1308. Free access at all times.

Denny Abbey TL 4965

Denny Abbey is on the A10 between Cambridge and Ely. It is managed by English Heritage and is open from 12.00 each day between April and October. This is one of the best standing examples of a Templar house.

Duxford TL 4746

Lies off the M11. The chapel by Whittlesford Bridge is sometimes mistaken for a Templar chapel, but in reality was a chapel of the Hospital of St John.

Great Wilbraham TL 5557

The Templar property can be identified as Temple End but there are no standing remains.

Essex

Cressing Temple TL 7920

The Templar site is on the B1018, three miles north of Witham. It is managed by Essex County Council and is open to the public on Sundays from March to October and Wednesdays to Fridays from May to September, from 10.30am to 4.30pm, and all bank holidays.

Witham TL 8125

The Templar new town site can be identified as Newlands.

Herefordshire

Garway SO 4522

Garway church with its Templar nave and mysterious carvings lies in the centre of the village. The preceptory probably lay beside the church, and there is a dovecote built in 1326 by the Hospitallers.

Hertfordshire

Baldock TL 2433
The layout of the Templars' town is still visible in the town centre, bounded by the square of the High Street, Hitchen Street, White Horse Street and North Street.

Dinsley TL 1824
The preceptory site is now the Princess Helena College for Girls and is not open to the public. The stone fragments from the effigies can be seen in the parish church of St Mary, Hitchen.

Royston TL 3540
The cave lies under the crossroads of Ermine Street and the Icknield Way in the centre of the town. It is open to the public on a Sunday afternoon.

Kent

Dover TR 3141
Knights Templar church on the Western Heights above Dover. The foundations of a small circular church. Managed by English Heritage. Open all reasonable times.

Strood TQ 8532
Manor house on the site of the Templar preceptory. Managed by Rochester City Council for English Heritage. Open 1 April–30 September, 10.00am–6.00pm.

Leicestershire

Rothley SK 5812
The preceptory and its chapel are restored and standing. Now known as Rothley Court, the complex is a hotel.

Lincolnshire

Temple Bruer TF 0054
Temple Farm is a listed building. The Templars' tower is still visible, and there is Templar work in the walls and barns. This is still a working farm, but Lincolnshire County Council have produced a booklet on it, and there is limited access.

Lincoln Castle stands opposite the cathedral at the top of Steep Hill overlooking the plain. It is open to the public. The house of Aaron the Jew that the Templars may have owned is at the bottom of the final slope of Steep Hill. It is distinguished as being a first-floor entry house and probably dates from soon after the Norman Conquest.

London

The Temple Church is open to the public from 12.00 Wednesdays to Saturdays with services at 8.30am and 11.15am on a Sunday. The nearest underground station is at Temple or Chancery Lane.

The Knights of St John, St John's Gate, Clerkenwell, has a museum with a section on the Templars.

Oxfordshire

Sandford on Thames SP 5301
Temple Farm is on the site of the preceptory. The barn incorporates the chapel.

Somerset

Templecombe ST 7022
The wooden panel that may be associated with the Templars is on the south wall of St Mary's parish church.

Warwickshire

Temple Balsall SP 2076
The Templars' preceptory, now known as the Old Hall, lies next to the parish church. This is in private ownership, but there are illustrations of its interior and reports of excavations in the area in E. Gooder, *Temple Balsall* (Chichester: Phillimore, 1995).

Yorkshire

York SE 6055
Clifford's tower is the remaining evidence of York Castle where the Templars were imprisoned. Open daily. Managed by English Heritage.

Penhill SE 0486
Ruins of a chapel, with stone altar and coffins visible in a field known as Temple Bank in the Yorkshire Dales National Park.

Temple Hirst SE 6025
The Temple remains incorporated into Temple Farm.

SCOTLAND

Mary Culter NO 8599
The ruins of the Templars' chapel are on the south bank of the River Dee at Kirkton of Mary Culter on the B1099.

Roslin Chapel NT 2763
Six miles south of Edinburgh off the A701 to Penicuik. From Edinburgh take the Straiton exit from the by-pass. Continue west through the village. The chapel is open 10.00am–5.00pm all year and 12.00 to 4.45pm on Sundays. There is an admission charge.

Temple NT 3158
Twelve miles from Edinburgh on the B6372. The Templar chapel ruins are by the South Esk in the valley below the village.

WALES

Llanmadoc SS 4493
On the Gower peninsular on a cul-de-sac. The nearest A road is A4118. Llanmadoc is reached through Reynoldston, Burry Green and Cheriton.

Templeton, Dyfed SN 1111
On the A478. The planned village can still be identified within the modern layout.

IRELAND

'The remains of the Irish establishment of the once mighty Knights Templars, or their successors, the Hospitallers have vanished or are hardly recognisable'.[1]

There are many place-names incorporating the word Temple in Ireland that have nothing to do with the Templars but stem from the Irish word *Teampull* or church.

Cooley J 2205 and Templetown J 2105
Two ruined churches in the graveyard. One is probably the Templars' chapel.

Kilclogan and Templetown, Wexford S 7603
The nineteenth-century church is connected by a corridor to the tower of the Templars' church, half a mile from Kilclogan Castle which was a square keep, now in ruins.

Kilsaran O 0595 Louth

Kilsaran lies on the old coach road from Dublin to Belfast. The preceptory lay south-west of Castle Bellingham. Only the foundations remain.

NOTE

1. Leask, H.C. (1955) *Irish Churches and Monastic Buildings*, Dundalk: W. Tempest Ltd (Vol. 11), 23.

BIBLIOGRAPHY

PRIMARY SOURCES — MANUSCRIPTS

Hertfordshire Record Office

67118–67122   *Sale Particulars Temple Dinsley*
D/Ex169/M1   *Survey of Temple Dinsley, 1664*

Scottish National Archives

GD160/112/4   *Grant of Robert de Turville to Christine of Perth, c. 1278*
RH6/17   *Grant of Robert de Sandford of land in Falkirk, c. 1230*
RH6/114–15   *Grant of land in Ballancrodok, 1345*
RH6/118   *Confirmation of purchase of land in Temple, 1350*
RH6/120   *Adjudication on Templar lands in Scotland, 1353/54*
RH6/122   *Adjudication in the court of Blancrodok on a tenement in Esperston, 1354*
RH6/161   *Notification of seisin of land at Ballyncrodok, 1344*
RH11/23/1   *Charter Book of the Earl of Haddington, 1732*

National Archives

E142   *Exchequer: King's Remembrancer: Extents and Inquisitions and Valors of Land*

E142/9   *Enrolled inquisitions taken on behalf of claimants to corrodies and rents issuing from Templar lands, 1308–14*

E142/10–18   *Extents and inquisitions (with writs) of lands and goods, 1308–9*

E142/10   *Essex*

E142/11   *Northumberland and Cumberland*

E142/12   *Nottinghamshire*

E142/13   *Berkshire and Oxfordshire*

E142/14   *Hampshire*

E142/15   *Surrey and Sussex*

E142/16–18   *Yorkshire*

E142/19–22   *Writs and inquisitions as to corrodies, pensions and rents granted from Templars lands, 1308–13*

E142/89–118   *Exchequer: King's Remembrancer: Extents and inquisitions (with writs) of lands and goods of the Knights Templar*

E142/89–90   *Bedfordshire*

E142/91–93   *Cambridgeshire*

E142/94–102   *Essex*

E142/103   *Huntingdonshire*

E142/104–105   *Leicestershire*

E142/106   *Lincolnshire*

E142/107   *London*

E142/108   *Northamptonshire*

E142/109–110   *Oxfordshire and Berkshire*

E142/111   *Dorset and Somerset*

E142/112   *Suffolk*

E142/113–114   *Wiltshire*

E142/116–118   *Yorkshire*

E142/119   *Inquisitions (with writs) of debts due to the Knights Templar, 1308–9*

E164/16   *Exchequer: Kings Remembrancer: Miscellaneous Books Series 1 1185 Survey of possessions of the Knights Templar taken by order of Geoffrey Fitz-Stephen, master*

E358/18–20   *Exchequer: Pipe Office: Miscellaneous Enrolled Accounts. Accounts for the lands of the Knights Templar confiscated by the crown.*

Ind 1/7029   *Index to E358/18–20*

Scottish National Library

Acc. 8090, Maidment, J. (1833) *A Rental of all the Annual Rents of Temple Lands throughout the Kingdom of Scotland.*

Mss 21196 *A large new historical catalogue of the Bishops of the several Sees within the Kingdom of Scotland* (1755)

Mss 26287 *Temple Village, Midlothian, Twentieth Century*

PRIMARY SOURCES — PRINTED

ARNOLD, T., ed. (1879) Henry of Huntingdon, *History of England*, London: HMSO (RS 74)

ASPIN, I., ed. (1953) *Anglo-Norman Political Songs*, Oxford: Blackwell

BAIN, J., ed. (1884) *Calendar of documents relating to Scotland in the PRO*, Edinburgh: HMSO

BARRACLOUGH, G., ed. (1988) *The Charters of the Anglo-Norman Earls of Chester*, Gloucester: Alan Sutton, Record Society of Lancashire and Cheshire (CXXVI)

BREWER, J.S., ed. (1873) *Giraldi Cambrensis Opera*, London: HMSO (RS 21, IV)

BROOKE, J. and S. FLOOD (1998) *Hertfordshire Lay Subsidy Rolls 1307 and 1336*, Hertfordshire Record Society Publication (14)

Calendar of the Charter Rolls, 1226–1257 (1903) London: HMSO

Calendar of the Charter Rolls, 1257–1300 (1906) London: HMSO

Calendar of the Charter Rolls, 1300–1326 (1908) London: HMSO

Calendar of the Close Rolls, 1227–1231 (1902) London: HMSO

Calendar of the Close Rolls, 1231–1234 (1905) London: HMSO

Calendar of the Close Rolls, 1234–1237 (1908) London: HMSO

Calendar of the Close Rolls, 1237–1242 (1911) London: HMSO

Calendar of the Close Rolls, 1256–1259 (1932) London: HMSO

Calendar of the Close Rolls, 1279–1288 (1902) London: HMSO

Calendar of the Close Rolls, 1288–1296 (1908) London: HMSO

Calendar of the Close Rolls, 1296–1302 (1906) London: HMSO

Calendar of the Close Rolls, 1302–1307 (1908) London: HMSO

Calendar of the Close Rolls, 1307–1314 (1892) London: HMSO

Calendar of the Fine Rolls, 1272–1307 (1911) London: HMSO

Calendar of the Liberate Rolls, 1226–1240 (1918) London: HMSO

Calendar of the Liberate Rolls, 1245–1250 (1937) London: HMSO

Calendar of the Liberate Rolls, 1251–1260 (1959) London: HMSO

Calendar of the Liberate Rolls, 1260–1267 (1961) London: HMSO

Calendar of the Liberate Rolls, 1267–1272 (1964) London: HMSO

Calendar of the Patent Rolls, 1215–1225 (1901) London: HMSO

Calendar of the Patent Rolls, 1225–1232 (1903) London: HMSO

Calendar of the Patent Rolls, 1238–1246 (1906) London: HMSO

Calendar of the Patent Rolls, 1247–1254 (1908) London: HMSO

Calendar of the Patent Rolls, 1255–1265 (1910) London: HMSO

Calendar of the Patent Rolls, 1266–1272 (1913) London: HMSO

Calendar of the Patent Rolls, 1272–1281 (1901) London: HMSO

Calendar of the Patent Rolls, 1292–1301 (1895) London: HMSO

Calendar of the Patent Rolls, 1307–1313 (1894) London: HMSO

Cartae et alia monumenta quae ad Dominum de Glamorgania (1910) Cardiff: William Lewis

CHANDLER, J. (1993) *John Leland's Itinerary*, Stroud: Alan Sutton

CHENEY, C.R. (1973) *Medieval Texts and Studies*, Oxford: Clarendon Press, for text of Corpus Christi Mss 250.

CHENEY, C.R. and E. JOHNS, eds (1986) *English Episcopa Acta III: Canterbury 1193–1205*, London: British Academy

CLAY, C. (1935) *Early Yorkshire Charters*, Wakefield: Yorkshire Archaeological Society (Extra series 1)

CLEW, H. and M. WEINBAUM, eds (1960) *The London Eyre of 1244*, London Record Society (VI)

COLE, H., ed. (1847) *Documents Illustrative of English History in the Thirteenth and Fourteenth Centuries*, London: Eyre & Spottiswood

COSS, P. (1980) *The Langley Cartulary*, Warwick: Dugdale Society

COWAN, I.B., P. MACKAY and A. MACQUARRIE (1983) *The Knights of St John of Jerusalem in Scotland*, Edinburgh: Scottish Historical Society (4th Series, Vol. 19)

Curia Regis Rolls, Richard I and John (1903), London: PRO

Curia Regis Rolls 1202–3 (1902) Newcastle upon Tyne: Records Committee Publication (11)

D'ALBON, M. (1927) *Cartulaire General de l'Ordre du Temple*, Paris: 1913 and 1922

Duchy of Lancaster (1897) *Ministers Accounts, 1322*, North Riding Records (NS IV)

EBDEN, E.P., ed. (1972) *The Great Roll of the Pipe, 1218*, London: Pipe Roll Society

EKWALL, E. (1951) *Two Early London Subsidy Rolls*, Lund: Utg. K. Humanist. Vet. Samfulent I Lund

FARRER, M., ed. (1920) *Feudal Cambridgeshire*, Cambridge: Cambridge University Press

FORESTER, T., ed. (1858) *The Chronicle of Henry of Huntingdon*, London: HMSO (RS 74)

FOSTER, C.W., ed. (1920) *Final Concords of the County of Lincoln*, Lincoln: Lincolnshire Record Society (17)

FOWLER, G.H. (1919) *Calendar of Feet of Fines, Bedfordshire*, Bedford: Bedfordshire Record Society (6)

FOWLER, G.H. (1925) *Roll of the Justices of the Eyre, Bedfordshire, 1240*, Bedfordshire Record Society (9)

FOWLER, G.H. (1930) *Cartulary of Old Warden Abbey*, Bedford: Bedfordshire Record Society (13)

FOWLER, G.H. (1935) *Roll of the Justices of the Eyre, Bedfordshire, 1247*, Bedford: Bedfordshire Record Society (17)

FRANKLIN, P., ed. (1993) *The Taxpayers of Medieval Gloucestershire*, Stroud: Alan Sutton

GABRIELI, F., ed. (1984) *Arab Historians and the Crusades*, London: Routledge

GARMONSWAY, G., ed. (1986) *The Anglo-Saxon Chronicle*, London: Everyman

GAVIGNAN, J.J., ed. (1948) Oliver of Paderborn, *The Siege of Damietta*, Philadelphia: University of Pennsylvania Press

GAYDON, A.T. (1958) *The Taxation Rolls of 1297, Bedfordshire*, Bedford: Bedfordshire Record Society (39)

GERVERS, M., ed. (1996) *The Cartulary of the Knights of St John of Jerusalem in England*, London: British Academy, Records of Social and Economic History of England and Wales (NS VI)

The Great Roll of the Pipe, 1184–88 (1913), London: Pipe Roll Society

GREENWAY, D., ed. (1977) *Charters of the Honour of Mowbray*, Oxford: Oxford University Press, British Academy Records of Social and Economic History (NS I)

HALL, H., ed. (1894) *The Red Book of the Exchequer*, London: HMSO (RS 99)

HAMILTON, H.C., ed. (1865) Walter of Hemingburgh, *Chronica Domum Walteri de Hemingburgh, De Gesta Regum Angliae*, London: HMSO (RS 82)

HARDY, T.D., ed. (1835) *Rotuli Litterarum Patenti in Turri Londonesis asservati*, London: George Eyre (Vol. 1)

HARDY, T.D., ed. (1844) *Rotuli Litterarum Clausam in Turri Londonesis*, London: George Eyre

HARTLAND, F.S., ed., JAMES, M.R., trans. (1923) Walter Map, *De Nugis Curialium*, Cymmrodian Record Series, IX

HEWETT, H., ed. (1887) *The Flowers of History by Roger of Wendover*, London: HMSO (RS 84)

HOWLETT, R., ed. (1886) *Chronicles of Stephen, Henry II and Richard I*, London: HMSO (RS 82)

HUGHES, A., A. GOUGE and C. JOHNSON, eds (1902) *Dialogues de Saccarios*, Oxford: Oxford University Press

HUGHES, M., ed. (1940) *A Calendar of Feet of Fines for the County of Buckinghamshire*, Aylesbury: Buckinghamshire Record Society (Vol. 4)

HUNTER, J., ed. (1835) *Feet of Fines AD 1195–AD 1214*, London

ILLINGWORTH, W. and J. CALEY (1812–18) *Rotuli Hundredorum in Turri Londensis*, London: Record Commission

JOHN, T., ed. (1992) *The Warwickshire Hundred Rolls, 1279–80*, Oxford: Oxford University Press

KIRK, R., ed. (1928) *Feet of Fines for Essex*, Colchester: Essex Record Society

La Fille du Comte de Ponthieu (1923), Paris: Societe des Anciens Textes Français

LARKING, L.B. (1857) *The Knights Hospitallers in England. The 1338 Inquest*, Camden Society (Vol. 65)

LECLERQ, J. and H.M. ROCHAIS, eds (1963) Bernard of Clairvaux *De Laude Novae Militae* (S. Bernardi Opera, Vol. 111), Rome: Editiones Cisteriensis

LEES, B., ed. (1935) *Records of the Templars in England in the Twelfth Century. The 1185 Inquest*, London: British Academy, Records of Economic and Social History of England and Wales, IX

LEYS, A. (1938) *The Sandford Cartulary*, Oxford: Oxfordshire Record Society (Vols 19, 22)

Liber St Marie de Calcho (1846), Edinburgh: The Bannatyne Club (Vol. 182)

LUARD, H., ed. (1864) *Annales Monastici*, London: HMSO (RS 36)

LUARD, H., ed. (1883) Matthew Paris, *Chronica Majora*, London: HMSO (RS 57)

LUNT, A. (1926) *The Valuation of Norwich*, Oxford: Clarendon Press

MACNIOCIALL, G. (1967) 'Documents relating to the Suppression of the Templars in Ireland', *Analecta Hibernica* (Vol. 24)

MACRAY, W.D., ed. (1886) *Chronicon Abbatiae Ramensciensis*, London: Longman (RS 8)

PAGE, W., ed. (1891) *Pedes Finum*, Cambridge: Cambridge University Press

PHILLIMORE, W., ed. (1909) *Rotuli Hugonis de Wells*, London: Canterbury and York Society

Receipts and Issue Roll 1241–1242 (1992), London: Pipe Roll Society

Registrum Episcopus Glasguensis (1846), Edinburgh: The Bannatyne Club

RILEY, H., ed. (1865) *William of Rishanger's Chronicles of St Albans*, London: Longman

RYMER, T. (1757) *Foedera* (2nd edition), London: J. Tonson

SALTER, H.E., ed. (1930) *Feet of Fines for Oxfordshire*, Oxford: Oxfordshire Record Society

SAYERS, J. (1999) *Original Papal Documents in England and Wales from the Accession of Innocent III to the Death of Pope Benedict XI (1198–1304)*, Oxford: Oxford University Press

SHIRLEY, W., ed. (1862) *Rerum Britannia Medii Aevi Scriptori*, London: HMSO (RS 27)

STENTON, D. (1949) *The Great Roll of the Pipe, 1209*, London: Pipe Roll Society

STEVENSON, J., ed. (1875) *Ralph of Coggeshall Chronicon Anglicorum*, London: HMSO (RS 66)

STEVENSON, J.S., ed. (1870) *Documents Illustrative of the History of Scotland 1286–1306*, Edinburgh: HM Register House

STOW, J. (1971) *The Survey of London*, London: Kingsland

STUBBS, W., ed. (1861) *Chronica Magister Rogeri Hovedene*, London: HMSO (RS 51)

STUBBS, W., ed. (1868) *Gesta Regis Henrici Secundi*, London: HMSO (RS 49)

THOMAS, A.P., ed. (1924) *Calendar of the Mayor's Court Rolls*, Cambridge: Cambridge University Press

THORPE, L., trans. (1978) Gerald of Wales, *The Journey Through Wales*, London: Penguin

TOULMIN-SMITH, L., ed. (1907) *The Itinerary of John Leland 1535–43*, London: George Bell

UPTON-WARD, J., trans. (1992) *The Rule of the Templars*, Woodbridge: The Boydell Press

VAUGHAN, R., ed. and trans. (1984) *The Chronicles of Matthew Paris*, Gloucester: Alan Sutton

WALKER, M.S., ed. (1954) *Feet of Fines, County of Lincolnshire*, London: Pipe Roll Society

WEINBAUM, M., ed. (1976) *The London Eyre of 1276*, London Record Society (XII)

WILKINS, D. (1737) *Conciliae Magnae Britannae et Hiberniae*, London (Vol. 2)

WILKINSON, J., with J. HILL and W.F. RYAN, eds (1988) *Jerusalem Pilgrimages 1099–1185*, London: The Hakluyt Society (2nd Series, Vol. 167)

William of Tyre (1943) *A History of Deeds Done Beyond the Sea*, trans. Babcock, E.A. and A.C. Krey, New York: Columbia University Press

WILSON, A., ed. (1961) *Custumals of the Manors of Laughton, Willingdon and Goring*, Lewes: Sussex Record Society

SECONDARY SOURCES – BOOKS

ADDISON, C.G. (1842) *The History of the Knights Templar* (2nd edition), London: Longman

ADDISON, C.G. (1843) *The Temple Church*, London: Longman

AMT, E. (1993) *The Accession of Henry III in England*, Woodbridge: The Boydell Press

ANDREWS, D. (1993) *Cressing Temple*: Chelmsford: Essex County Council

ANON (1822) *The Templar*, London: T. & G. Woodward

BAIGENT, M.K., R. LEIGH and H. LINCOLN (1982) *The Holy Blood and the Holy Grail*, London: Cape

BAIGENT, M.K. and R. LEIGH (1998) *The Temple and the Lodge*, London: Arrow

BARBER, M. (1978) *The Trial of the Templars*, Cambridge: CUP

BARBER, M., ed. (1994) *The Military Orders*, London: Variorum

BARBER, M. (1994) *The New Knighthood*, Cambridge: Canto

BARROW, G. (1981) *Kingship and Unity, Scotland 1000–1306*, Edinburgh: Edinburgh University Press

BARTLETT, R. and A. MACKAY, eds (1989) *Medieval Frontier Societies*, Oxford: Clarendon Press

BAYLIS, T.H. (1900) *The Temple Church*, London: George Philip

BEAMON, S. (*c.* 1992) *The Royston Cave*, Ashwell: Cartrey Publications

BLAKE, P. and P. BLEZARD (2000) *The Arcadian Cipher*, London: Sidgwick and Jackson

BLOCH, M. (1989) *Feudal Society*, London: Routledge (reprint)

BOAS, A.J. (1999) *Crusader Architecture*, London: Routledge

BOGG, E. (1908) *Richmondshire*, Leeds: J. Miller

BOSWELL, J. (1980) *Christianity, Social Tolerance and Homosexuality*, Chicago: Chicago University Press

BOTHWELL-GOSSE, A. (1918) *The Templars*, no publication details

BRADLEY, S. and N. PEVSNER (1997) *The Buildings of England, the City of London*, London: Penguin

BROWN, D. (2003) *The Da Vinci Code*, London: Corgi

BURMAN, E. (1986) *The Templar Knights of God*, no publication details

BURNES, J. (1840) *A Sketch of the History of the Knights Templar*, Edinburgh

CALCRAFT, J. (1825) *Ivanhoe*, Edinburgh: John Anderson

CAMPBELL, G.A. (1937) *The Knights Templar, Their Rise and Fall*, London: Duckworth

CARLIN, M. (1996) *Medieval Southwark*, London: The Hambledon Press

CARPENTER, D.A. (1996) *The reign of Henry III*, London: The Hambledon Press

CHARPENTIER, J. (1945) *L'Ordre des Templiers*, Paris: Editions du Vieux Colombiers

CHARPENTIER, L. (1972) *The Mysteries of Chartres Cathedral*, London: Thomson

CLARK, P. and P. SLACK (1976) *English Towns in Transition, 1500–1700*, Oxford: Oxford University Press

CLUTTERBUCK, R. (1815) *The History and Antiquities of Hertfordshire*, London: Nichols

COHN, N. (1973) *Europe's Inner Demons*, London: Pimlico

COMPTON, P. (1973) *The Story of Bisham Abbey*, Reading: Thames Valley Press

COOPER, A., ed. (1987) *A New History of Ireland*, Oxford: Clarendon (Vol. 11)

COSS, P. and S. LLOYD, eds (1986) *Thirteenth-Century England*, Woodbridge: The Boydell Press

COWAN, I.B. and EASON, D. (1976) *Medieval Religious Houses in Scotland*, London: Longman

CROWDEN, S. (1986) *Scottish Medieval Churches*, Edinburgh: John Donald

CUNNINGHAM, H. (1845) *The Templars*, no publication details

CURRER-BRIGGS, N. (1987) *The Shroud and the Grail*, London: Weidenfeld and Nicolson

DAVIES, R.R. (1978) *Lordship and Society in the March of Wales, 1282–1400*, Oxford: Clarendon Press

DAVIES, R.R. (2000) *The First English Empire*, Oxford: Oxford University Press

DENHAM, T. and J. LAST (1997) *Multi-Period Finds, Great Wilbraham, Cambridgeshire*, Cambridge: Cambridgeshire County Council

DIBDIN, T. (1820) *Ivanhoe*, London: Roach and Co.

DOUBLEDAY, A., ed. (1972) *The Victoria County History of England and Wales, Bedfordshire*, Oxford: Oxford University Press (Vol. 3)

DUBY, G. (1968) *The Rural Economy and Country Life in the Medieval West*, Columbia: University of South Carolina Press

DUBY, G. (1980) *The Three Orders*, Chicago: University of Chicago Press

DUNKING, J. (1823) *The Hundred of Bollington*, Oxford: Harding, Mavor and Lepard

DYER, C. (1989) *The Standard of Living in the Later Middle Ages*, Cambridge: Cambridge University Press

ECO, U. trans. W. WEVER (1989) *Foucault's Pendulum*, London: Secker and Warburg

EDBURY, P.W. and D.W. METCALF (1980) *Coinage in the Latin East*, Oxford: BAR International Series

ELLIOTT, P. (1995) *Warrior Cults*, London: Blandford

ELLIS, C. (1952) *Hubert de Burgh*, London: Phoenix House

ESDAILE, K. (1933) *Temple Church Monuments*, London: George Baker

EYTON, R.W. (1854) *Antiquities of Shropshire*, London: J. Russell Smith (Vol. 1)

FORD, R. (1979) *Dramtisations of Scott's Novels*, Oxford: Oxford Bibliographic Society

FOREY, A. (1973) *The Templars in the Corona de Aragon*, Oxford: Oxford University Press

FROUDE, J.A. (1892) *The Spanish Story of the Armada and other essays*, London: Longman

FRYDE, E.B., ed. (1986) *Simon de Montfort and Baronial Reform*, London: The Hambledon Press

GALBRAITH, V.H. (1982) *Kings and Chroniclers. Essays in English Medieval History*, London: The Hambledon Press

GERVERS, M., ed. (1992) *The Second Crusade and the Cistercians*, New York: Peter Lang

GIES, F. (1986) *The Knight in History*, London: Hale

GOODER, E. (1995) *Temple Balsall*, Chichester: Phillimore

GOODICH, M.S., S. MENARCHE and S. SCHEIN, eds (1995) *Cross-Cultural Convergence in the Crusader Period*, New York: St Martins Press

HAAGENSON, E. and H. LINCOLN (2000) *The Templars' Secret*, Moreton in the Marsh: The Windrush Press

HALLAM, H.E. (1998) *The Cambridge Agricultural History of England and Wales 1042–1350*, Cambridge: Cambridge University Press

HAMMER-PURGSTALL, J. von (1853) *Die Schuld der Templier*, Vienna: Akad der Wissenschaft

HANCOX, J. (1992) *The Byrom Collection*, London: Cape

HARRISON, C. (1986) *Essays on the History of Keele*, Keele: Keele University Press

HENDERSON, D. (1892) *Annals of Lower Deeside*, Aberdeen: D. Wylie

HINE, R. (1927) *The History of Hitchen*, London: Allen and Unwin

HODGSON, J. (1827) *Northumberland*, Newcastle upon Tyne: T. & J. Pigg

HOLT, R. and G. ROSSER (1990) *The Medieval Town 1200–1540*, London: Longman

HORE, P.H. (1904) *History of the Town and County of Wexford*, London: Eliot Stock

HUYSHE, W. (1906) *The Royal Manor of Hitchin*, London: Duckworth

JECKS, M. (1995) *The Last Templar*, London: Headline

KEDAR, B.Z. (1992) *The Horns of Hattin*, Rome: Variorum

KEDAR, B.Z., H. MAYER and R. SMAIL, eds (1982) *Outremer*, Jerusalem: Yad Izhtak Ben-Zvi Institute

KIRSHNER, J., ed. (1974) *Business, Banking and Economic Thought in Late Medieval and Early Modern Europe*, Chicago: University of Chicago Press

KNIGHT, C. and R. LOMAS (1997) *The Second Messiah, Templars, the Turin Shroud and the Great Secret of Freemasonry*, London: Arrow

LAIDLER, K. (1998) *The Head of God*, London: Weidenfeld and Nicolson

LEA, H.C. (1888) *The History of the Inquisition in the Middle Ages*, London: Sampson Low

LEASK, H.C. (1955) *Irish Churches and Monastic Buildings*, Dundalk: W. Tempest Ltd

LEGGE, M.D. (1963) *Anglo-Norman Literature and Its Background*, Oxford: Oleander Press

LEVETT, A. (1938) *Studies in Manorial History*, Oxford: Clarendon Press

LINCOLN, H. (1997) *The Key to the Sacred Pattern*, Moreton in the Marsh: The Windrush Press

LITTLE, A.G. and F.M. POWICKE, eds (1925) *Essays in Medieval History*, Manchester: Manchester University Press

LITTLE, L.K. (1978) *Religious Poverty and the Profit Economy in Medieval Europe*, London: Paul Elek

LLOYD, S. (1988) *English Society and the Crusades 1216–1307*, Oxford: Clarendon Press

LUCAS, H. (1830) *Manual of the Order of the Temple*, Liverpool: David Marple

MACINNES, C. and W. WHITTARD (1955) *Bristol and Its Adjoining Counties*, Bristol: British Association for the Advancement of Science

MACQUARRIE, A. (1985) *Scotland and the Crusades 1095–1560*, Edinburgh: John Donald

MARTIN, E. (1928) *The Trial of the Templars*, London: Allen and Unwin

MATARASSO, P. (1971) *Aucassin and Nicolette and other tales*, London: Penguin

McDONALD, K. (1968) *Medieval London Suburbs*, Chichester: Phillimore

McKINLEY, R. (1988) *The Surnames of Sussex*, Oxford: Leopard's Head Press

MEYNOTT, W. (1881) *An Historical Record of the Parish Church of Christ Church, Surrey, with a Short History of the Manor of Old Paris Gardens*, privately printed by the author

MILLER, E. and J. HATCHER (1978) *Medieval England, Rural Society and Economic Change, 1086–1348*, London: Longman

MITCHELL, J. (1977) *The Walter Scott Operas*, Alabama: University of Alabama Press

MORANT, P. (1768) *History and Antiquities of Essex*, no publication details

MORSHEAD, J. (1888) *The Templars' Trials*, London: Stevens

NEWTON, K. (1970) *The Manor of Writtle*, Chichester: Phillimore

NICHOLS, H. (1804. Fasc. Edn, 1971) *The History and Antiquities of the County of Leicestershire*, Leicester: Leicestershire County Council

NICHOLSON, H., ed. (1992) *The Military Orders*, Andover: Ashgate Press

NICHOLSON, H. (1992) *Templars, Hospitallers and Teutonic Knights: Images of Military Orders, 1128–1291*, Leicester: Leicester University Press

OWEN, D. (1971) *Church and Society in Medieval Lincolnshire*, Lincoln: History of Lincolnshire (Vol. IV)

Oxford Essays in Medieval History presented to H. Salter (1934), Oxford: Oxford University Press

PAINTER, S. (1982) *William Marshal*, Toronto: University of Toronto Press

PARKER, T.W. (1965) *The Knights Templar in England*, Tuscon: University of Arizona Press

PARSONS, C.O. (1964) *Witchcraft and Demonology in Scott's Fiction*, Edinburgh: Oliver and Boyd

PARTNER, P. (1982) *The Murdered Magicians*, Oxford: Oxford University Press

PETERS, E. (1978) *The Magician, the Witch and the Law*, Philadelphia: University of Pennsylvania Press

PICKNETT, L. and C. Prince (1997) *The Templar Revelations*, London: Bantam Press

PIQUET, J. (1939) *Les Templiers. Etude de leurs operations financière*, Paris: Librairie Hachette

PLATTS, G. (1985) *Land and People in Medieval Lincolnshire*, Lincoln: History of Lincolnshire Committee

POSTAN, M. (1975) *The Medieval Economy and Society*, Cambridge: Cambridge University Press

POWICKE, F.M. (1947) *Henry III and the Lord Edward*, Oxford: Oxford University Press

PRUTZ, J. (1888) *Entwicklung und Untergang des Tempelhenenorden*, Berlin: G. Groeriche Verlagbuch

RANKIN, I. (2000) *Set in Darkness*, London: Orion

RANKIN, I. (2001) *The Falls*, London: Orion

READ, P.P. (1998) *Knights of the Cross*, London: Phoenix

READ, P.P. (1999) *The Templars*, London: Weidenfeld and Nicolson

REES, W. (1947) *A History of the Order of St John of Jerusalem in Wales and the Welsh Border*, Cardiff: University of Wales Press

REES, W. (1924, repr. 1964) *South Wales and the March 1285–1415*, Bath: Chivers

REEVES, A. (1979) *The Newport Lordship*, Ann Arbor, MI: University Microfilms

RILEY-SMITH, J. (1993) *The First Crusade and the Idea of Crusading*, London: The Athlone Press

RILEY-SMITH, J. (1997) *The First Crusaders 1095–1131*, Cambridge: Cambridge University Press

ROBINSON, J. (1989) *Born in Blood – The Lost Secrets of Freemasonry*, London: Century Books

RODWELL, W. (1993) *The Origins and Development of Witham, Essex*, Oxford: Oxbow Monograph

ROKCEDI, Z. (2000) *Medieval English Jews and Royal Officials*, Jerusalem: Hebrew University Press

ROUND, J. (1892) *Geoffrey de Mandeville*, London: Longman

ROUND, J. (1899) *The Commune of London*, London: Constable

Royal Commission on Ancient and Historical Monuments of Scotland (1929) *Mid and West Lothian*, Edinburgh: HMSO

Royal Commission on Historical Monuments of England (1911) *An Inventory of the Historical Monuments of Hertfordshire*, London: HMSO

Royal Commission on Historical Monuments of England (1922) *An Inventory of the Historical Monuments of Essex*, London: HMSO (Vol. 3)

Royal Commission on Historical Monuments of England (1929) *An Inventory of the Historical Monuments of London*, London: HMSO (Vol. IV) The City

Royal Commission on Historical Monuments of England (1931) *An Inventory of the Historical Monuments of Herefordshire*, London: HMSO (Vol. 2)

Royal Commission on Historical Monuments of England (1987) *Houses of the North Yorks Moors*, London: HMSO

SCOTT, W. (1825, 1968 edn) *The Talisman*, Ipswich

SCOTT, W. (1819, 1994 edn) *Ivanhoe*, London: Penguin

SEWARD, D. (1972) *The Monks of War*, London: Penguin

SINCLAIR, A. (1995) *The Sword and the Grail*, London: Century Books

SINCLAIR, J. (1771) *The Statistical Account of Scotland, The Lothians*, Edinburgh

SMITH, B. (1999) *Colonisation and Conquest in Medieval Ireland*, Cambridge: Cambridge University Press

SMYTH, F. (1991) *Brethren in Chivalry*, London: Lewis Masonic Books

SPUFFORD, P. (1986) *Handbook of Medieval Exchange*, London: Royal Historical Society

SPUFFORD, P. (1988) *Money and Its Use in Medieval Europe*, Cambridge: Cambridge University Press

THOMAS, H.M. (1993) *Vassals, Heiresses, Crusaders and Thugs*, Philadelphia: University of Pennsylvania Press

TOUT, T.F. (1920) *Chapters in the Administrative History of Medieval England*, Manchester: Manchester University Press

TREHARNE, R.F. (1972) *The Baronial Plan of Reform 1258–1263*, Manchester: Manchester University Press

TROLLOPE, T. (1872) *Sleaford and the Wapentake of Flaxwell*, Sleaford: Fairfield

TURNER, R.N. and R. HEISER (2000) *The Reign of Richard the Lionheart*, London: Longman

TYERMAN, C. (1988) *England and the Crusades 1095–1588*, Chicago: University of Chicago Press

The Victoria County History of England and Wales, Bedford (1972), ed. Page, W., London: Institute of Historical Research (Vols 2–3)

The Victoria County History of England and Wales, Berkshire (1972), ed. Page, W. and P. Ditchfield, London: Institute of Historical Research (Vols 2–4)

The Victoria County History of England and Wales, Buckinghamshire (1969), ed. Page, W., London: Institute of Historical Research (Vols 1, 3, 4)

The Victoria County History of England and Wales, Cambridgeshire (1967), ed. Elrington, C., London: Institute of Historical Research (Vol. 2)

The Victoria County History of England and Wales, Cambridgeshire (1973), ed. Elrington, C., London: Institute of Historical Research (Vol. 6)

The Victoria County History of England and Wales, Essex (1966), ed. Pugh, R., Oxford: Institute of Historical Research

The Victoria County History of England and Wales, Essex (1977), ed. Page, W. and J. Read, London: Institute of Historical Research (Vol. 2)

The Victoria County History of England and Wales, Essex (1983), ed. Powell, W.R., Oxford: Institute of Historical Research

The Victoria County History of England and Wales, Gloucestershire (1972), ed. Page, W., London: Institute of Historical Research (Vol. 2)

The Victoria County History of England and Wales, Gloucestershire (1972), ed. Page, W., Oxford: Institute of Historical Research (Vol. 6)

The Victoria County History of England and Wales, Hertfordshire (1971), ed. Page, W., London: Institute of Historical Research (Vols 2–4)

The Victoria County History of England and Wales, Huntingdonshire (1974), ed. Page, W., G. Proby and S. Ladds, London: Institute of Historical Research (Vols 1–3)

The Victoria County History of England and Wales, Kent (1974), ed. Page, W., London: Institute of Historical Research (Vol. 2)

The Victoria County History of England and Wales, Leicestershire (1969), ed. Hoskins, W.G., London: Institute of Historical Research (Vol. 2)

The Victoria County History of England and Wales, Leicestershire (1964), ed. Hoskins, W.G., Oxford: Institute of Historical Research (3)

BIBLIOGRAPHY

The Victoria County History of England and Wales, Lincolnshire (1906), ed.
Page, W., London: Archibald, Constable and Co. (Vol. 2)

The Victoria County History of England and Wales, Middlesex (1964), ed.
Cockburn J.S., H. King and K. McDonnell, Oxford: Institute of
Historical Research (Vol. 1)

The Victoria County History of England and Wales, Middlesex (1972), ed. Pugh,
R., Oxford: Institute of Historical Research (Vol. 3)

The Victoria County History of England and Wales, Middlesex (1980), ed. Baker,
T., Oxford: Institute of Historical Research (Vol. 6)

The Victoria County History of England and Wales, Middlesex (1989), ed. Baker,
T., Oxford: Institute of Historical Research (Vol. 9)

The Victoria County History of England and Wales, Middlesex (1995), ed. Baker,
T., Oxford: Institute of Historical Research (Vol. 10)

The Victoria County History of England and Wales, Northamptonshire (1970),
ed. Sergeantson, R. and W. Atkins, London: Institute of Historical
Research (Vol. 2)

The Victoria County History of England and Wales, Northamptonshire (1970), ed.
Page, W., London: Institute of Historical Research (Vol. 3)

The Victoria County History of England and Wales, Northamptonshire (1970), ed.
Salzman, L.F., London: Institute of Historical Research (Vol. 4)

The Victoria County History of England and Wales, Oxfordshire (1907), ed.
Page, W., London: Archibald, Constable and Co. (Vol. 2)

The Victoria County History of England and Wales, Oxfordshire (1957–1967),
ed. Lobel, M., Oxford: Institute of Historical Research (Vols 5–7)

The Victoria County History of England and Wales, Oxfordshire (1964), ed.
Lobel, M., Oxford: Institute of Historical Research (Vol. 8)

The Victoria County History of England and Wales, Oxfordshire (1969), ed.
Lobel, M. and A. Crossley, Oxford: Institute of Historical Research
(Vol. 9)

The Victoria County History of England and Wales, Oxfordshire (1972), ed.
Crossley, A., Oxford: Institute of Historical Research (Vol. 10)

The Victoria County History of England and Wales, Oxfordshire (1983), ed.
Crossley, A., Oxford: Institute of Historical Research (Vol. 11)

The Victoria County History of England and Wales, Oxfordshire (1990), ed.
Crossley, A., Oxford: Institute of Historical Research (Vol. 12)

The Victoria County History of England and Wales, Oxfordshire (1996), ed. Crossley, A., Oxford: Institute of Historical Research (Vol. 13)

The Victoria County History of England and Wales, Shropshire (1973), ed. Gaydon, A., Oxford: Institute of Historical Research (Vol. 2)

The Victoria County History of England and Wales, Somerset (1969), London: Institute of Historical Research (Vol. 2)

The Victoria County History of England and Wales, Somerset (1978), ed. Dunning, R., Oxford: Institute of Historical Research (Vol. 4)

The Victoria County History of England and Wales, Staffordshire (1970), ed. Greenslade, M., Oxford: Institute of Historical Research (Vol. 3)

The Victoria County History of England and Wales, Surrey (1967), ed. Malden, H., London: Institute of Historical Research (Vol. 3)

The Victoria County History of England and Wales, Surrey (1967), ed. Page, W., Oxford: Institute of Historical Research (Vol. 4)

The Victoria County History of England and Wales, Sussex (1973), ed. Page, W., London: Institute of Historical Research (Vol. 2)

The Victoria County History of England and Wales, Sussex (1973), ed. Salzman, L., London: Institute of Historical Research (Vol. 7)

The Victoria County History of England and Wales, Wiltshire (1956), ed. Pugh, R. and E. Crittall, Oxford: Institute of Historical Research (Vol. 2)

The Victoria County History of England and Wales, Wiltshire (1980), ed. Crowley, D., Oxford: Institute of Historical Research (Vol. 11)

The Victoria County History of England and Wales, Wiltshire (1983), ed. Crowley, D., Oxford: Institute of Historical Research (Vols 11, 13)

The Victoria County History of England and Wales, Yorkshire (1974), ed. Page, W., London: Institute of Historical Research (Vols 2–3)

The Victoria County History of England and Wales, Yorkshire, East Riding (1974), ed. Allison, K., Oxford: Institute of Historical Research (Vol. 2)

The Victoria County History of England and Wales, Yorkshire, East Riding (1976), ed. Allison, K., Oxford: Institute of Historical Research (Vol. 3)

The Victoria County History of England and Wales, Yorkshire, East Riding (1979), ed. Allison, K., Oxford: Institute of Historical Research (Vol. 4)

The Victoria County History of England and Wales, Yorkshire, East Riding (1984), ed. Allison, K., Oxford: Institute of Historical Research (Vol. 5)

The Victoria County History of England and Wales, Yorkshire, North Riding (1968), ed. Page, W., London: Institute of Historical Research (Vols 1–2)

WALKER, A. (1887) *The Knights Templar in and around Aberdeen*, Aberdeen: Aberdeen University Press

WARREN, W.L. (1961) *King John*, New Haven, CT: Yale University Press

WESTON, J.L. (1913) *The Quest for the Holy Grail*, London: G. Bell and Sons

WESTON, J.L. (1957) *From Ritual to Romance*, New York: Doubleday

WILLIAMS, E. (1927) *Early Holborn and the Legal Quarter*, London: Sweet & Maxwell

WILLIAMSON, J.B. (1924) *The History of the Temple in London*, London: John Murray

WILSON, I. (1998) *The Blood and the Shroud*, London: Weidenfeld and Nicolson

WOODHOUSE, F.C. (1879) *Military Religious Orders*, London: SPCK

WORLEY, G. (1911) *The Church of the Knights Templar in London*, London: G. Bell and Sons

ZARNECKI, G. (1979) *Studies in Romanesque Sculpture*, London: The Dorian Press

SECONDARY SOURCES — ARTICLES

AITKEN, R. (1898) 'The Knights Templar in Scotland', *The Scottish Review* (July)

ANDREWS, H. (1940–44) 'Remarks on the Place Name Baldock', *East Herts Archaeological Society Transactions* 11

AYLOTT, P. (1906) 'Earthworks at Temple Chelsing and Rennesley', *East Herts Archaeological Society Transactions* (111, Pt 11)

BALDWYNE, R.C. and H. O'Neill (1958) 'A Medieval Site at Chalk Hill, Temple Guiting', *Bristol and Gloucestershire Archaeological Society Transactions* (VLXXXVII)

BARBER, M. (1970) 'The Origins of the Order of the Temple', *Studia Monastica* (XII)

BARBER, M. (1982) 'The Templars and the Turin Shroud', *The Catholic Historical Review* (LXVIII, 2)

BARBER, M. (1984) 'The Social Context of the Templars', *Transactions of the Royal Historical Society* (5th Series, 34)

BARBER, M. (1992) 'Supplying the Crusader States', in B.S. Kedar, ed., *The Horns of Hattin*, Jerusalem and London: Variorum

BARROW, G. (1978) 'The Aftermath of War: Scotland and England in the Late 13th and Early 14th Centuries', *Transactions of the Royal Historical Society* (5th Series, 28)

BEAUMONT, G.F. (1925) 'The Manor of Borley, AD1308', *Transactions of the Essex Archaeological Society* (18)

BLACKMORE, L. and I. SCHWAB (1986–87) 'From the Templars to the Tenement: A Medieval and Post-medieval Site at 18 Shore Road, E9', *London and Middlesex Archaeological Society Transactions* (37–8)

BRAITHWAITE, W. (1909) 'Discovery of Ancient Foundations and Human Remains at Temple Newsom', *Thoresby Society Miscellany* (XV)

BRITNELL, R. (1968) 'The Making of Witham', *History Studies* (1)

BRITNELL, R. (1983) 'Agriculture in a Region of Ancient Enclosure, 1185–1500', *Nottingham Medieval Studies* (XXVII)

BULST-THIELE, M.L. (1992) 'The Influence of St Bernard of Clairvaux on the Formation of the Order of the Knights Templar', in M. Gervers, ed., *The Second Crusade and the Cistercians*, New York: St Martin's Press

BURTON, J. (1991) 'The Knights Templar in Yorkshire in the 12th Century: A Reassessment', *Northern History* (XXVII)

CARPENTER, D. (1988) 'The Gold Treasure of Henry III', in P.R. Coss and S. Lloyd, *Thirteenth-Century England*, Woodbridge: The Boydell Press

CERRINI, S. (1992) 'A New Edition of the Latin and French Rule of the Temple', in H. Nicholson, ed., *The Military Orders*, Andover: Ashgate Press (Vol. 2)

CHETWYND-STAPYLTON, A. (1887–89) 'The Templars at Temple Hirst', *Yorkshire Archaeological and Topographical Society Transactions* (X)

CHRISTIE, R.M. and J.G. COAD (1980) 'Excavations at Denny', *Archaeological Journal* (137)

CLARK, G.T. (1882) 'The Customary of the Manor and Soke of Rothley in the County of Leicstershire', *Archaeologia* (47)

CONSTABLE, G. (1982) 'Financing the Crusades in the Twelfth Century', in B.S. Kedar, H. Mayer and R. Smail eds, *Outremer*, Jerusalem: Yad Izhtak Ben-Zvi Institute

CROSSLEY, E.W. (1918–20) 'A Temple Newsam Inventory, 1565', *Yorkshire Archaeological and Topographical Society Transactions* (25)

Current Archaeology (1968)

DERMOT, B. (1960–62) 'The Knights Templar in County Louth', *Seanchas Ardmacha* (4)

DOVE, W. (1967) 'The Temple Church and its Restoration', *London and Middlesex Archaeological Society Transactions* (Vol. 21, No. 3)

EDBURY, P.W. (1992) 'Looking Back on the Second Crusade', in M. Gervers, ed., *The Second Crusade and the Cistercians*, New York: St Martin's Press

EDWARDS, J. (1909) 'The Templars in Scotland in the Thirteenth Century', *Scottish Historical Review*

FERRIS, E. (1902) 'The Financial Relations of the Knights Templar to the English Crown', *American Historical Review* (VIII)

FINCHAM, H.W. (1976) 'The Bailiff of Eagle and His Bailliwick', *First Aid and St John Gazette* (Oct)

FLEMING-YATES, J. (1927) 'The Knights Templar and Hospitallers in the Manor of Garway, Herefordshire', *Woolhope Natural History Field Club, Transactions*

FOREY, A. (1986) 'Recruitment to the Military Orders, mid 12th–mid 14th Centuries', *Viator* (17)

FOREY, A. (1987) 'Women and the Military Orders in 12th and 13th Centuries', *Studia Monastica* (29)

FOREY, A. (1994) 'Towards a Profile of the Templars in the Early Fourteenth Century', in M. Barber, ed., *The Military Orders*, Rome: Variorum

FOSBROOKE, T.H. (1921–22) 'Rothley – The Preceptory', *Leicestershire Archaeological Society Transactions* (12) 2–32

GALLOWAY, J. and M. MURPHY (1991) 'Feeding the City: Medieval London and its Agrarian Hinterland', *London Journal* (Vol. 16, No. 1)

Gentleman's Magazine, (1857) (NS. III)

GODFREY, W. (1951) 'Recent Discoveries at the Temple and Notes on the Topography of the Site', *Archaeologia* (XIV)

HEWITT, C. (1967) 'The Barns at Cressing Temple and Their Significance in the History of English Carpentry', *Journal of the Society of Architectural History* (XXVI)

HINE, R. (1937) 'The Early History of Temple Dinsley', *East Herts Archaeological Society Transactions* (9)

HODGSON, J. (1895) 'Temple Thornton Accounts, 1308', *Archaeologia Aeliana* (XVII)

HUNTER, J. (1993) 'Historic Landscape of Cressing and its Environs', in D. Andrews, ed., *Cressing Temple*, Chelmsford: Essex County Council

KASTNER, L.E. (1906) 'Some Old French Versions of the Anti-Christ', *Modern Language Review* (Vol. 1, No. 4)

KEENE, D. (1989) 'Medieval London and its Region', *London Journal* (Vol. 14, No. 2)

LEES, B. (1933–37) 'The *Humbra* and *Quabba* of Hackney and Leyton', *London and Middlesex Archaeological Society Transactions* (7)

LLOYD, S. (1986) 'Crusader Knights and the Land Market in the Thirteenth Century', in Coss, P. and S. Lloyd, eds, *Thirteenth-Century England*, Woodbridge: The Boydell Press

LUNT, A. (1915) 'Papal Taxation in England in the Reign of Edward I', *The English Historical Review* (CXIX)

MACINERY, M.H. (1913) 'The Templars in Ireland', *The Irish Ecclesiastical Review* (5th Series, 11)

MARTIN, E.J. (1927–29) 'The Templars in York', *Yorkshire Archaeological and Topographical Society Transactions* (29)

MARTIN, W. (1929–33) 'Notes upon the History and Topography of the Temple, London', *London and Middlesex Archaeological Society Transactions* (6)

MCKERRACK, A. (1991) 'Bruce's Secret Weapon', *The Scots Magazine* (June)

Menache, S. (1993) 'The Templar Order: A Failed Idea', *The Catholic Historical Review* (LXXIX)

MENACHE, S. (1995) 'Re-writing the History of the Templars according to Matthew Paris', in M.S. Goodich, S. Menache and S. Schein, eds, *Cross-Cultural Convergence in the Crusader Period*, New York: Peter Lang

METCALF, D.W. (1980) 'The Templars as Bankers and Monetary Transfers between West and East' in P.W. Edbury and D.W. Metcalf, *Coinage in the Latin East*, Oxford: BAR International Series

MORDAUNT-CROOK, J. (1965) 'The Restoration of the Temple Church: Ecclesiology and Recrimination', *Architectural History* (8)

NICHOLSON, H. (1991) 'Templar Attitudes towards Women', *Medieval History* (1)

NICHOLSON, H. (1992) 'Steamy Syrian Scandals, Matthew Paris and the Templars and Hospitallers', *Medieval History* (Vol. 2, No. 2)

Notes and Queries (1854) (10)

Notes and Queries (1855) (11)

OLIVER MINOS, R. (1899) 'The Knights Templar Chapel at Garway', *The Reliquary and Illustrated Archaeologist* (V)

Pall Mall Gazette (1910), 5th March

PANTIN, W.A. (1970) 'Minchery Farm, Littlemore', *Oxoniensia* (35)

PERKINS, C. (1909) 'The Wealth of the Knights Templar in England and the Disposition of it after their Dissolution', *American Historical Review* (I, XV)

PERKINS, C. (1910) 'The Knights Templars in the British Isles', *English Historical Review* (XCVIII)

POSTAN, M. (1928) 'Credit in Medieval Trade', *Economic History Review* (Series 1, 2)

POSTLES, D. (1993) 'Some Differences between Seigniorial Demesnes in Medieval Oxfordshire', *Oxoniensia* (58)

PRYOR, J. (1982) 'The Transportation of Horses by Sea in the Era of the Crusades', *Mariners Mirror* (68)

REES, W. (1949) 'The Templar Manor of Llanmadoc', *Bulletin*, Board of Celtic Studies, University of Wales (XIII)

RILEY-SMITH, J. (2001) 'The origins of the commandery', Proceedings, Larzac Conference, 2000

RITOOK, S. (1994) 'The Architecture of the Knights Templar in England', in M. Barber, ed., *The Military Orders*, London: Variorium

ROBERTS, E. (1963) 'The Boundary and Woodlands of Shotover Forest', *Oxoniensia* (23)

RYAN, P. (1993) 'Cressing Temple: Its History from Documents', in D. Andrews, *Cressing Temple*, Chelmsford: Essex County Council

SACHS, J. (1904) 'Discoveries Made during the Excavations for the Foundation of the Safe Deposit Bank, Chancery Lane', *London and Middlesex Archaeological Society Transactions* (NS 1)

SANDYS, A. (1925) 'The Financial and Administrative Importance of the London Temple in the Thirteenth Century', in A.G. Little and F.M. Powicke, eds, *Essays in Medieval History*, Manchester: Manchester University Press

SCHEIN, S. (1995) 'The Miracles of the Hospital of St John and the Carmelite Elianic Tradition – Two Medieval Myths of Foundation', in M.S. Goodich, S. Menache and S. Schein, eds, *Cross-Cultural Convergence in the Crusader Period*, New York: Peter Lang

Somerset Notes and Queries (1935), (XXI)

Spottiswode Miscellany (1845), (2), Edinburgh: The Spottiswode Society

ST JOHN HOPE, W. (1908) 'The Round Church of the Templars at Temple Bruer, Lincolnshire', *Archaeologia* (61)

STRINGER, K. (1993) 'North East England and Scotland in the Middle Ages', *The Innes Review* (XLIV)

TAYLOR, B.V. (1881–82) 'Ribston and the Knights Templar', *Yorkshire Archaeological and Topgraphical Journal* (11)

WAITES, B. (1967) 'Moorland and Vale-land Farming in North-East Yorkshire: The Monastic Contribution in the 13th and 14th Centuries', *Borthwick Papers* (32)

WARD, J. (1983) 'The Fall of the Templars: A Review Article', *The Journal of Religious History* (13)

WEBB, J. (1844) 'Notes on the Preceptory of the Tempars at Garway in the County of Herefordshire', *Archaeologia* (XXI)

WOOD, H. (1906) 'The Templars in Ireland', *Proceedings of the Royal Irish Academy* (XXV) Section C.

UNPUBLISHED MATERIAL

ELDERS, J. (2000) *Temple Dinsley Archaeological Project Report*

'SHALLOW, J.' (J. MORSHEAD), *Conjectures on the Templars Proces*, Typewritten notes, 1918. CUL Syn.4.91.47

INDEX

Wales (*continued*)
  Newport 146, 148
  Pembroke Castle Mill 146
  Templeton 148–9, 316
Warwickshire 93, 120, 123, 175
  Barston 122–4
  Flechamstead 124
  Harbury 123–4, 126
  Hardwick 126
  Newbold 124, 126
  Shireburn 124, 126
  Temple Balsall 94, 105, 119, 122–6, 255, 314
  Tysoe 123–4, 126
  Warwick 123–4, 126, 250
Welsh Marches 142–4, 175
Wiltshire 22, 134, 309
  Lockeridge 152–3
  Temple Rockley 151–3, 170
Women 152, 161–3

Yorkshire 22, 25, 90–1, 93–4, 99, 103–4, 106, 109, 112–14, 118, 120, 309
Copmanthorpe 105, 107, 115
Faxfleet 25, 105, 114, 252, 253
Foulbridge 105–6, 112
Hunsingore 111
Osmanthorpe 107
Penhill 93, 105, 112, 114, 314
Ribston 105, 111
Temple Cowton 25, 93, 105, 110, 114
Temple Hirst 25, 105–7, 114–15, 252, 263, 314
Temple Newsam 105, 107, 109–10, 114–15, 263
Westerdale 105
Wetherby 105, 111
York 104–5, 117, 250–1, 254–6, 314